SUPPORTING WORKPLACE
LEARNING FOR
HIGH PERFORMANCE WORKING

David Ashton is Professor and founder of the Centre for Labour Market Studies of the University of Leicester in the United Kingdom, where he developed one of the first Master's courses in training and human resource development. He has published extensively in the field of international human resource development and has advised national governments and international bodies on human resources development policy.

Johnny Sung is currently Director of the Centre for Labour Market Studies at the University of Leicester in the United Kingdom. He has published extensively on national education and training systems, workforce development, workplace learning and learning technology.

SUPPORTING WORKPLACE LEARNING FOR HIGH PERFORMANCE WORKING

David N. Ashton and Johnny Sung

International Labour Office, Geneva

ISBN 92-2-112801-6

Printed in France   SAD

ACKNOWLEDGEMENTS

A large number of people have been involved in the production of this book. John Stevens provided an initial impetus on behalf of the Chartered Institute of Personnel and Development in the United Kingdom and the International Federation of Training and Development Organizations. Trevor Riordan and Torkel Alfthan of the International Labour Organization provided further inspiration and then helped to make it a reality; their critical comments on earlier drafts were extremely valuable. Tony Twigger and Barrie Oxtoby helped with the research on the case studies and have been an important source of support and encouragement. Maureen Ashton proofread the entire text and helped make sense of the ideas.

We are also grateful to the personnel of the various companies we visited during the course of this research who provided time and help in our attempt to understand their operations. As ever, the authors are responsible for any mistakes.

PREFACE

The ILO's recent interest in high performance work organizations (HPWOs) arose out of comments from our constituents - governments, workers' and employers' organizations - on the ILO's 1998-99 World Employment Report: Employability in the Global Economy - How Training Matters. While this report was generally acknowledged as making a substantial contribution to the role of training in promoting employability and concentrated more on public policy, it was felt that the discussion on workplace learning could be taken further. The ILO, therefore, joined together with the International Federation of Training and Development Organizations (IFTDO) to conduct a number of case studies on workplace learning and training and, in particular, how these are conducted in the newly emerging HPWOs. Nine of these studies were conducted and were placed on the ILO's InFocus Programme on Skills, Knowledge and Employability (IFP/SKILLS) website, along with a research project overview. These studies were presented at the IFTDO International Conference in London in March 2000 and generated substantial interest. The ILO has taken up the challenge of this widespread interest and produced this book, written by David Ashton and Johnny Sung.

The book looks at many aspects of workplace learning and training and considers these aspects from the perspective of workers as well as employers, including the prospective benefits for the different parties. It also looks at the role government can play in fostering high performance work practices, and in particular encouraging enterprises to make better use of the skills of their employees. In practical terms, it is possible to do this by, for example, changing the rules of accounting to place investment in people on a level footing with investment in plants and equipment. For the ILO, this book contributes to our strategic objective of creating greater opportunities for women and men to secure decent work. The HPWOs create the scenario for a win-win outcome: the companies benefit through increased productivity, and the employees gain through improved quality of working life - decent employment - with increased remuneration compared to more traditional enterprises. The recent research, for the first time, effectively shows the linkages between the use of high performance work practices (HPWPs) and increased productivity. The book also shows that employees in HPWOs often have more stable employment and that equity issues are dealt with in a more open and fair manner. Workers are usually provided with greater opportunities to have their skills recognized and certified under national qualifications frameworks.

The use of HPWPs also provides the opportunity for workers to develop their capabilities, and range of skills, through the introduction of job rotation, multi-skilling and learning in teams. Through these approaches, learning does not remain a one-off event, as is the case in many traditional companies, but becomes a continuous process throughout the individual's working life - a genuine approach to lifelong learning. In addition to increasing workers' skills, it also provides higher levels of remuneration and material rewards. Work becomes a more personally satisfying pursuit.

The discussion on HPWOs, however, is not just about training. It involves a major commitment from managers and workers alike - mutual trust is an essential part of the reorganization of the workplace. The reward of performance and involvement in decision-making processes are an essential part of high performance work practices. Where other management innovations, such as quality circles, only achieved marginal success in many companies and were later dropped when this lack of success became evident, the high involvement necessary in HPWOs has contributed to sustainable long-term improvements, both in productivity and the quality of goods produced.

It is hoped that this book will stimulate further debate on the subject of workplace learning and training and contribute to the promotion of greater opportunities for decent work for all. I would like express my sincere appreciation to David Ashton and Johnny Sung for working with us on this project, and writing this book, and to Trevor Riordan of IFP/SKILLS who managed the project.

Pekka Aro, Director
In Focus Programme on Skills, Knowledge and Employability
International Labour Office

CONTENTS

OVERVIEW

The objectives of this book are twofold. The first objective is to increase the awareness among governments, employers and unions of the importance of workplace learning as a means of enhancing both work performance and the quality of working life. The second is to explore the ways in which public policy can be used to encourage organizations to make more effective use of the skills of all their employees.

The growing importance of workplace learning is manifest in two ways. First is the growth of those occupations which are devoted to the application of specialist professional and scientific knowledge in the workplace. For example, across the globe we have seen an increase in the proportion of professional, scientific, managerial and technical workers in the workforce. While these groups have grown most rapidly in the more advanced industrial economies, they are also growing as a proportion of the labour force in many of the developing societies. Second, the growth of the new high performance work organizations (HPWOs) has meant that where these organizations have been fully established all employees have become involved in workplace learning. There, the use of modern management techniques is making continual learning a reality. It is the growth of these new forms of work organization that provides the focus of this book.

In this brief introduction, we tackle a number of questions raised by the growing use of high performance working practices (HPWPs). What are these practices? Are they something new or just another management fad? What benefits do they create over and above other more traditional forms of organizing work? Why should an organization such as the International Labour Organization (ILO) be interested in them? Are they just another means of exploiting workers? If not, what benefits do they bring to workers? These are questions around which the main body of this text is centred, but we raise them to illustrate that HPWPs should be of interest not only to employers but also to workers and all groups for whom it is the agenda of the ILO to improve the quality of working life.

High performance working practices consist of new ways of organizing work, rewarding performance and involving employees in the decision-making process in the workplace. Some of these practices, such as job rotation, performance-related pay and self-directed work teams, have been around for a number of decades. Others, such as 360-degree appraisal and personal development plans, are relatively recent innovations. What is new is the way in which these practices have been combined to create a working environment which not only provides the potential for developing the personality of the worker, but also raises the productivity of the organization. This does not eradicate differences in the interests of management and workers, but it does minimize the conflict of interest and provide a significant improvement in their combined ability to increase wealth and the prospect of an increase in the standard of living for all.

This may sound almost too good to be true, and indeed we must be wary of any claim that we have suddenly created a utopia in which all parties stand to gain. Indeed, in researching this topic the authors have been acutely aware of the possibility that this is simply a new management fad. Over the years, we have seen many such fads come and go: business process re-engineering, quality circles and more recently the learning organization, to name just a few. These all contain one "good idea", which is why they are adopted in the first place. Thus, quality circles provided an opportunity for employees to make suggestions of ways in which quality could be improved. This made sense, as it is the workers doing the everyday tasks who are closer to the manufacture of the product or the delivery of the service, and it is they rather than the more remote managers who can readily see how the product or service can be improved. However - and this is the snag - if the managers are unwilling to devolve responsibility to the workers or to listen and act on the advice of the workers, then there is in no incentive for the workers to continue to be involved in such practices. Similarly, if the workers are not rewarded for their suggestions and improvements, then once again they should not bother: behaviour that improves performance must be rewarded if it is to be sustained. These are just some of the reasons why quality circles failed in some organizations. Yet we must not forget that in some organizations they did work.

Where quality circles and other initiatives did work, they were often part of a more general attempt by management to involve the employees in the decision-making process of the organization. In these organizations, managers were willing to devolve power and decision-making to employees, to trust the employees to make the correct decision and to ensure that they were rewarded for their efforts. Thus, while many managers abandoned quality circles because in their organizations they did not deliver the goods, others did not and built on their success. They introduced systems of continuous improvement where the employees became involved in more than just improving quality but making decisions about how the whole process of production or service delivery could be improved.

The introduction of total quality management (TQM) underwent a similar fate. In many organizations based on the traditional managerial system of command and control, where all authority and decision-making is vested in the senior managers who tell those below them how to perform their jobs, systems of TQM failed abysmally for many of the same reasons that quality circles failed. Where they were successful was in organizations which had moved away from the old style of management toward a more participative style. Managers consulted with employees, work was organized on a team basis and the employees were involved in making many of the decisions about how work was organized.

In these new styles of organization, it is not unusual to find a number of the old "fads" as an integral part of management practices. There they can be found alongside each other in the form of quality circles, TQM, self-managed work teams, gain sharing and team briefings. In fact, in these organizations the employee, rather than being the recipient of orders and directions from above, is now part of a broader more inclusive team whose objective is to improve the performance of the organization as a whole. This is a very different work environment. Here all the employees are treated the same, all are involved in the process of continually improving how they produce the goods or deliver the service. All are consulted or are involved in decisions about how their work is organized. A sustained effort is put into developing the skills of all employees and making training and learning continuous activities, not just one-off events. Systems of reward are in place to ensure that the gains which flow from this method of organizing production are distributed throughout the organization. What we see here is a totally different way of organizing production from anything found in traditional command and control organizations. These are the high performance work organizations.

Changes of this magnitude in the way in which we organize production do not happen overnight. They are not the result of the manager going off to a training course and coming back with a totally new concept or idea on the basis of which he or she will make a mark in the organization. These changes can take years to introduce and require a substantial shift in the attitudes and behaviours of both management and other employees. However, as they are successfully introduced, they do provide major gains for all those involved. The most fundamental change is the gain in efficiency and productivity. In HPWOs human beings produce higher-quality goods and services using less human labour. They represent a way of improving our ability to generate wealth. For organizations that successfully introduce them, they produce major improvements across a range of outputs in the form of increased productivity, customer and employee satisfaction and in the private sector in the form of profitability.

Again, this may sound like good common sense, but we now have firm scientific evidence that this is the case. Put plainly, investment in these practices and the skills associated with them pays off on the bottom line. This statement is not just based on the results of a small number of studies. Over the last decade, evidence has been steadily accumulating across a number of countries on the link between the use of high performance practices and organizational performance. Research on large samples of employers in the United States, Canada, the United Kingdom and Germany has produced the same results. The fact that such findings have been produced independently in a range of countries and are statistically robust suggests that this is no one-off management fad but rather a more efficient way of utilizing human resources.

However, if this is just a means of making more money for employers, why should workers be interested? The exciting fact is that these practices increase opportunities for employees to develop their capabilities while at the same time providing them with higher levels of income and material rewards. The introduction of job rotation and mutli-skilling increases the range of tasks and technical skills required by employees. The use of teamworking and self-managed work teams means that workers develop better communication and decision-making skills: they learn to cooperate and participate in the decision-making process. The devolution of responsibility to individual workers and teams, together with the need for continuous improvement in the delivery of the product or service, means that employees are constantly faced with new challenges and learning opportunities. Learning becomes a continuous process - not something that one "does" on a training course. Work becomes a more satisfying experience and one which provides opportunities for personal development.

On the material level, the use of these practices when successfully implemented in an organization also provides more security of employment. The fact that these organizations are more efficient in their use of human labour means that they stand a better chance of survival and growth in the market place, which translates into more secure jobs. Finally, we now have solid evidence from the United States that workers also benefit directly from the increased profitability of companies in the form of higher wages - the gains are distributed to the workers. On all fronts, in terms of work satisfaction, employment security and wages, workers stand to gain.

If these are the benefits, what are the drawbacks? Surely, no system of work organization can be all light and roses. Do some employers merely use this technique of work organization as a means of squeezing more out of employees without distributing the gains? One of the main drawbacks is the length of time it can take to implement these practices. As with any major innovation, the introduction of these practices, if they are to be successful, has to be done over a period of time. This is not a quick fix. It requires months and often years to introduce these practices. It also requires a strong commitment from both managers and employees. One group cannot do it without the consent and help of the other; it is a collective endeavour in the real sense of the word. Moreover, as we shall see later, these practices do not work in isolation. By this, we mean that practices have to be introduced as bundles. For example, if teamworking, quality circles and continuous improvement systems are put in place but the workers are not rewarded for improvements in organizational or company performance, then the attempt will fail. Workers will withdraw their commitment and without this improvements in performance will fall, and the experiment will be seen as just another in the list of management failures.

For the high performance system to work effectively, changes are required in four main areas. First, jobs have to be designed in such a way that they use the full intellectual and practical experience of all employees and engage them in the decision-making process (e.g. practices such as teamworking and self-managed work groups). Second, employees at all levels will not be able to make use of their new situation to improve performance if they do not have the requisite knowledge of the business environment. Therefore, the second set of practices must include those which are associated with the dissemination of knowledge within the organization (e.g. regular meetings of the workforce, the regular dissemination of business information to all employees). In order to make the most effective use of this information, the employees must be committed to the values and objectives of the organization, and they must want to use that information to improve their performance. Third, they must be supported in the process of learning the requisite skills, hence the importance of regular coaching or mentoring sessions, feedback on performance through appraisals and the opportunity for further training to acquire and practice the new skills. Finally, as we have already mentioned, none of this is likely to produce improved results unless the employee is rewarded, both financially in the wage packet as well as in the everyday process of learning, through acknowledgement by colleagues and superiors. To put all four sets or bundles of practices in place takes a tremendous amount of effort, energy and time.

The fact that putting these bundles into place requires the active commitment of employees means that, while some employers have been able to impose these systems on employees in the short term, they have not been able to sustain them over time. Without the commitment of employees, the kind of long-term gains in productivity and profitability which high performance work systems (HPWSs) are capable of generating do not materialize. We document such cases in the main text. This in itself is a guarantee that HPWSs cannot be used in the long term as a means of merely intensifying the work effort.

This is not to say that there are no new strains and stresses associated with HPWPs. While scientific evidence on this is still relatively thin at this stage, it is fair to say that there are always stresses associated with new ventures, with introducing change and disrupting people's expectations. The main issue is whether the use of techniques such as self-managed work groups, multi-skilling and continuous improvement produce new and potentially harmful stresses on employees. However, while it was initially thought that workers would suffer stress from group pressure on them to improve performance, recent research has found that this is not the case. Workers in HPWOs are no more likely to experience stress than those in more traditional organizations.

If the benefits of this way of organizing work are so all-pervasive, why is not every organization adopting them? Again this question is dealt with at length in the main body of the text, but here we would make two important points. First, there is widespread ignorance about the potential of HPWOs. Many employers and union officials are not aware that there are very different ways of organizing work to those command and control systems which they have personally experienced over their lifetime. One of the purposes of this book is to increase awareness of the alternative provided by HPWOs.

Second, and perhaps of greater significance, is the fact that HPWSs are based on mutual trust between employer and employee. The economic and productivity gains which these organizations generate are only possible because they make full use of the intelligence and practical skills of the whole labour force. To get all employees continually to improve their performance requires not only that there is the appropriate work design in the form of teamworking and multi-skilling in place, but also that all employees are continually and consciously seeking ways of improving their performance. Furthermore, high levels of performance also require creativity. Employees have to feel secure enough to experiment and try new behaviours and learn from mistakes. All this requires the worker to be fully committed to the objectives and values of the enterprise.

Of course, a basic precondition for this commitment on the part of both worker and manager is trust. Trust cannot be achieved by orders, threats and commands from above, which is the stock in trade of the traditional command and control organization. All that produces is minimal compliance: "You do what you have been told to do in order to safeguard your back. There is no point in doing more, because you will not be rewarded for that and may risk the wrath of the boss if you step out of line." That type of organization works because average levels of performance are sufficient to generate the output necessary to remain competitive in what are often sheltered markets or where a monopoly position may guarantee profits. The creativity and commitment which is characteristic of HPWPs can only be sustained when employees have the trust of their managers, where managers feel free to let employees develop new ideas and where in developing new ideas or trying out new practices employees are secure in the knowledge that mistakes will be tolerated and achievements rewarded. To embed these practices in the organization therefore requires sustained commitment from both management and workers and can only be done effectively in an atmosphere of mutual respect and trust.

This type of trust is not created overnight. It requires more than fine words and glossy brochures to sustain it. It requires consistent and sustained behaviour from senior managers which can only be observed by employees over time; in the jargon of the business world, it requires senior managers to "walk the talk". As those involved in any aspect of management and industrial or employee relations are acutely aware, this is not an easy task. Thus, while HPWOs provide substantial benefits to both parties, they are by their very nature fragile because the trust which takes so much time to build can be destroyed overnight. It has taken us two decades to learn how to create HPWOs, but the gains they provide are soon lost if either party loses his/her commitment to the collective goals.

In spite of the difficulties in creating these organizations, they are spreading rapidly across the globe. In part this is because, once established, their benefits are obvious to all concerned. At one stage, it was believed that these organizations were a product of the rich man's club and could only function in the more advanced economies of the world. This assumed that they were some form of luxury that the poorer nations could not afford. Ten years ago, that might have appeared to be the case. These practices first appeared in Japan, partly as a product of the special relationship of trust which characterized Japanese manufacturing companies with their "guarantee" of lifetime employment. From there, they spread to the West, especially the United States where, in the face of Japanese competition, US companies had to adapt HPWPs and raise their own productivity or risk going under. Since then, they have, in part through the behaviour of multinational organizations, spread throughout the world. As we demonstrate in the text, they are just as likely to be found in Jamaica, the Gambia, South Africa and China as in the United States, Singapore, the United Kingdom or Germany. Where they appear to have been slower to take root is in the public sector, but even there we are now witnessing an increasing number of governments finding ways of pushing public sector organizations in the direction of HPWOs.

Finally, we can now answer the question we asked at the beginning. Why should the ILO be interested in these developments? The answer is simple. For decades, the ILO has been something of a lone voice in advocating the adoption of what it would term "sound labour-management practices". These have consisted of not just minimum contractual standards designed to prevent the exploitation of workers, but also the use of joint consultation between management and workers, the building of trust and the encouragement of worker participation in the decision-making process. These are all issues integral to the establishment of HPWOs. What we now know is that these also improve business performance. In a very real sense, both management and workers stand to gain from the adoption of these practices.

CHAPTER 1

THE GROWING IMPORTANCE OF WORKPLACE LEARNING

Introduction

Workplace learning has become increasingly important during the last decade. There are of course a number of different types of workplace learning, but we are especially interested in that which takes place in high performance work organizations (HPWOs). These organizations are relatively new phenomena, which have arisen in large part as a consequence of the process of globalization. We explore the characteristics of these organizations in some detail in Chapter 2. Our concern here is to understand the reasons behind their growth and the benefits they offer for both employers and employees. Although they are still somewhat unusual, they do provide a range of benefits for both groups, ranging from higher levels of profitability and productivity for employers to higher earning and more challenging work for employees. The purpose of this chapter is to demonstrate that these are not just the result of another management fad, but rather represent a major change in the way in which we organize the production of both goods and services.

Types of workplace learning

Over recent years, the use of the workplace as a learning experience has been transformed. There are three main reasons for this. The first relates to the growth of the knowledge economy. The second refers to the impact of the "new economy" and information and communications technology (ICT) in improving productivity. The third and related reason is the growing use of high performance working practices (HPWPs) that are transforming the ways in which work is organized. This is being facilitated by developments in ICT.

A great deal of space has been devoted to the growth of the so-called knowledge economy in recent years. Keep (2000) argues that there are at least two definitions present in the literature and public discussion, the first of which is based on the high-tech industrial clusters in the United States along the lines of those which developed in California. This provides knowledge-based jobs for the labour force, but these jobs only represent a minority of the total Californian and US labour force. The second is a broader definition which is more inclusive, suggesting a realm of economic activity characterized by a foundation of mutually reinforcing factors which together form the core of a high value-added economy where knowledge is a key to economic success and where skills and learning are valued and productively employed. These factors include, among others, a general demand for sophisticated products, high levels of research and development (R&D) especially in new technology, a high value on learning throughout life and an efficient and open educational system and labour market. Central to this definition is a highly skilled and knowledgeable workforce.

The growth of the "new economy" is also seen as a reason for the expansion of knowledge-based jobs. The idea of a "new economy" focuses attention on the role of ICT and its impact on technological progress. Here we are talking about technology-driven change leading to the knowledge-based economy or, as a minimum, providing support for more rapid knowledge creation and diffusion (OECD, 2001). However, the OECD report on the "new economy" points out that our knowledge of the impact of ICT is still largely confined to its impact on the US economy (OECD, 2000). While it does not identify any major impact of the "new economy" on employment, it does point to the importance of the accumulation of knowledge and human capital and the importance of government action in expanding the knowledge base required for the "new economy". This serves as a note of caution, for while the new high-tech economy is growing it still forms only a small proportion of total employment. As such, it is not as yet a major cause of the growth of knowledge-based jobs.

The third, and most important, source of the growing importance of workplace learning is the spread of HPWOs. The spread of HPWPs which characterize these organizations has created the opportunity for all employees within them to develop their skills, not just those in professional, managerial or craft occupations. The growth of these organizations has been facilitated by both the spread of the knowledge economy and the use of ICT associated with the "new economy". However, the dissemination of these HPWOs cannot be explained away just by reference to these factors. As we shall see later, they are linked to equally profound changes in the nature of competition in world markets.

The consequence of all three factors has been the growth in the proportion of the working population who utilize the application and manipulation of knowledge in their everyday work tasks. Here we are referring primarily to the professionals, scientists and managers. While we encounter difficulties in identifying precisely who are these "knowledge workers" (Scarbrough et al., 1998), we do know that as a group professional, scientific and managerial workers are increasing as a proportion of the total labour force. This shift in the direction of more highly skilled white-collar workers is of course part of the more general shift in the occupational structures of the advanced economies from manufacturing to the service sector. The ILO's World Employment Report 1998-99, after surveying the employment growth rates for a number of developed and developing countries, points out that in all countries the employment of skilled workers has been on the rise. In the advanced countries for the period 1981-96, the growth has been highest for professionals and technicians, while production employees (skilled and unskilled) either declined or did not increase very rapidly. The United States Department of Labor estimates that in the late 1990s occupations that required a college degree were growing twice as fast as others (Herman, 1999). In developing countries, professionals and technicians also grew as a proportion of the total labour force, not as great as in the developed countries, but nevertheless they still grew at a faster rate than production workers. Table 1.1 below illustrates the growth of professionals and technicians in selected countries. However, it should be noted that while this is a powerful trend affecting many countries, some countries have not experienced it. In the Philippines, the percentage of professionals and technicians remained static over that period, while in countries such as Paraguay there was a small fall. Even in Thailand where economic growth was rapid, there was only a small increase in the percentage of professionals and technicians.

The significance of the growth of HPWOs is that as well as employing more of these traditional knowledge workers they are extending the opportunity to experience continuous workplace learning to a new group of employees, namely the junior white-collar and manual workers, a much larger proportion of the total labour force. For the first time, we have the radical prospect of the majority of the labour force being presented with the opportunity to experience work as a source of lifelong learning.

For the traditional knowledge workers in professional, technical and managerial occupations, workplace learning has tended to be associated with formal courses. These are the most highly educated workers who also have the greatest chances of further education and training once they enter work (Ashton and Green, 1996). It is therefore not surprising that they are pioneering continuous professional development, encouraged by the activities of professional associations. However, while formal training courses are an important component of continuous professional development, they may represent only the tip of the iceberg when it comes to lifelong learning and development. Recent research by Eraut et al. (1998) has shown that for technicians and professionals most learning is informal, taking place through everyday interaction in the workplace. Thus, recent research is revealing that for this group the workplace may well be the most important source of learning.

Table 1.1: Growth of professionals and technicians in selected countries, 1980s-90s (%)

Country	1980s	1990s
Canada	15.6	32.8
United States	16.1	17.9
Peru	14.1	16.5
Chile	7.2	8.8
Japan	7.9	12.4
New Zealand	16.1	24.6
Korea, Rep.	4.0	14.0
Thailand	2.5	3.5
Philippines	6.0	6.0
Belgium	18.9	22.5
Norway	18.6	25.5
Spain	6.7	19.1
Egypt	10.1	16.7
Swaziland	9.4	12.9

Note: Adapted from the ILO *World Employment Report 1998-99*, table 7, p. 232.

Apart from professionals, the other groups who have traditionally experienced the workplace as a source of learning are the craft workers. In the past, craft workers in their initial years at work combined both off-the-job theoretical learning with on-the-job practical experience. Indeed, for many years the German dual system, which was the most highly developed form of apprenticeship system, was seen as the model to which all forms of training should aspire. However, with the increased speed of technological and economic change, especially the impact of ICT together with the introduction of new working practices, the apprenticeship system is now being subject to modifications. There is a growing body of opinion that it is no longer possible to provide all the necessary knowledge and skills on a one-off basis at the start of a person's career. The speed of technological change and the application of ICT to the workplace mean that this type of "front-loaded" learning experience is no longer sufficient on its own, even for this group. Given the speed of change, it is now seen as increasingly important that employees should continue to learn throughout their working life. As we shall see in Chapter 7, governments throughout the world are now introducing reforms to support the use of the workplace as a source of lifelong learning.

For those employees in semi-skilled and unskilled work in the manufacturing and service sectors, the situation has been very different. They have never experienced much in the way of either initial training or of formal work-based learning. This is not to say that they did not learn at work. Indeed, the textbooks are full of examples of workers who have learned to impose their own controls on the workplace, in spite of attempts by employers to control their behaviour. Studies dating back to the Hawthorne experiments (Roethlisberger and Dickson, 1939) have shown how workers developed their own norms of behaviour, either increasing or restricting output and controlling their working environment, sometimes at the expense of the economic efficiency of their organization (Roy, 1952). Apart from this informal activity, these jobs have short learning times and are characterized by few other opportunities for the acquisition of skills or personal development.

The introduction of HPWOs is now transforming these occupations. The use of ICT has provided the basis for more effective ways of sharing information and introducing devolved management. In addition, practices such as multi-skilling and use of self-managed work groups, all characteristics of HPWOs, have meant that in these organizations the workplace has become a source of continuous learning for all employees. In addition to any technical skills they acquire, workers have to use their intellectual faculties to tackle unexpected problems for which there is no immediate recourse to technical specialists. They have to resolve day-to-day production problems, they have to communicate solutions to colleagues and clients and they have to learn how to work effectively in teams. Unlike employees in more traditional organizations who can legitimately claim that any problem which affects their job and is outside the operation of their narrowly defined tasks is not their responsibility, this new breed of high performance worker has to take these and other problems and issues on board. It is the use of these practices which are making the workplace a crucial source of learning for all employees in modern organizations.

High performance work organizations and high performance working practices

Characteristics of HPWOs

HPWOs are relatively new; indeed, many managers and human resource practitioners are not familiar with the term. Even some of those who have introduced what we term here as high performance working practices would not have described the practices in these term.[1] In view of this, it is not surprising that there is some confusion in the public debate over the labelling of both the practices and the organizational forms in which they are embedded. In the late 1990s, the American Society for Training and Development (ASTD) used the term high performance work systems to refer to "…those organizations which organized workflow around key business processes and often create teams to carry out those processes" (Gephart and Van Buren, 1998). Also in the United States, the Center for Creative Leadership uses the term high performance work organizations (Kirkman et al., 1999), while the United Kingdom Chartered Institute of Personnel and Development refers to high performance working, emphasizing the outcome of such practices in generating a differentiated product or service (Stevens, 2000). Academics and consultants tend to be more confusing. Reviewing this literature, Wood (1999) traces the debate from the use of the term high commitment management by Walton in 1985 to high involvement management as popularized by Lawler in 1986 through to the current concept of high performance management or high performance organizations (Lawler et al., 1998). While this debate about terminology may seem confusing to the practitioner, it is of more than academic importance.

By and large, the authors are talking about the same things, but as Wood (1999) points out, talk of high performance management or high performance work systems implies that the link between the working practices and performance has been proved. However, some academics still doubt whether that link has been established, and when this is the case then they argue that it is more useful to talk of high involvement management practices (HIMPs). As is clear in our discussion of the evidence on this point later in this chapter, we believe that link has now been established, so we use the term high performance work organizations to refer to organizations which utilize high performance working practices in a systematic manner.[2]

After some initial confusion, there is now a growing consensus on what we mean by high performance working practices. What runs throughout all this literature is the concern on the part of employers with developing their labour force and making use of practices such as teamworking, job redesign, employee involvement in decision-making, extensive communication and performance-related pay to enhance organizational performance. However, we still do not have anything approaching unanimity. Pfeffer (1998) talks of seven practices of successful organizations: employment security, selective hiring, self-managed teams and decentralization of authority, comparatively high compensation, extensive training, minimal status distinctions and extensive sharing of financial and performance information. Pil and MacDuffie (2000), looking at the automobile industry worldwide, restrict their use to five key practices affecting work: "on-line" work teams, "off-line" employee involvement practices and problem-solving groups, job rotation, suggestion programmes, and the decentralization of quality efforts. These practices generally entail the despecialization of resources, the integration of conception with execution and a decentralization of information.

Guest (2000) reflects all these in the following 18 practices used in research into HPWOs in the United Kingdom.

High performance working practices (Guest, 2000)

1. Realistic job previews
2. Psychometric tests for selection
3. Well developed induction training
4. Provision of extensive training for experienced employees
5. Regular appraisals
6. Regular feedback on performance from many sources
7. Individual performance-related pay
8. Profit-related bonuses
9. Flexible job descriptions
10. Multi-skilling
11. Presence of work improvement teams
12. Presence of problem-solving groups
13. Information provided on the firm's business plan
14. Information provided on the firm's performance targets
15. No compulsory redundancies
16. Avoidance of voluntary redundancies
17. Commitment to single status
18. Harmonized holiday entitlement

Note: In recent research in the United States, Becker and Huselid (1998) have extended these to more than 30 practices.

We can move beyond the listing of practices and make more sense of them by thinking in terms of a series of four dimensions: employee autonomy and involvement in decision-making, support for employee performance, rewards for performance, and the sharing of information and knowledge. These four dimensions tend to be present in almost all the lists proposed in the literature. We explore the use that organizations make of these in later chapters. Here it is also important to note that these underlying dimensions are manifest in sets or bundles of practices.

The first dimension and associated practices refer to the structuring of opportunities for the exercise of employee skills, for example the use of self-managed work teams and multi-skilling which provide the employee with the opportunity to develop teamworking and decision-making skills, as well as a range of technical skills. The second refers to the use of practices designed to support continuous learning acquisition of skills, for example appraisal systems, mentoring and coaching and train-the-trainer provision. The third refers to the use of systems designed to reward performance and motivate the employee, namely individual and group-based performance pay. Finally, if the workers are to have the requisite knowledge to inform their decision-making and participation in the management of the work process, the organization must have systems in place to communicate this information to all employees and also to ensure that feedback from employees reaches those responsible for the organization's strategy. For the ASTD, these management practices come together in the form of a high performance work system which consists of " a particular configuration of working practices and processes with overlapping human resource policies and practices supported by communication, information system, technology system and measurement" (ASTD, 2000). The ASTD argument is that, when taken together, these create the conditions for much higher levels of performance than we have hitherto been able to achieve with previous management practices.

Essentially, these "new" working practices and the organizations in which they are embedded are perceived to have abandoned their Taylorist heritage. In this sense, they represent a new way of organizing production (Wood, 1999). The Taylorist or traditional way of organizing production was to rely on rigid command and control forms of organization with a highly specialized division of labour. These were characterized by numerous levels of authority, each precisely specified. Knowledge resided with senior managers and technical specialists, and workers were not expected to make any contribution beyond that prescribed by their job description. Workers' jobs were clearly demarcated, with tightly defined job descriptions, a restricted range of tasks to complete and with little or no discretion exercised by the worker (e.g. the bellboy in the hotel with a narrow range of tasks, the assembly-line workers with specific highly routinized tasks performed at a speed determined by the movement of the line, or the call centre telephonist with strict time limits governing the dialogue). Such jobs are learned in minutes rather than months or years, and there is no scope for the development of work-related skills. In the United States, Ichniowski and Shaw (1995) refer to these as "traditional" systems featuring narrow job classifications, no work teams, communication confined largely to grievance procedures, training only through on-the-job learning, and incentive pay-based output.

These characteristics of jobs in Tayloristic organizations are important because they have a profound impact on the personality of the worker. For four decades, Kohn and his associates have been researching the impact of work on the personalities of workers. Using longitudinal data, comparing the personalities of the same workers ten years apart, Kohn demonstrated that those who worked in jobs that were free from close supervision that involved complex operations and independent judgement, such as those of managers and professionals, had a lasting impact on the personality. In this case, those who could exercise self-direction at work became self-confident themselves and exhibited greater flexibility in handling ideas. Those in routinized jobs with little self-direction and subject to close supervision had lower levels of self-confidence, were more fatalistic, were more likely to experience psychological distress and were less flexible in dealing with ideas (Kohn and Schooler, 1983). In later work (Kohn and Slomczynski, 1990), the same results were found in both Poland and in the United States. Clearly the way we organize work has powerful effects on the personality.

The contrast between work in the traditional organization and that in the new HPWOs is just as dramatic. In the latter, the workplace is designed to facilitate the development of workers' skills and to tap into their emotional capital and tacit knowledge in order to enhance organizational performance. In addition to the technical skills acquired through multi-skilling, the need for ongoing problem-solving, communication and teamworking requires the continuous exercise of discretion and day-to-day learning. Here we are starting to create the kind of work or work environment which can lead to the development of self-confidence and the flexibility to handle ideas that Kohn speaks of. With the spread of these organizations, we are starting to see the prospect of lifelong learning becoming a reality for a substantial part of the labour force that has hitherto been denied these opportunities. This is an issue we explore further in Chapter 4.

Reasons for the growth of HPWOs

If these HPWOs do represent new ways of organizing production, why should they suddenly appear at this point in time? What are the factors that are responsible for their growth? The somewhat glib answer is globalization, the spread of new technologies and the intensification of competition in world markets.[3] At its most elementary level, the economists' use of the term globalization refers to the increased mobility or flow of goods and factors of production, especially capital and professional labour between countries. However, for this to occur, a number of other non-economic changes have to have taken place. At the political level, following the Second World War new countries opened their economies to world markets. First, the Latin American and later the high-performing economies of East Asia made a significant impact on European and US markets. In the case of the East Asian economies, these initially provided a new source of cheap goods for the American and European consumers. Later, they moved up the value-added chain and were replaced by the second-generation newly industrializing countries (e.g. Thailand and Indonesia) as the main providers of cheap goods. With the end of the cold war, China and, to a lesser extent, the Russian Federation entered world markets as major players, again operating mainly at the lower end of the product market but with abundant supplies of low-cost labour. Thus, not only are there more countries competing, but also those countries are increasingly opening up their own markets to international capital, a process in part spearheaded by international agencies such as the International Monetary Fund and the World Bank. In addition, changes in international regulations, especially the deregulation which is taking place in areas such as telecommunications, information and financial services, have further opened up markets and intensified competition. This has been aided by improvements in information and communications technology, of which the Web is but the latest example.

Associated with the opening up and growth of these new markets has been the spread of multinational corporations (MNCs). Again, aided by the new information and communication technologies, these provide one of the means whereby capital and productive capacity can be rapidly transferred from one country to another. It should therefore be no surprise that MNCs provide one of the main means by which new forms of management are also spread across the globe. This has certainly been the case with the introduction of HPWPs, with multinational organizations such as Procter and Gamble introducing HPWPs in all its subsidiaries, including those in China. Research findings from the OECD (1999) and the United Kingdom (Cully et al., 1999) also suggest that it is the MNCs which are more likely to be introducing HPWPs into their subsidiaries than indigenous companies. However, as our case studies show, this is not the only means by which these practices can be spread. In many cases, they appear in indigenous enterprises which are striving to enhance performance.

While the intensification of competition associated with globalization may have been a necessary condition for the spread of HPWPs in organizations, it is not sufficient in itself. We still have to explain why this particular combination of practices came into being and not others. Why could companies not continue with the use of Taylorist techniques to intensify production and achieve higher levels of productivity? Why did they develop these new high performance working practices?

In chronological terms, it was the Japanese companies which first introduced the new working practices on a wide scale. Although many of the techniques they adopted originated from western ideas such as Deming's on total quality management, they were only fully developed by Japanese companies after the Second World War. With their highly skilled labour forces tied to the company with an assurance of lifetime employment, companies used just-in-time inventory systems and innovative quality control systems to raise the levels of productivity of labour beyond that of their American and European competitors. This sent shock waves through established western manufacturers. The 1980s then witnessed initial benchmarking activities by US corporations anxious to establish the basis of the Japanese competitive advantage. This led some, such as Womack, Jones and Roos (1990), to advocate that the Japanese model of lean production should be applied to all industries.

Out of this flurry of activity came a concern with new techniques to improve quality in the form of quality circles and total quality management (TQM). These blossomed in the United States and the United Kingdom in the 1980s. However, there remain many instances where attempts to introduce quality circles and TQM failed (Kirkman et al., 1999; Hill, 1991; Hill and Wilkinson, 1995). At the same time, some US companies such as IBM, Cummins Engines and Texas Instruments were developing what is sometimes referred to as the US human resource model. This draws on organizational psychology to build incentive programmes and improve communication, providing the basis for what later became known as performance management (Applebaum and Batt, 1994).

While companies were experimenting with these and other techniques such as re-engineering to improve productivity, the increasing intensity of competition was leading to the shedding of labour – downsizing or rightsizing, as it is sometimes euphemistically called. This was sometimes done through a process of delayering as firms sought to reduce the number of management levels and shed labour to stay in business. In the 1990s, this was given further impetus with the advent of "shareholder capitalism" as companies in the Anglo-Saxon world were obliged to ensure maximum short-term returns to shareholders. This placed pressures on managers to reduce costs and cut their use of labour, which further intensified the delayering and downsizing as layers of management were eradicated and workers laid off, leaving the remainder facing an intensification of work. The result was a period of massive delayering of organizations to make them leaner and in the process to introduce "flat" hierarchies. This was a painful process of change in many western societies, as economic and labour market restructuring took place with some employees displaced and others rewarded with higher wages (Froud et al., 2000).

One consequence of this reduction in the headcount and associated delayering was that responsibilities tended to get pushed down the line. As there were fewer employees left to perform the same amount of work, multi-skilling was encouraged and work teams became the obvious source of decision-making. If the teams were capable of organizing the production process, then that eradicated another layer of management. The intellectual justification for this came from a number of sources. First, the Japanese had used the work group as a source of input into the decision-making process (Dore, 1973) while the British through the work of the Tavistock Institute in London had experimented with the use of self-managed work teams (Kelly, 1978). Meanwhile the Swedes were also using self-managed work teams in Volvo's Uddevalla plant.

At the same time, there was growing interest in quality of working life programmes (Krahn and Lowe, 1993) followed by interest in the use of employee involvement schemes (Sisson, 1997). The latter were being used by companies to increase the participation of their employees in the organization of their work. As the production and service workers had the most detailed knowledge of the work process, it made sense to try to utilize this uncodified and often intuitive or tacit knowledge in pursuit of performance improvements. After all, the Japanese had been doing this for decades through their skill formation system (Koike and Inoki, 1990; Koike, 2000) while the Germans had achieved similar results through their Works' Councils and the tripartite governance of the apprenticeship programme (Streeck, 1989).

The result of these various initiatives and trends was the gradual adoption of some of these practices by an increasing number of companies in an attempt to remain competitive. This process of adoption was also aided by the spread of information and communications technology as computer and telecommunications technologies merged. Reduced transaction costs transformed the handling of data and the transmission of knowledge. The resultant transformation was evident first in manufacturing, as computers were used to control the manufacturing process, but later in the financial and business services sector and also in retailing and tourism. The speed with which information could be processed and transmitted facilitated the delayering of organizations and the pushing down of responsibility to the lower levels, as the requisite knowledge and information required for decision-making could be made instantly accessible. All this has enabled companies to respond to market changes by introducing more highly differentiated goods and services with shorter product life cycle times and to react more rapidly to changes in customer preferences. We can see the evidence for this in the vast increase in the range of models of automobiles that are available to customers and in the service sector the range of services now provided by the banks. These changes have in turn created the conditions under which management has to rely more and more on the tacit knowledge of the workers to secure a competitive advantage.

When it came to the introduction of these new management practices, they were often implemented in an ad-hoc fashion as a once-and-for-all solution to management's problems and equally often discarded at the first hurdle. This was a process which led many in management to perceive such techniques as management "fads" of no lasting significance. However, for those companies which persevered, the use of bundles of these practices were starting to produce results. In individual firms, levels of productivity were achieved which were comparable to and sometimes surpassed those of the Japanese and the Germans (Wickens, 1999). Together these practices came to form the basis for high performance work systems. Thus in the year 2000, the ASTD State of the Industry Report (McMurrer et al., 2000) identified the three most widely used practices in the United States designed to increase performance as: task forces, problem-solving teams or quality circles; job rotation or cross training; and employee access to key business information. This ad-hoc and incremental growth of HPWPs helps explain why there is no universally accepted definition of what constitutes a high performance organization. The extent to which these practices are embedded in organizations across the globe is an issue we discuss in Chapter 6.

Why are HPWOs important?

We have already argued that HPWOs are important because they provide more efficient ways of organizing human labour as well as offering the prospect of extending learning opportunities to all their employees. We now examine the proposition that they also deliver higher levels of productivity and profitability. Earlier we showed how some academics were inclined to use the term "high involvement organizations" because they were sceptical of the link with productivity and profitability. However, as we show below, recent research has confirmed such a link. There is now evidence of a robust link between HPWPs, productivity and profitability and a range of other performance measures. Unlike some of the individual techniques that now comprise the range of high performance working practices, HPWOs are clearly not a one-off management fad but signify underlying changes in the ways in which we organize production. In the light of the evidence presented below, we argue that HPWOs are here to stay for the foreseeable future. We put forward a number of reasons to substantiate this claim.

First and foremost, stringent scientific research has now established a strong link between the use of these human resource practices and enhanced performance across a range of indicators, but especially in productivity and, crucially, profitability. Put plainly, investment in these practices and the skills associated with them pays off on the bottom line. Over the last decade, we have had a number of studies which independently report the use of these new "innovative" working practices being linked to improved performance. What is even more interesting is that while these studies were conducted in different countries, the results all pointed in the same direction. In the United States, these include studies by Kling (1995), Ichniowski et al. (1997), Becker and Huselid (1998) and Applebaum et al. (2000) to name just a few, which established this link between HPWPs and organizational performance. Similar findings were produced in the United Kingdom by Patterson et al. (1997) and Wood (2001), where the same link was established, while in Canada the work of Betcherman et al. (1997), in Taiwan, China the work of Tung-Chun Huang (1997) and in New Zealand the work of Guthrie (2001) also reached similar conclusions. It suggests that these new working practices are embedded in organizations throughout the world and are producing the same or similar results. This is a conclusion reinforced by MacDuffie's (1995) study of 57 auto assembly plants in a number of countries, including the United States, Japan, Australia, Korea, Mexico, Brazil and some in Europe, where once again the same relationships were noted. This would imply that what we are observing is a real change in the organization of production, one that is producing significant and lasting results which represent a step change in the productivity of human labour.

Not only were the same findings coming from studies in and between different countries; they were also coming from studies using different methodologies. If they had all been using the same methodology, there is always the fear that the results were an artefact of the method. For example, if they had all relied for their measures of company performance on the replies from managers on how well their companies had done compared with others, then it could be argued that managers would tend to paint a rosy picture of their own enterprise's performance. This is because they are responsible for them - "They would say that, wouldn't they?". However, as some studies have used hard measures of performance, derived from published data on the companies' results as well as stock market valuations (Ichniowski et al., 2000), this suggests that the links are more than the product of the managers' imagination.

If they had all been studies of single firms, such as Ichniowski's (1992) study of a paper mill, or even single industries such as the Berg et al. (2000) study of the apparel industry or the Ichniowski et al. (1997) study of the steel industry, there would also have been doubt about the extent to which these findings were generalizable. However, not only were the results of studies in different industries throwing up similar results, cross-sectional studies which examined the relationship between innovative HPWPs and performance across a range of industry sectors were also producing the same results: for example, Huselid (1995), Ichniowski (1990), Ichniowski and Shaw (1995), Huselid and Becker (2000) in the United States and Betcherman (1997) in Canada. In the United Kingdom, similar results were emerging from Wood's (2001) analysis of the large Workplace Employee Relations Survey. The researchers found the same relationship between the use of HIWPs/HPWPs and performance in both the public and private sectors. A similar relationship was also established for small and medium-sized enterprises (SMEs) in the United Kingdom. There, Cosh et al. (2000) found a correlation between human resource management (HRM) practices such as consistent investment in training, total quality management, quality circles, job rotation and performance-related pay and employment growth.

Finally, given all this evidence, it could still be argued that what we are witnessing is a correlation, a link between the use of these practices and higher levels of performance, but this does not necessarily tell us anything about the direction of causation. It could be that these companies were all producing good financial results and therefore had the extra resources necessary to invest in these "expensive" human resource practices. Hence, the practices could be a result of the prior performance. This is a perennial problem with social science research based on cross-sectional data. However, we now have a number of studies in different countries which have used a longitudinal methodology; they have followed the same firms through time and been able to observe the effect of the implementation of these practices on the performance of the organizations. In the United Kingdom, Patterson et al.(1997) followed through 60 manufacturing companies and found that it was the implementation of HPWPS that produced the improvements in performance, not vice versa. Ichniowski et al. (1997) also found that the implementation of the practices was followed by financial and productivity improvements in the United States. What these longitudinal studies also suggest is that there is a "lagged effect"; the practices once implemented take time to produce an improvement in productivity, profitability and long-term stock market valuation (Huselid and Becker, 2000).

The other finding which appears equally robust is that these performance improvements only come from the implementation of bundles of practices. The use of individual practices such as work teams or quality circles is not enough in itself to produce sustained performance improvement. Katz, Kochan and Keefe (1987) report that plants which changed traditional job classifications into teams without changing other practices performed worse than those which had not made such changes. Inchiowski and Shaw (1995) also found that the use of single working practices did not improve productivity and was sometimes associated with a decline. Similar findings were reported by Wood (2001) for the United Kingdom. This is an important point, precisely because previous innovations had tended to focus on individual practices such as quality circles or total quality management. The practical lesson is that these practices work most effectively when they are implemented as mutually reinforcing "bundles" of practices - what the aforementioned ASTD report refers to as a high performance work system. Applebaum et al. (2000) argue that these practices cluster around certain areas such as worker participation in decision-making, enhanced workforce skills and incentive systems. For example, the introduction of self-managed teams requires that team performance is rewarded through some form of group-based performance pay, while company information must also be made available to the team and training provided for the new skills. The one set of practices needs to reinforce the effect of the other, and all need to be focused on performance. Earlier in this chapter, we identified four such bundles, each of which is associated with an underlying dimension of the learning process. The first referred to the autonomy to practice and exercise skills, the second to the support required for the continuous development of skills, the third to the rewarding of skills and the fourth to the information and knowledge required to underpin the successful execution of skills. These four dimensions will be used to structure the discussion in Chapters 4, 5 and 6.

As for the magnitude of the effect of these practices on productivity and profits, these can be substantial. In the United Kingdom, Patterson et al. (1997) identified two dimensions of HRM which are systematically linked to improved performance, namely the "acquisition and development of employee skills" and "job design". These account for 19 per cent of the variation between companies in the change in profitability and 18 per cent of the variation between companies in the change in productivity, both of which are statistically significant findings. Job design and the development of skills are the most significant predictors of change in both profitability and productivity.

In the United States, Huselid's 1993 survey found "support for the hypothesis that an HPWS will have a positive effect on multiple measures of firm performance". Using the one-standard deviation shift in HRM practices as a benchmark, the implied economic effects were increases in sales/employee of more than $27,000 and market value/employee of more than $18,000 (Becker and Huselid, 1998:72). Their latest research indicated that there is a lagged effect on both the market value and accounting profits, but it is greater for the gross rate of return on assets. The 1994 survey used a broader range of HRM practices (more on compensation, strategy and implementation) and again found that one standard deviation in the index is associated with a 11-13 per cent range in market value per employee. The 1996 survey had 24 items, but again there was the same impact on profits: "one standard deviation higher value on the high performance work system (HPWS) measure has 24 per cent higher market value of shareholder equity and 25 per cent higher accounting profits in 1995" (Becker and Huselid, 1998:81). In their comparison of plants with one specific steel-making production process, Ichniowski and Shaw (1995) also came up with large effects, estimating that production lines with a full complement of innovative practices are about 7 per cent more productive than those with traditional practices, a productivity difference which corresponded to annual revenues of $2.5 million for one production area (Ichniowsli et al., 2000).[4]

What benefits do employees derive from these practices?

While there are clear benefits to employers who use these practices, the next question must be whether there are similar benefits to employees. Here again we have some solid evidence; Patterson et al. (1997) reported a link between the use of these practices and higher levels of job satisfaction. Applebaum et al. (2000) found that having autonomy over task-level decision-making, membership of self-directed production and off-liner teams, and communication with people outside the work group are associated with workers trusting their managers more and experiencing intrinsic rewards. Trust and intrinsic rewards in turn have a strong positive impact on organizational commitment and job satisfaction. What is more surprising, in view of earlier suggestions that HPWPs are linked to work intensification and enhanced stress levels, is that Applebaum et al. could not find any evidence to support these negative effects. They found no negative effects on work-related stress; nor is the use of techniques such as worker participation linked to a speed-up of work. In the United Kingdom, Wood et al. (2001) found that work intensification as perceived by employees is not related to the use of HPWPs and improved performance. In short, the improvements in performance are not achieved at the expense of workers working harder.

In the area of earnings, evidence is starting to mount of a clear link between involvement in HPWOs and earnings. In general, workers involved in high performance work systems earn more. The OECD (1999) found evidence of a link between some high performance working practices and earnings in Australia and the United States. Cappelli (1996, 1998) found that in the United States the presence of a TQM programme is associated with higher salaries for some employees, as is the involvement in self-managed work teams. Osterman (1998) was unable to identify a clear link between high performance work organizations and earnings.

However, Applebaum et al. (2000) found an unambiguous link between involvement in high performance practices and earnings. After controlling for personal characteristics such as race, education, and gender, among others, they found that workers in the apparel and steel companies who are involved in high performance working practices still earn more. However, the effect is not as strong in the medical electronics instrument companies they studied.[5]

Another benefit for employees is higher levels of skills. Numerous studies have found higher levels of training in establishments with HPWPs, for example Osterman (1995), Lynch and Black (1998) and OECD (1999). As one would expect, this higher level of training tends to produce higher levels of skills among the workforce. Cappelli and Rogobsky (1994) and Cappelli (1996) report higher levels of skills in HPWOs, while Felstead and Ashton (2000) found that workers in HPWOs in the United Kingdom report higher levels of the "new" skills in information technology, problem solving, communication and teamworking. Moreover, these skills are higher for all employees, even among the relatively "unskilled". Similar findings have emerged from more detailed studies based on direct observation of employees in the United States. Thus, Stasz (1998) found that where these practices are used throughout the organization employees not only have more technical skills, but they also develop the skills required to work with others, to communicate effectively with others and make problem-solving decisions either themselves or in collaboration with others. These are precisely the work conditions which Kohn and Schooler (1983) revealed as having beneficial impacts on the personality, facilitating a growth in self-confidence. These jobs provide the opportunity to stretch the employees' intellectual development and therefore offer more opportunity for long-term personal development.

These are all very positive outcomes for the workers, but because the workers' experience has not been studied as intensively as the impact on organizational performance we cannot have the same degree of confidence in these results in all instances. For example, we only have data from the United States on the impact of these practices on work-related stress and earnings (Applebaum et al., 2000). Ideally we need these findings to be replicated in other societies to provide the same degree of confidence in them that we have for the organizational performance outcomes. Nevertheless, these remain important and very solid findings.

Conclusions

In this chapter, we have examined the reasons for the growing importance of HPWPs and the benefits they have produced for companies and employees. However, we must close this section with some words of caution. First, most of the work on HPWOs has been done on firms in the private sector and, within that, more specifically in the manufacturing sector. As manufacturing employment is declining as a source of employment, this is an important consideration. In the next chapter, which deals with the case studies of HPWOs, we attempt to counter this by concentrating more on the service sector. The other area which large-scale studies of HPWOs has neglected is of course the public sector, where there are no hard measures of success in terms of profitability, although equally hard measures are available of productivity and employee and customer satisfaction.

A second important limitation of current research is that it is almost invariably concerned with companies in the older industrial economies. Even within that group, the Anglo-Saxon economies of the United States and the United Kingdom are over-represented. In order to counter this, we have deliberately taken many of our case studies from the East Asian societies and the developing economies. A third limitation is that these large-scale studies have also tended to focus on larger organizations, and so we have sought to include a number of SMEs in the case studies.

Finally, we would remind the reader that while we have focused on the contribution HRD can make to profitability and employee satisfaction, we would point out that the success of companies depends on factors other than HRD. These include a range of factors such as business and product market strategy and research and development expenditure. As Lloyd (2000), Keep and Coleman (2001) among others have argued, we must not forget that broader issues such as mergers and acquisitions, economies of scale, relationships with government and politics are also major determinants of business success: within this overall configuration, HRD strategy is just one factor. However, as the evidence documented here shows, it is an important factor.

Notes

[1] During the field work for this book, some of the organizations we visited as exemplars of high performance work organizations were not seen by the senior executives as high performance organizations; rather, the executives saw themselves as merely implementing good human resource management practices.

[2] The ASTD uses the term "high performance work systems" to refer to those organizations which have introduced these practices across a range of dimensions in a systematic manner. These are distinguished from those organizations which have only introduced high performance work practices in a limited manner, perhaps only in one area such as work design or rewards.

[3] The academic literature contains an extensive debate on the concept of globalization, with each discipline adopting its own definition of the concept. Here we are using it to refer to the intensification of competition between companies which have been associated with the opening up of world markets. We make no assumptions that this is leading to a convergence of institutions or to the death of the nation state or to the establishment of a single market. Here we are speaking of a process of change in the direction of more open markets, the reduction of trade barriers and the increasing mobility of capital between countries. This is not to deny the existence of centrifugal forces. We fully recognize that existing trade relations are still largely within the triad bloc of North America, the European Union and Japan (Rugman, 2000).

[4] The complexities of the impact of HPWPs on performance are dealt with in greater depth in Chapter 3.

[5] Some earlier studies have found a relationship; others have not. Some of the ambiguity in these findings may be explained by the fact that as Applebaum et al. (2000, p. 211) point out, earlier studies related a measure of average wage for the firm or establishment to data on average characteristics of the organization. Their data, by contrast, matched the earnings of individuals to individual characteristics, including whether they work in HPWOs.

CHAPTER 2

CHARACTERISTICS OF HIGH PERFORMANCE WORK ORGANIZATIONS

Introduction

The purpose of this chapter is to further our knowledge of HPWOs through the use of case studies to explore the nature of these organizations and the practices which characterize them. We also seek to identify the form taken by the various bundles of practices. This will enable us to examine whether these practices vary systematically between companies and industries.

In the last chapter, we established what quantitative research has identified as the salient characteristics of HPWOs. These include more complex job design, devolution of responsibility, use of teamworking, mechanisms to ensure employee access to key business information and forms of compensation which link rewards to performance. We now move beyond this and explore how these practices manifest themselves in specific organizations and how they were introduced. Here we face a new set of questions and issues. Does teamworking perform the same functions in all organizations, or is it more important in some rather than others? How do companies go about introducing teams? Does performance-related pay take the same form in all organizations, or do some organizations rely on it more than others? Does the compensation always take the form of wage or salary payments, or are there other means of rewarding performance in relation to business objectives? In short, what do these practices look like when they are implemented?

In addition to these questions, there are a series of others which these quantitative studies have not been able to explore. Are the practices the same across all industries? Are they applicable in the service sector and especially in the public sector where performance cannot be so easily measured in terms of profitability? Do these practices apply equally to small and medium-sized organizations, or are they only to be found in large organizations with specialized HR departments? What is the link with technology? Are these practices only found in organizations which have introduced new technology? If we are talking about bundles, are the basic bundles we identified above always found together, or are some bundles more applicable to some industries than to others? Does the introduction of HPWPs always involve delayering?

Are there other characteristics of high performance work organizations which the methodologies employed by these studies have missed?

To provide some tentative answers to these questions, we use a series of case studies. These have been primarily drawn from research sponsored by the ILO in association with the International Federation of Training and Development Organizations (IFTDO). Full details of these are available on the ILO website. The studies were designed to cover the service sector as well as the manufacturing sector and within the service sector to include studies of public as well as private organizations. They were also designed to include organizations from developing countries.

To tackle these questions, we have divided this chapter into three main sections. The first examines these questions in relation to the manufacturing sector, the second deals with the service sector and the third with the public sector.

High performance working in the manufacturing sector

Thorn Lighting, Ltd.

Perhaps the best way of understanding these practices is to look at a medium-sized company which operates in a global market and which introduced them over the last decade. The company in question is Thorn Lighting, Ltd. in the United Kingdom. In order to survive in a very competitive market, the company had to undergo radical change. It shifted its emphasis from a command and control functional structure to one where the employees were empowered to take ownership of the work process, thereby enhancing the quality of the output and guaranteeing a continuing focus on the requirements of the customer. The result was a doubling of market share, but it took considerable ingenuity and effort to change the culture of the company with leadership coming from the head of the human resource management function operating in partnership with the managing director.

Building trust

This was a company on an old industrial site. The introduction of HPWPs was part of an attempt to focus more effectively on the requirements of the customer and product excellence. To this end, the company determined to introduce new technology and more flexible working practices. Effectively this meant transforming the culture of the organization - all this against a background of mistrust between the union and the company. The main tools for this transformation were the building of trust with the workforce, the introduction of new technologies and associated working practices, especially teamworking, and the creation of open channels for the flow of business information and knowledge. It also meant realigning rewards with business performance. The following is a brief account of how this was done.

The plant where this case study was conducted employs just over 1,000 in the north of England. In the eyes of the company, product and quality, technology and innovation, and global capabilities were the three main driving factors behind the innovations implemented.

This emphasis on technological innovation is reflected in the fact that approximately 40 per cent of group sales are generated from products introduced in the last three years.

The immediate trigger for the introduction of HPWPs was a management buyout. The company faced a difficult market situation, and productivity had to be improved if it was to stay in business. This meant accelerating the pace of change, including the introduction of cellular-based manufacturing technology and new working practices. For the vast majority of the workforce, this involved a radical change as teamworking and multi-skilling was introduced across the whole business. The employees all had to acquire new skills and adjust to new relationships as they moved toward more flexible working practices and self-managed teams.

The building of trust was, from the outset, seen as a crucial basis for the free flow of information within the organization. To this end, the company set out to transform its relationship with the trade union. To start this process, senior management opened the books to the unions and introduced a "Partners in Change" programme. This involved holding regular management and union workshops. In addition, the union and senior management now meet annually for a business review and planning workshop. The company provides the trade unions with details of performance, market conditions and the forthcoming strategy for the year. This provides the basis for the development of a joint action plan to enable the trade unions to play a positive role in the business. One measure of the impact of this change is that the annual wage negotiations have been reduced from eight months to less than one month.

Work design

The introduction in the early 1990s of cellular-based manufacturing on the shop floor allowed for better management of the product range. The layout within the factories was changed so that all operations relating to a product could be done in one area. A cell has anything between 20 and 200 employees, depending on the product, with larger cells divided into smaller teams. Associated with this was the devolution of authority to teams. As team leaders were developed as supervisory or first-line managers, the company was able to reduce the number of management levels. Here self-managed work teams and delayering went hand in hand.

Teams now typically have up to 20 members and are led by a working team leader. The team members are multi-skilled operators and carry out their own maintenance. To a large degree, operators rotate around jobs, although not every team member is able to complete every task. One operator is typically competent in three jobs. Team leaders may be working day to day with the team or may have a wider planning role, depending on the product. The payment system was realigned and simplified to support teamworking.

As teams were introduced and employees started making decisions about their own work processes, it was essential that they were fully informed about all facets of the business. To facilitate this, the company diverted resources from an "outdoor" team-building exercise for managers to create an internal programme for all employees through which they participated in simulated business activities. The "UK Team Building" business awareness programme, as it was called, exposed employees to all of the main functions of the business to give them a rounded view. This was a two-day programme, which ran every two weeks for14 people at a time, over a four-and-a-half year time span. This awareness is reinforced by business awareness sessions that cover every aspect from cash flow to material inflation and the state of the market place. In addition, line managers provide monthly team briefings for their staff. This ensures that information cascades down through the tiers of teams and thus throughout the organization as a whole. In this way, consistent information is cascaded through the business to shop-floor level. The pursuit of an open and transparent style of leadership is seen as a never-ending process.

The line managers played a crucial role in this transformation. The initial team-building programme was facilitated by line managers who were perceived as role models for the new ways of working. They were invited to make presentations on the functional role of their departments and the external market place during the business awareness programme. This helped emphasize the fact that the line manager is in the leadership role for the development of employees. For this, they had the support of the human resource function. This key supporting role was to design, develop and facilitate innovative practices, as well as to develop the line managers themselves. The head of the HR function sees his role as aligning HR with business objectives.

Sharing information

The upward flow of information is facilitated through the use of confidential attitude surveys amongst employees. They are conducted regularly and thereby help managers understand the employees' perspective. Finally, team leaders across three shifts have a "shift hand-over" to help maintain communication and continuity of production. As for feedback on individual performance, this is provided through appraisals that are conducted with employees to develop their skills, knowledge and awareness of the business. Appraisals also serve to review employee performance as individual members of their own team and of the broader UK "team".

Supporting learning

Sustaining these practices requires a significant training input. Line operators undergo a basic assessment and are given skills in teamworking. Team leaders have a three-day course that also covers management skills. Potential leaders are assessed not only on their technical skills but also on their interpersonal and team-leading abilities. In addition to the training programme for all employees which is provided to ensure they understand the teamworking concept, there is also in-house training for multi-skilled line operators. Team leaders receive further training, especially in team skills, which includes leading meetings and managing people. However, individual training is sometimes difficult to coordinate in areas working a three-shift system. Training sessions are also held for the team as a whole.

Rewarding performance

Rewards in the form of wage increases are, as we have seen, collectively negotiated. However, the company does not have a bonus scheme based upon team or individual performance. Senior managers feel that team reward actually detracts from teamwork. This is because it leads to competition between teams who can become preoccupied with their own performance rather than concentrating on working with other teams for the achievement of the overall organizational objectives. It is also argued that teamworking does not take place in a vacuum and that other factors influence whether a team is able to reach its target or not. However, team performance can be recognized in other ways. Teams receive individual badges and certificates for quality, while managers also publicize team achievements in the company magazine. When Thorn wins awards, for example on training or environmental improvements, line operators and supervisors often represent it at the awards ceremony.

As we have seen, the rewards for the company have been enhanced performance and a larger market share. For the employees, the result has been more satisfying work and crucially, in an area of high unemployment, job security.

South African Breweries, plc.

We now turn to a large multinational company (MNC), South African Breweries (SAB), the fourth largest manufacturer of alcoholic beverages in the world. Like Thorn, SAB has progressively introduced HPWPs over the last decade but on a much larger scale. Here again, the introduction of teamworking plays a crucial role, although there has not been the same transformation of the technological base witnessed at Thorn. However, the use of the new working practices at SAB did involve substantial downsizing as the company strove to place itself at the leading edge of world markets.

What the case study illustrates is the progressive implementation of these practices in the four areas identified in Chapter 1. Here we are looking at the way in which the company introduced employee involvement through teamworking and multi-skilling. It provides support for employee performance through systematic feedback via appraisals and extensive training. It also carries out an extensive programme of change aimed at creating a common culture in which the two-way flow of information is central. Finally, it sets about rewarding performance through pay and other techniques.

SAB is listed in London as a FTSE 100 organization with beer, beverage, hotel, and gaming interests that span 21 countries across Africa, Asia and Europe. This case study focuses on the SAB operation in South Africa, which is the largest single country operation and the original basis from which the international interests have grown.

One of the key features of the SAB experience was that the end of apartheid meant that South Africa was exposed to the full weight of international competition. The entry of the South African market into the world market meant abandoning the protectionist policies that had previously characterized the economy. For SAB this meant that it had to act rapidly and effectively to bring its costs into line with that of its international competitors.

This meant downsizing and redundancies. It was also the occasion for the introduction of HPWPs.

The task facing the company was made even more complex because of its size. Conservatively, the up-and-downstream impact of SAB's operations translates into responsibility for approximately 400,000 jobs, the majority of these being in black-owned retail and on-premise outlets. Given its size and dominance in the home market, it also had to be seen to be acting in a socially responsible manner, especially in its handling of equity issues. Economically, it faced and still faces a sluggish home market, an acute shortage of skills and a national labour force potentially devastated by the impact of HIV/AIDS.

Over the last decade, the company has introduced a number of key changes which involved the use of HPWPs, starting in 1990 with what it termed the Integrated Management Process (IMP). This was to initiate changes in the realm of business planning, communication and performance management. Compared with the process of change in Thorn, that in SAB was much more highly structured from the beginning, as would be expected in such a large organization. Here we can only deal with aspects of it.

Building trust

Like Thorn, SAB realized that it had to build the trust of its workforce, a task made all the more difficult following the use of institutionalized racism in the form of apartheid. The implementation of the IMP was therefore initiated with an exceptionally inclusive process of value sharing, during which approximately 6,000 employees from all organizational levels participated in facilitated workshops. These workshops encouraged open discussion about the history of South Africa, the damaging effects of apartheid, and the important role of shared values in creating a sense of community. The result was the definition and publication of ten values ranging from customer service participation to empowerment. This formed the backdrop to the sharing of information necessary for the effective implementation of the other HPWPs.

Having ensured that the employees "bought in" to the change, the objectives of the IMP were to: cascade the business goals throughout the organization; ensure an objective process of performance management for teams and individuals; and drive appropriate levels of participation and interdependence in the organization. Each of these areas of change was treated in a very systematic manner. Taking first the business goal, this was to be in the top five brewers in the world by the year 2004. This goal was to be achieved through systemic change involving the three key success factors in which the company invests, namely growth, people and corporate reputation or image. These were operationalized through four core strategies: marketing, manufacturing, sales and distribution, and managing the environment.

Sharing information

Improvements in the area of communication and information sharing were achieved in two ways. The first was through ensuring effective top-down communication about the "big picture", i.e. strategy, progress against strategy, global acquisitions, etc. The second way was by ensuring effective bottom-up communication about delivery against strategically aligned goals, concerns, suggestions, etc. Teams were used to facilitate this communication process. In addition, a vast number of communication tools were and still are used, e.g. newsletters, newsflashes, regional visits by directors, feedback sessions, and normal team meetings across the regional team tiers.

The other area of change, performance management, was the means whereby the strategy was translated into team and individual goals across all levels. These goals are informally reviewed in monthly one-to-one meetings between managers, as well as in team meetings. Biannual formal performance reviews also take place for individuals and teams. For the IMP to be an effective culture driver, it was important to stress the spirit of performance management (i.e. it is not a paper-driven mechanistic process). As part of performance management, a set of desired management and self-management practices was also introduced; among others, these encouraged managers to practice participative goal setting and provide development opportunities. Team members were also encouraged to set and obtain ongoing agreement to performance goals and develop themselves. In addition, an IMP survey was developed to obtain feedback from employees on the application of IMP in their areas. These surveys were conducted on an annual basis from 1993 to 1998. The communication of survey feedback resulted in regional IMP renewal plans, which again were aligned with team and individual goals.

Securing union commitment

As was the case with Thorn, another crucial element of change was in the relations with the trade unions. Here, SAB and the Food and Allied Workers' Union (FAWU) have committed tremendous time and resources to build strong relationships. Following the communication of the Manufacturing Strategy in 1992-93, the parties undertook a joint World Class Manufacturing (WCM) study tour, which included visits to Volkswagen in Germany, Miller Trenton in the United States, the Coke Wakefield plant in the United Kingdom, etc. One of the functions of these trips was to generate a common understanding and appreciation between management and workers of the problems facing the organization and the kind of steps that have to be taken to rectify them.

Work design

A joint manufacturing task force then carried out an analysis on the impact of WCM on the organization. The task force functioned within the assumption that WCM itself is not negotiable, but that the manner of its implementation is. This meant downsizing. The team then explored the implications of greater workforce flexibility, the need for higher skill levels, the impact of multi-skilling on manning levels, etc. Following this work, a joint visit to the ILO in Geneva took place to prepare for the establishment of a project entitled Project Noah. Noah provided a support structure for those SAB employees who were made redundant and who were encouraged to establish their own businesses.

Keeping the system going – constant change

No one programme, no matter how well conceived, is sufficient to ensure the effective operation of HPWPs. Therefore, over the last nine-year period, there has been a constant struggle to align structures with strategies; after all, this is an ongoing process. This first attempt in 1992-93 was called Best Operating Practice (BOP1) and involved the introduction of team-based structures in manufacturing. It meant redesigning work, the establishment of work teams, shop-floor problem solving, and the introduction of performance measures, all supported by the use of new technology to streamline the administration. This resulted in the establishment of a four-tier team structure: the regional executive team, the departmental management team, the unit/section team, and the shift team. At the same time (1993), the human resource management function was restructured to ensure that line managers were directly accountable for all aspects of people management. The role of the departmental HR specialist and training specialist was transformed to provide professional support to the line manager.

In 1995 there was a further realignment of structure and strategy with the decision to "outsource" the driving of distribution trucks to SAB employees. This was done through a structured process, so that in excess of 50 per cent of SAB's distribution is currently conducted through its owner-driver network.

The second phase in the attempt to align structures with strategy, BOP2, involved revised team-based structures in packaging. This took place from 1997 onwards and was focused on enhancing the skills of the team members. Following a pilot project, the basic-level 1 team now consists of four "building block" positions, designed on the assumption that maintenance is the core competence in packaging and that product quality is key. Therefore, each team now plays four key roles, each with its own outputs, qualifications and attributes. The four key roles are team leader, process artisan, process operator and BOP operator. All roles require appropriate technical skills, team skills and problem-solving skills. These teams are now fully self-sufficient in that there is no external support for them in the form of artisans or quality-control technicians. The teams are autonomous and equipped for the full range of their outputs.

Equity as a priority

One other area where SAB has been very active in creating change concerns the issue of equity. In 1971, 1 per cent of all salaried staff were Black, Asian or Coloured (hereinafter referred to as Black). By 1978, Black employees constituted 13 per cent of salaried staff. This was achieved by appointing Black employees into real jobs, avoiding either tokenism or the existence of dual standards. Today, 55 per cent of the total salaried staff and 22 per cent of all executives are Black. The third phase of SAB's equity programme was launched in 1998. The aim was to place SAB in the top five organizations in South Africa in terms of the race and gender headcount. It also involved action in three other areas: ensuring that people development practices included everyone from the executive to shop floor; removing subtle forms of discrimination; and finally, commercial equity, to be achieved through the use of Black-owned small/micro/medium enterprises as preferred suppliers. What is particularly interesting here is that the same performance management techniques have been employed to ensure continuous improvement in this as in other areas. For example, annual assessments against regional Equity 3 plans are monitored by regional structures, referred to as Employment Equity Consultative Committees (EECCs).

The training and development activities used to support the implementation of these practices were organized around a set of SAB competences. These were introduced during 1994-95 and form the basis for a systematic process of employee development. The competences are aligned with the requirements of the South African Qualifications Act, 1995. The aim is to create high performance opportunities and a form of certification that is nationally recognized.

Overall, this case study illustrates the ways in which changes were made in all four areas identified above: employee involvement, supporting employee performance, sharing information, and linking performance to organizational objectives. What it also demonstrates is that, like the situation at Thorn, these four sets of practices may not be sufficient on their own to guarantee results. A backdrop of trust and shared values may be essential if these practices are to be effective. The case of SAB also illustrates the ways in which the alignment of practices with business objectives is always an ongoing process. HPWPs are not a cure-all that can be applied and then left to work their magic; they require constant fine tuning and adjusting in the same way that gaining the acceptance of organizational values and maintaining trust have always to be worked at. Finally, we should note that this is an interesting example of the use of HPWPs to achieve broader social and equity objectives, in this case changing the ethnic composition of the labour force.

High performance working in the service sector

Comfort Driving Centre

In moving on to examine HPWOs in the service sector, we have taken this opportunity to introduce a small company. Here we can examine the differences between the conditions facing companies in the two sectors while also exploring differences that the size of the organization may have on the use of HPWPs. The company in question is the Comfort Driving Centre (CDC), a new company with 145 employees which has succeeded in obtaining 24 per cent of the market of trainee drivers in Singapore in the space of three years. Here there is the same emphasis on establishing shared values, aligning rewards with performance against company objectives, involving employees in their work, supporting the capabilities of staff at all levels and sharing knowledge and information. Once again, teamworking is the main mechanism for driving the process of learning at work. However, this has all been achieved without the kind of formality in procedures that characterizes the large firms.

The other obvious difference between CDC and companies in the manufacturing sector is that the focus of the company is not on achieving excellence with a concrete product; rather, what is being delivered here is quality not in a "thing" but in a relationship with the customer/client. In this case, the quality is "the Comfort learning experience" which the company seeks to differentiate from that provided by its main competitors.

Unlike the previous two companies, this is a new company on a "greenfield site"; therefore, there is no baggage to be eliminated - it does not have to transform an old culture, merely build a new one. For this reason the general manager deliberately recruited young employees who could be moulded in the ways of the new company. However, the technology it uses, the cars, motor bikes and basic learning track, are more or less the same as its competitors. If the company was to deliver a different product, it had to find ways of creating a different and better quality of learning experience. It was to achieve this objective that the company used HPWPs.

In countries such as Japan and Singapore, it is not possible to practice and learn initial driving techniques on public highways. All learners must have their initial experience on off-the-road circuits, specially designed for learner drivers. To obtain a driving licence, a person must pass two written tests and a practical test.

From the outset, the strategy of CDC was to gain market share through providing value-added services with a strong focus on customer service. The goal is to produce both technically competent and socially responsible drivers: drivers who can drive defensively and therefore anticipate hazards and reduce the risk of being involved in accidents, a growing public problem resulting from increased road congestion.

This added value takes a number of forms, including a relaxed supportive learning environment and a systematic programme of instruction that speeds up the process of learning and makes learning a positive experience while creating socially responsible drivers. The approach adopted by CDC may be termed "learner centred". The instruction is grounded on basic learning theory, gearing training to the learner's knowledge and skill at the point of entry to the programme and then using explanation, demonstration and practice as the principles to guide the learning process. The instructors are treated as the experts who guide this learning process, and it is their activities and behaviour which play a large part in creating the added value by improving the learning experience of the customers. The company's pass rate is two-and-a-half times higher than that of private instructors.

Generating commitment and supporting performance

A determined effort has been made to ensure that all staff are committed to the goals and vision of CDC. In part, this is a result of the fact that all instructors are trained within the company. However, there is also a culture of incremental change and continuous improvement that starts with the initial training. The generation of this culture stems from the leadership of the director/general manager. It is his vision, commitment to service and continuous search for improvements in the learning process that drives the culture of CDC. Responsibility has been devolved to junior staff, and there is a tolerance of mistakes insofar as these are an inevitable part of the learning process. However, there is also an emphasis on accountability in order that responsibility for performance can be identified and rewarded. As part of the learning culture, there is an ongoing attempt to make the links between learning, improvement and performance as transparent as possible.

CDC constantly attempts to emphasize that learning is not just about the acquisition of knowledge and skills, but also about shaping attitudes. The aim is to change the mindset of the staff from one of skills training, which is task oriented, to a broader concept of learning, for example encompassing learning about and using a computer and developing problem-solving skills. It is also about enhancing communication and service skills to ensure that interaction with the clients/customers is handled in a supportive rather than in a didactic manner. The intention is to move the staff away from their role as instructors to one in which they facilitate learning on the part of the client/customer.

CDC has a small management team, with an average age in the late 20s, but it is characterized by a total commitment to the company's objectives. There has been a conscious attempt to sustain a flat hierarchy, with only one layer of management below the senior executive. Given that this is still a small organization, communication is direct through management team meetings, and the information is then conveyed to the rest of the staff.

Work design

Extensive use has been made of project teams to tackle management problems, for example to develop the computer-based theory package, to redesign the track layout to incorporate motorcycle instruction, and to redesign the registration system. Access to the project teams is open to all staff on the basis of individual initiative and enthusiasm.

The project team responsible for the introduction of the computer-based training (CBT) system for the learning of theory consisted of a group of instructors who were interested in developing their skills in this area. All had only a basic secondary education, entering the job with a minimum requirement of an "N" level or National Trade Certificate Level 2. None had any previous experience of computing. They worked collectively, with the services of a consultant computer program designer, to design a package which would not only instruct the learner in the theory required for the driving test but would also provide feedback and support in a learner-friendly environment. Extensive use was made of video clips, graphics and animation to make the learning pleasurable. The result has been well received by the customers, and competitors have sought to purchase it from the company. Instruction is available from a menu of three languages. The project team continues to meet with the purpose of continually modifying the programme and enhancing its effectiveness as a learning tool. Provision is now being made for access to be available via the Internet so that learners can log on at their convenience and do not have to go to the centre.

Staff teams have also redesigned the layout of the driving circuit to incorporate motorcyclists. This was considered by experts in the field to be impossible, as they argued that the circuit was not large enough. Staff have also further improved the circuit by introducing advanced digital sensory timers to allow motorcycle riders to check the times of their manoeuvres during practice and testing. This is important, because manoeuvres have to be completed within specific time frames as a demonstration of rider competences. This form of participation is one of the main means through which problem-solving skills are acquired. This principle of teamworking is now being used as the main means of organizing work throughout the company at all levels. This is a major change that has required considerable preparatory work, involving the redesign of the registration and other IT packages to incorporate the use of teams as the main focus of management.

Supporting learning and performance

Feedback on performance is provided through appraisals. There is also a mentoring system in which senior staff act as guides and coaches for their younger colleagues. Other support for enhancing performance is through a strong commitment to training, driven by its focus on customer service and enhancing the technical and learning-to-learn skills of the staff. Thus, most training is either customer-service or technical training. In 1998, 131 staff attended 23 courses, while in 1999 145 training opportunities were provided and 107 staff trained. In 1998, all staff were put through a course on customer service training delivered by a local training consultancy group. Because the company was growing fast, it could not afford - either in terms of cash or time away from work - to send staff to external courses for intensive off-the-job training. Instead, the consultancy group produced a course that was tailor-made for the company. On-the-job instructor training has also been focused on developing the skills in customer service and facilitating learning among the clients, as well as those required to teach socially responsible and defensive driving. In addition, it is also concerned with engendering a sense of professionalism and pride in the instructors' appearance. Every shift has a five-minute briefing session to cover operational issues before it starts. Every month, one hour is spent to reflect on and reinforce the company message with a different theme each month. The company also has a resource room where staff can enhance their skills and knowledge.

Most of the management training is also informal and on the job. None of the management team apart from the director/general manager had prior experience of management, so he adopted a "logical approach" with the aim of engendering a sense of ownership of the company among the staff. So far, for management all training has been on a need-to-know basis, but the director/general manager has never turned down a request for work-related training. In addition, some staff are also undertaking their own work-related studies outside work, such as diploma/degree programmes in relevant disciplines. Extensive use is made of management meetings to work collectively through the management problems facing the company. These meetings focus on problems such as "creating a customer-based organization" and "the management of change".

Benchmarking

Comfort benchmarks against its Japanese partner from which it also receives training for its instructors in advanced driving techniques. The Japanese company concerned also has many driving schools and access to knowledge from the professional racing circuit on how to develop teaching methodology and driving techniques. This type of technical knowledge is not available to CDC in Singapore, and therefore this is seen as a valuable link. However, the general manager estimates that the company still has some ground to cover to improve staff commitment to the organization and the customer, as well as in improving technical knowledge.

The director/general manager is conscious of the fact that he is moving his staff away from a focus on task performance toward more problem-solving, communication and teamworking skills, while encompassing the new technology and exploring its possibilities. The aim is to make everyone multi-skilled, a strategy that has also increased the overall productivity of the organization.

Here then is a small company seeking to introduce HPWPs. Like other small companies, it does not have the resources to develop elaborate programmes and cannot afford the disruption to the day-to-day running of the organization caused by sending staff on external courses. In the absence of an HR director, the process of implementing HPWPs is driven by the general manager who has to maximize the use of the workplace as the means through which the requisite skills are acquired by the staff. Some formal procedures associated with appraisals and mentoring are already in place, but most of the learning takes place through the everyday interaction of the employees. It is this that the general manager structures in order to ensure that performance is in line with organizational objectives.

The Laiki Bank, Ltd.

One of the areas where high performance working practices have made a major impact is in financial and business services (Becker and Huselid, 1998). In this area, the use of these practices appears to have been closely associated with the impact of ICT. Here the product to be delivered is the management of finances. Nevertheless, the emphasis is still on delivering quality to the customer. These organizations have traditionally been large and bureaucratic in their operation. Therefore, the introduction of HPWO has involved considerable cultural change. We examine this through the case of the Laiki Bank in Cyprus.

The executive chairman has played a crucial role in transforming this somewhat traditional bank into a high performance organization. His vision was to differentiate the Laiki Bank's products though using the Bank's human resources and continuous technological advancement to generate high levels of customer satisfaction and service excellence. Once again, the same pattern appears, namely the creation of shared values as a backdrop against which employee involvement is maximized through the use of teamwork; extensive support is provided for the achievement of high levels of performance, information flows are opened up and a system of rewards is put in place which ensures the link between business objectives and the performance of staff.

Sharing values

The Bank puts considerable effort into ensuring that all employees share its values. These are to care for all employees, to invest in new technology and products and to constantly strive for excellence in customer service. It propagates these values by widespread distribution and discussion of its mission statement and by determined efforts to ensure that the conditions listed in the statement are clearly implemented. It also encourages social activities amongst the staff through use of the Residential Training Centre as a means of cementing internal relationships. The aim is to create an environment in which employees are supported and encouraged to achieve these collective objectives.

In 1991, the Laiki Bank took a policy decision to differentiate its customer service provisions from those of its competitors and thereby to increase market share. The areas targeted for the service differentiation included more effective use of the latest technology. Here teams were set up to examine best-practice use of the latest technology to improve customer service, with the result that the Bank was the first organization to install automated teller machines (ATMs).

Another area where the Bank differentiated its services was with regards to quality standards. The need for the introduction of quality standards for customer service was identified, and standards were duly defined. Comprehensive training arrangements were introduced on a "cascading" basis, starting with the managers and including all staff. Similarly, in the area of continuous improvement an ongoing dialogue has been set up whereby staff discuss the meaning of "fair treatment" and "values" at each level and for each job. Finally, in the area of innovation, a wide scope for innovation in improving customer service was recognized, and means for encouraging staff to come up with innovative ideas were developed. The payoffs for this approach can be seen in the quality of the group's technology projects. Here teams have succeeded in improving customer service through non-traditional channels. Examples include the introduction of the teleservice option through a call centre and the Internet banking facilities.

Work design

Clearly, one of the main means through which these objectives have been achieved is by drawing on the abilities of all staff through the use of project teams. Work has been redesigned to provide the most efficient means of achieving these business objectives. It is the high-calibre workforce of young, aggressive, forward-looking employees brought together in teams who have provided the unconventional ideas which have led to the Bank becoming dominant in Cyprus. The Bank trusts its professional staff, gives them appropriate accountability and responsibility, and encourages prudent risk taking. It is their imaginative use of technology that is seen to be the key to success.

Like Comfort DC, much use is made of new technology to deliver improvements in customer service through the use of teams, but in this instance it is on a much larger scale. The Bank then provides extensive support to maximize the performance of project teams through the provision of training and learning support targeted at improving specific competences. In addition to the provision of financial incentives that link performance with business objectives, the delivery of the organization's competences provides another means for ensuring that employees' behaviours are focused on achieving business objectives. Finally, the Bank makes strenuous efforts to ensure that the requisite information is available to inform the decisions of the project teams.

Supporting performance

Given the investment the Bank makes in its staff, considerable resources are devoted to the selection process. Here the Bank uses recruitment and development centres, based on models used by the Hong Kong and Shanghai Banking Corporation (HSBC) (which has a share in Laiki Bank). Twenty-five per cent of the employees are university graduates, and 10 per cent have post-graduate qualifications. As part of their development, selected staff may be attached to the human resource development (HRD) department for up to two years to deliver lectures, organize training and act as HRD facilitators.

Considerable resources are devoted to training in order to support staff in the achievement of these objectives. Employees spend an average of three days per year on formal learning activities. One such programme is entitled "Customer service, communications and promotion of services" and covers excellent service skills, negotiation skills for retail credit officers, product knowledge, product promotion, effective presentation skills, sales skills, and communications and interpersonal skills. Other training programmes focus on specific areas of bank activity, such as current account or exchange business, credit facilities, and commercial business. An extensive human resource development programme includes coaching, training of on-the-job facilitators, performance appraisal, the role of managers in excellent service, time management, and stress management.

As with many other high performance work organizations, the Bank has identified the competences or abilities required for employees to achieve organizational objectives. For managers, these include the following abilities: written and verbal communication, teamworking, interpersonal sensitivity, leadership, management planning, analytical reasoning, problem solving, decision-making, creativity, entrepreneurial spirit, dynamism, energy and initiative and stress management. For all employees, it is recognized that changes in work organization require the learning of new competences by the staff who have to acquire them. Such competences encompass the requirement to perform individual tasks (task skills); manage a number of different tasks within the job (task management skills); respond to irregularities and breakdowns in routine (contingency management skills); and develop skills to deal with the responsibilities and expectations of the work environment (job/role environment skills).

Having established the competences, the Bank then makes sure that provision is in place to ensure that there is effective feedback on performance in relation to those competences. This is done through an appraisal system based on the HSBC model. When it comes to decisions on promotion, these are made through the development centre. This is also based on an HSBC-proven model that allows for detailed individual assessments to be made. Data from the appraisal and assessment systems are fed into the processes that culminate in promotion decisions being made. All of the managers are involved in such decisions, first in a discussion forum, then through second-level discussions at which final decisions are made.

Rewarding performance

Rewards are closely linked to performance. At the Board Meeting in January 2000, it was agreed that stock options would be offered to employees meeting certain criteria, whereby shares can be purchased at very favourable prices in quantities depending on the individual's length of service and position in the company. The belief is that as employees become stakeholders in their own company, this will strengthen their commitment and identification with the group, resulting in enhanced efforts for the maximization of group performance. An additional incentive scheme was also offered in January 2000, whereby employee savings over a five-year period are converted into shares at a favourable price. Both these schemes have been based on successful models already in operation in the HSBC. Individual ideas are rewarded through a suggestion scheme.

At the organizational level, the Bank makes active efforts to ensure that its policies and practices meet with customer approval and with national and international banking standards. Representatives of an external consultant assess customer service and customer reactions before issuing feedback in the form of a report to the Bank. The Bank also has its own method of assessing the performance of its branches. Anonymous customers (known in the Bank as "mystery shoppers") visit the branches on behalf of the Bank's headquarters and rank each branch in terms of its customer service performance. Prizes are awarded to the branch or branches that receive the highest ratings.

High performance working in the hotel industry

A major part of the service sector employment is the hospitality industry. Traditionally companies in this sector have been based on the old command and control system, with many layers of authority. Although new technology has been introduced into the industry, unlike banking where the ATMs provide the service, in the hospitality industry the service is still delivered personally through the behaviour of employees interacting with the customer. In this context, improvements in work design and employee behaviour play a more central role in delivering a higher quality of service. Nevertheless, in the next case study we still observe changes along the same four dimensions of employee involvement, support for performance, information sharing and the linking of rewards to the achievement of organizational objectives. It is the balance between the use of these different dimensions that is different and in particular the radical redesign of the work process. Here substantial improvements were made in terms of employee flexibility, operating efficiency and employee knowledge and skills. To make better sense of these changes we first examine the changes taking place in other parts of the industry.

Changes in the hospitality industry

The traditional command and control system that characterized the hotel industry in the past utilized top-down vertical communication, often with little horizontal communication. The management structure typically consisted of many layers of authority, frequently as many as 25. People with few skills and a low level of educational achievement were recruited into the industry. It was characterized by low salaries, but it did offer the prospect of upward career progression. However, this progression was usually within a specific function such as catering, with some progression from waiter to general manager. Jobs were tightly demarcated, from the bellboy to waiter to receptionist. An employee's experience was frequently limited to just one functional area and then perhaps did not include all the jobs within that area. Those who progressed, for example within the catering function, did not necessarily have business acumen. People who stayed in the industry had to be committed and ready to work the long hours demanded by systems that had to operate 24 hours per day, 365 days per year. Human resource practices were often rudimentary, for example with decisions about promotion and recruitment often made on the basis of subjective judgements and assumptions.

Delayering

In the Pacific region, this change started in the late 1980s. Ideas for change came from SAS Airlines and Blackmores' in Australia, while the Sheraton in Singapore pioneered the concept of continuous improvement. What happened there amounted to a re-engineering of the industry with the introduction of many high-performance work practices. Hotel management was delayered from 25 to ten levels. A fresh look was taken at the distribution of jobs. Rather than organizing work tasks in terms of functions, they were restructured in terms of bands. These bands consisted of jobs that were clustered in line with the customer skill set required. Those with the same customer skill set were clustered into broad bands with similar skill levels. This produced the ten levels from the entry jobs, Level 1, to the general manager at Level 10; Levels 8, 9 and 10 were all the decision-making grades; Levels 5, 6 and 7 were the trainee managers and department heads; Levels 1, 2, 3 and 4 were the operational levels, with the regular waiter at Level 2 and the supervisor at Level 4; Level 1 entry jobs consisted of those of the bellboy and the room attendant.

Work design

Once the bands were established, employees were multi-skilled within each band. They were expected to master all the skills within the band. Training and job progression were then determined by the need for all the staff to become proficient in all the jobs within their band. This involved moving staff through all the jobs in their existing band. Once they were multi-skilled within their band, having become proficient in three or four different jobs, they would then be ready for promotion to the next band, other things being equal. There the process would start again, and the person would be skilled in the tasks within that band before moving up to the next level. At department-head level, it meant that department heads were skilled in all functions from finance to HRD. It also meant that staff were not only more flexible in terms of the functions they could perform, but they were also more highly skilled in the sense that they had a much broader range of knowledge about the ways in which the organization operated.

Ideas of continuous improvement were taken from the Deming tradition, although Deming's ideas on statistical quality control could not be transferred into the hospitality industry very effectively. The basic idea of process mapping was applied within these broad bands. Using a consultative process and external consultants, the traditional triangle was effectively inverted putting the operation staff at the top, with those with direct customer contact driving the process.

This process delivered a number of advantages. It made the jobs more demanding and satisfying for the employees. It provided all future managers with training in the full range of functions and ensured that they had a concrete knowledge of all aspects of the business, including the necessary business acumen. In addition, for those who moved up within the organization, who became "career spiralists", they achieved a considerable depth of knowledge, acquiring very high levels of skill, having knowledge in both breadth and depth. Of course, not all staff could be climbers, and in fact the ideal position is that about only 40 per cent are climbers and therefore motivated to move between bands, with the remaining 60 per cent of staff as clingers, i.e. content to remain within their band.

The other advantage of the process was that at each level staff were interchangeable. If there was a rush in the coffee shop and waiters were under pressure with the associated risk of a fall in customer service and individual productivity, then staff could be redeployed from another function and levels of customer service and satisfaction sustained. All the staff member had to do was to change his/her uniform. For the manager of the coffee shop, this would cost more, but for the organization as a whole, this was a far more productive and efficient use of staff resources.

Supporting performance

For innovations such as this to be successful required substantial improvements in the support for staff both in terms of the level of training and feedback on performance. Competences were introduced for staff at all levels, and these were used to drive the training. Also, successful attempts were made to empower staff by giving them the right to make decisions and adopt courses of action that would enhance the quality of service provided. In the Australian experience, this empowerment was seen as an important reason for the success of the system. In terms of employee relations, this new system was consolidated through the Enterprise Agreement.

Mandarin Hotel

The Mandarin is part of a larger hotel group operating at the top end of the market worldwide. It aims to be recognized as one of the top luxury hotel groups in the world, providing exceptional customer satisfaction in each of its hotels through a strategy of investing in facilities and people while maximizing profitability and long-term shareholder value.

The new ideas on HPWPs being pioneered in the industry were being used to drive change in the Mandarin Hong Kong, China. With the support of senior managers, the head of HR was implementing HPWPs progressively throughout the hotel and extending it to other hotels in the group. This was being done carefully, as the group had a strong brand image that had to be preserved as one of the main sources of competitive advantage. Also the company operates across the globe, and the different national contexts and institutional arrangements have important affects on the ways in which the strategy could be implemented. These will be discussed in Chapter 5.

One of the main ways in which other companies have been able to introduce this type of new structure in the past is through the direction of a chief executive officer (CEO). In many organizations, it has been the CEO who has driven the change. However, this runs the risk of the culture becoming too dependent on the CEO and collapsing if he or she should leave. The challenge here, as in most organizations, is to implement the culture change across all the hotels in such a way that it is deeply embedded so that, even if CEOs change, the culture would be sustained.

The strategy for introducing HPWPs

The Mandarin strategy has five separate but related dimensions: recruitment and selection; training and development; succession planning; compensation and benefits; and employee relations. The group director of HR is currently working on all five areas, but progress has been more rapid in some than others. The strategy is being implemented in a number of stages, with some of the dimensions in place before others, but with action taking place across all five dimensions. The group director of HR estimates that it will take three to four years for the culture change to be completed.

The first stage of the strategy has been to tackle the recruitment and selection of personnel entering the management cluster. In the past, recruitment was done in a fairly ad-hoc manner with decisions often made on the basis of subjective criteria without reference to all the competences required for the job. This has now been replaced with a structured process involving a full day's assessment, a redesigned, more sophisticated application form, a weighting index and a score for the interview process. The whole process now involves seven or eight managers from across the various functions. This has taken the subjectivity out of the process of management selection. As in the Bank, once there has been a commitment to invest in the development of staff, recruitment and selection are approached in a more systematic manner.

Central to the restructuring of the management cluster has been the introduction of core competences for the group as a whole. As we saw in the Bank, these not only provide support for the improvement of performance, but they also provide for linking behaviours to organizational objectives. These took time to develop but were eventually derived directly from the company mission statement. A firm of consultants has been used to develop an assessment centre using these competences as the base against which managers' strengths and areas of development could be identified. Once the process has been embedded in the management team, the next task is to move down to the next level. The decision was taken not to rush the changes because of the fear of destabilizing the brand.

Given the centrality of work redesign to the process of performance improvement, it is not surprising that training and development are regarded in many ways as the essence of the project. As skills and knowledge are enhanced, the aim is to introduce a learning environment into the hotel, i.e. a university within the hotel. Each of the job bands has its own competences and every job its own standards, and as the person acquires those competences he/she will be certified not just by the company but by an external authority, either a college or university.

As the staff work long and unsociable hours, the aim is to bring the university to them. Certification is delivered at every stage. From the staff's point of view, as they acquire the competences and are certified they will build up credits for a certificate qualification, then a diploma and for some a Master's qualification. The aim is to ensure that there is something in the process of learning for the staff, to encourage them to buy into it; this is the reason for incorporating some form of a recognized qualification. It is planned to make extensive use of development centres in implementing these changes. The approach will be piloted at one hotel in the year 2000 before being implemented throughout the group.

The next issue to be tackled is succession planning. At the moment, people are moved around to help broaden their experience, but no real structure has yet been put in place. Use is being made of external consultants to ensure that as much subjectivity as possible is taken out of the process, with the aim of demonstrating to senior staff how decisions can be made in a more objective manner.

Over the last six months, the group director of HR has been looking for an appropriate structure to ensure that financial rewards are linked to performance. Part of the problem this industry faces is that the system has to accommodate the movement of people across countries with very different terms and conditions.

Employee relations are being transformed through the use of the profit chain. This takes the form of the equation:

Employee satisfaction = customer satisfaction = increased profit.

A mechanism in the form of a new monthly survey has been put in place to track employee satisfaction through time. This survey is delivered to a sample of employees and provides a regular snapshot of the problems that have to be tackled. At the moment, the survey has revealed three areas crucial to the success of HPWPs where work is required: communication, recognition and reward, and leadership. The latter is being tackled though a leadership audit, although managers have encountered problems in using it. Once again, it has taken time to develop an instrument that is appropriate to the needs of the group.

This provides an interesting example of how the introduction of change has been systematically planned across all four dimensions. It also demonstrates the centrality of work design and, allied to this, the importance of providing the support in the form of training and learning experiences required for the full benefits of work design to be realized. The other feature that this case illustrates is the attempt to build a culture change, with the support of the CEO, but without over-reliance on the personality of the head of the organization to drive the process. Here considerable reliance was placed on transforming the recruitment process to ensure that appropriate personnel were brought on board as well as through introducing a permanent learning culture throughout the entire organization. Finally, it gives some indication of the length of time such a culture change can take to put in place as a permanent feature of the organization.

High performance working in the public and state-regulated sector

In this last section, we tackle the problem of introducing HPWPs in public sector organizations and those private sector organizations subject to government regulation.

The United States Social Security Administration (SSA)

The big difference between the public sector and the private sector is that control of some public sector organizations, especially those delivering government financial services, is firmly in the hands of politicians. It is therefore not the market which tends to drive change, but rather the ideologies and actions of politicians. Here we turn to the United States where the Government has made a deliberate attempt to introduce HPWPs into the public sector. This has involved changing the culture and working practices of one of the largest bureaucracies in government service, with 65,000 employees. The change was accomplished again from the top down in response to pressure from the President's Office. Here there has been less delayering and teamworking or work redesign. This organization is therefore low on our employee involvement dimension. Nevertheless, extensive use has been made of other HPWPs through the measurement of performance, employee development and improved communication, both within the organization and especially in relation to the customers. Of particular note here has been the role of the HR department in introducing and sustaining change.

The SSA is responsible for administering three major programmes: the Old-Age and Survivors' Insurance (OASI) and Disability Insurance (DI) programmes commonly known as "Social Security", and the Supplemental Security Income (SSI) programme. Disability and survivors' benefits make up about 30 per cent of all Social Security benefits paid. Social Security is a successful domestic programme and arguably the most effective anti-poverty programme ever created in the United States. Today, without Social Security, about 50 per cent of the elderly would be living in poverty. In addition to its basic programmes, the SSA also provides a significant measure of service delivery support to other programmes, for example Medicare and Medicaid.

The SSA integrates these activities across all programmes through a single national service-delivery structure. By doing so, the SSA is able to enhance efficiency, avoid duplication of effort and increase opportunities to provide one-stop services to its customers. The SSA's total administrative budget proposal for all programmes is US$6.89 billion, an amount equal to 1.6 per cent of total programme outlays. The service is delivered through 1,348 field offices.

Introducing HPWPs in the public sector

As mentioned above, the Government drove the initial introduction of HPWPs into government agencies. In 1993, President Clinton and Vice President Gore asked all federal agencies to become more customer focused - to find out what customers want from the Government, to stop assuming that they knew and to set customer service standards. Although federal legislation exists to govern how the agencies must work (e.g. pay and financial management), the Government has backed away from such constraints, and agencies have become much more free to decide their own mode of operation within the requirement of producing their own strategic plans. Oversight of agency operations has been much reduced.

The immediate pressure to introduce HPWPs came through the President's Management

Council (PMC) which is committed to improving the performance of the federal Government. The PMC sees human resource development as leading the way to improved federal performance. In April 1995, the PMC therefore asked for specific actions on making HRD more effective in improving the performance of the federal Government. The response of the government-wide Human Resource Development Council was to have high expectations of HRD - and to communicate and reinforce those expectations. The central expectation of HRD is that its contributions result in high-performing federal agencies. Thus, HRD is seen as the main driver within the organization and the central pivot through which HPWPs will be embedded in the organization. Unlike the private sector, there is less reliance on the charismatic chief executive to drive the process of change. In these circumstances, the HR department steps in to play a more central role as change agent.

Securing commitment

As in the private sector, great importance is attached to all employees understanding the goals and the strategic plan. The SSA mission statement is "to promote the economic security of the nation's people through compassionate and vigilant leadership in shaping and managing America's social security programmes". In order to accomplish its mission, the SSA's September 1997 strategic plan created a set of five strategic goals that encompass all of the SSA's programme activities and address the competing needs of the wide variety of SSA stakeholders. For example, these goals are to promote valued, strong and responsive social security programmes and conduct effective policy development, research and programme evaluation.

Each strategic goal is subdivided into performance objectives that are published and widely dispersed. Performance of the programmes is tracked using various traditional and new outcome measures to help the SSA and others assess whether the social security programmes and the SSI are achieving their intended outcomes. Here again, measurement of the organization's performance is seen as crucial. For this purpose, Syracuse University was asked to assess performance in a number of government agencies across five management areas. These were financial management; human resources management; information technology; capital management and managing for results. The SSA came out of this exercise with the award of an "A" grade.

Transforming the HRD function

In order to meet the challenge posed by the government directives, the HR department has had to extend its role well beyond its traditional concern with training to include career development, organizational development and performance improvement. The HRD function is central in ensuring that information and values are shared throughout the organization. It is therefore responsible for clarifying business goals and ensuring that all employees are aware of them. Here communications are important either in the form of publications or meetings. Communications have been improved through the use of both the Internet and Intranet.

The HRD function also has to identify the people and technology required to support the SSA's strategic business goals, the performance support function. To this end, it uses competency models to assess its current capability and includes in its assessment the capabilities of internal HRD professionals, others in the SSA and outside resources. This process enables the HRD function to be clear on the gaps between the skills and competences required to meet SSA aspirations and those that are currently available. It must also ensure that resources in the form of people, information, technology, facilities and materials are aligned to support the achievement of the SSA's goals.

In the realm of performance management, the SSA has to set ambitious but measurable performance goals and crucially ensure that the rewards are delivered to those who achieve them. The HRD function must also manage the learning process. This means delivering high levels of involvement among employees and providing mentoring systems and making sure that the appropriate skills are in place for self-improvement and increasingly team building, although as yet teams are not central to the delivery of the service as they were in other case studies.

Supporting the learning process

Given the magnitude of the changes involved in introducing HPWPs, the SSA has, like the hotel group, devoted considerable resources to support the learning process. Thus, in the field of training, the identified training needs indicate that learning opportunities have to be provided for 65,000 federal and 12,000 state employees with decreasing budget availability. To meet this challenge, the SSA is making use of learning technology to assist in the delivery of training. This takes the form of interactive video training (IVT) broadcast from two studios at SSA headquarters and three in SSA regions; stand-alone workstations at each SSA site offering customized, off-the-shelf CD ROM multimedia programmes for large audiences with common training needs. Intranet/Internet training available over the SSA's Office of Training Intranet Home Page and through a "Virtual Campus" offering all types of training is available to all SSA employees at their own workstations.

As we have seen in other organizations, feedback is crucial to ensure that objectives are being met, and for that reason the HRD function also has to encourage ongoing, multiple-source feedback from customers and stakeholders, including taxpayers and the general public who experience the agency's services. Annual satisfaction surveys, comment cards, focus groups and special surveys have helped the SSA understand the needs and satisfaction of most of its various customer groups. This system has recently been improved. In February 1998, Commissioner Apfel approved a new programme, called the Market Measurement Program (MMP), for the SSA. The SSA's MMP includes a variety of data collection activities that, taken together, should give the agency the information it needs to fully understand its customers, employees and stakeholders.

Like the hotel industry, the introduction of HPWPs into public administration requires a major culture change led by the HR department. However, unlike the hotel industry, this appears to have been accomplished without a major change as yet in the employee involvement dimension. Tremendous effort has been made on introducing competences and other support for performance in the form of training and feedback. Much more effort has also been made in ensuring that the business objectives are known and that the requisite knowledge for performance improvement is available. Finally, rewards have been restructured. This may well represent a model for other government agencies.

The state-regulated private sector

The final company in this study is a private sector organization providing airport security. This means that the delivery of its service is characterized by two distinct features. First, because it is essentially a police force, it is subject to strict government control but still operates on commercial principles. Second, it delivers a very distinctive service, one that is only appreciated in the absence of events. Thus, the quality of the customer experience is in the absence of the pilfering of baggage, of not being hassled in the airport by long waits to get through security, etc. The delivery of this service through a police force means that a hierarchy is essential; yet in contrast to the United States SSA, teamworking is a central feature of this company's approach to HPW. Therefore, one of the interesting features of this case study is how the two features - hierarchy and teamworking - were combined. Like the SSA and the hotel group, a major effort and considerable resources have gone into providing support in the form of training and other mechanisms such as appraisals that support employee involvement and performance.

SATS Security Services (SSS)

SATS Security Services (SSS) is a wholly owned subsidiary of Singapore Airport Terminal Services (SATS), which is itself a subsidiary of the Singapore Airlines group of companies. It encompasses an auxiliary police force engaged in providing security services to airlines and other related organizations at airports in Singapore. As its mission statement says, it "aims to provide outstanding security services at reasonable cost and at a profit to the company". SSS was established in 1965 and provides a wide range of security services for most airlines operating in Changi Airport and to other organizations in Singapore as well as overseas. The majority of its staff are police officers trained to utilize a wide range of sophisticated security equipment. The company has grown from a staff of 450 in 1989 to 760 in 1999.

Because of these distinctive features of its market, the general manager of SSS makes extensive use of benchmarking as a means of improving performance. Almost all of this benchmarking is with overseas organizations that face similar security problems. Because it is competing in terms of community criteria, e.g. reducing bomb threats, threats to public security and crime reduction, it is not always in competition against other providers and therefore can cooperate with agencies in other countries and in Singapore.

Introducing HPWPs

When the general manager took over the company in the early 1990s, SSS was suffering from low morale, low motivation and poor levels of service performance. The aim of his changes was to introduce higher levels of service and professionalism into the company. The focus was to generate higher levels of customer satisfaction through investing in the "company product", i.e. the security guard.

The general manager's basic belief is that managers should "develop your people, treat them well, motivate them, empower them, and they will take care of your problems for you". He sees the system he has introduced as reflecting these principles rather than any abstract concept of high performance working, although the systems and procedures he has put in place (team working, job rotation and multi-skilling, clear management objectives, performance-based rewards, leadership and business training) would be recognized as high performance practices.

The system produced results. Company performance is measured by profit and by a series of performance indices. As the level of performance has improved over the last five years, there has been more success in combating crime, and customers have become more satisfied with the company and therefore willing to pay more for the service, which has then fed back into the profitability of the company. As service levels have improved, clients have been willing to accept an increase in price. In addition, more consultancy opportunities have been created and the market widened, which have all fed into higher profits. The company customer satisfaction among clients has increased from 44.2 per cent in the early 1990s to 81.9 per cent in 1999.

In order to turn the company around, the general manager used his previous experience as head of HRM in the parent group Singapore Airlines to guide him. He initiated change on a number of fronts: building trust, transforming the attitude of managers toward their subordinates, increasing business awareness, introducing a TQM programme, redesigning jobs, improving feedback to employees, introducing performance-based rewards and revamping training to support a culture of continuous learning.

The process of change was similar to that observed in other organizations. First, an attempt was made to build up trust between management and staff on the basis of which a shared culture could be built. When he first started, the general manager introduced feedback sessions for all staff, what he termed "skip-level interviews", where he made himself available for private one-to-one discussions with staff who wished to raise problems in confidence. He then acted on these complaints without ever identifying the source. This provided the basis for the development of high levels of trust between management and employees within the organization. As there is no union for the police force, the general manager feels it important to continue to have these channels open. He continues to hold these one-to-one sessions on an annual basis.

At the same time, the general manager sought to change the attitudes of management and employees, which he saw as one of the biggest obstacles to change. The security industry is not one that has traditionally attracted highly qualified recruits. Indeed, recruitment has been a problem in the past, as SSS has to compete against the regular police force and finds that it cannot compete with some of the "softer" jobs outside. Thus, this is not a highly qualified set of recruits through which to build high performance work practices. To transform their level of performance, he first started by addressing the attitudes and behaviour of the senior officers.

The problem the general manager faced was typified by the attitude of the senior officers toward training. Hard-pressed police commanders often thought of training in a negative way.

It caused them problems by taking people away from operations, making arrangements for coverage and incurring additional costs. The problem facing him was how to change this perception. His solution was to introduce business concepts into police management, changing the perception of the police officer, to view the police officer as a product and training as product development. In his words, "once we take this approach, we are able to see why it is important not just to look at police training but at all processes that affect a police officer's performance". For him, these include areas that are traditionally not thought of as an organization's concern, such as a police officer's physical and medical fitness, his communication skills, his contribution to the community beyond mere policing and his long-term development. While it appears altruistic, he sees this as a very hard-nosed, practical approach to improving police officer performance and hence the organization's effectiveness. In this respect, the investment in training is seen as the equivalent of a manufacturer investing in research and development. The general manager sees performance in the service sector as requiring the full utilization of human potential.

Sharing information

Information sharing and business awareness have been improved by the introduction of an annual Strengths, Weaknesses, Opportunities and Threats (SWOTS) exercise. This involves all employees. Each department conducts its own SWOT analysis in confidence, and the results are passed to the section leaders who repeat the exercise, the results of which are then sent to the management team. The management team then moves to a hotel for three days to study the results and incorporate them into the company's goals and to set an action plan for the next year. In this way, the company encourages the upward flow of ideas and employee involvement in the decision-making process.

The downward flow of information is also taken very seriously. Members of the management team have responsibility for communication both across and within sections. Specific forms of communication used by the company are briefing sessions, which are held every three months at departmental and supervisor levels. The briefings include a review of company financial performance, as well as other matters of concern to the company as a whole. In addition, there is an extensive newsletter that contains announcements of commendable achievements by staff, as well as letters of complaints. There is a separate bulletin for supervisors, but this is largely for technical matters.

Work design

To improve the quality of service, the general manager launched a comprehensive Total Quality Management Programme with the help of Singapore's Productivity and Standards Board. It involved seminars on quality for all levels, beginning with his management team, the introduction of quality circles and a quality policy.

The other major change was the introduction of teams. There were a number of reasons for this. First, they ensure accountability in the delivery of services. Second, they enable performance measures to be used to reward excellence. Third, they enable management to act on poor practices across a range of areas - for example, absence rates, medical leave, and baggage and cargo pilferage rates. Data are collated on all of these and other items and then used to measure the performance of the groups responsible for cargo and baggage security, etc. Data on sick leave and absence are used to measure morale and thereby the performance of the leaders of different teams. Teams are also used for the implementation of TQM. Each of the teams acts as a quality circle in that it is a focus of discussion of performance issues and a forum for continuous improvement. The use of teams also provides a unit of personal identification and loyalty that is smaller and more meaningful than the company as a whole.

In addition to the use of teams, job rotation is an essential element of SSS, a practice introduced by the general manager from his experience in Singapore Airlines. Normally, after two years in one job, the person is moved on. No one is allowed to stay in any one job for more than five years. This practice ensures that officers move around and do not become too familiar with those they are guarding and hence fall prey to corruption. It also ensures that officers do not become too familiar with other employees and thereby become lax in their vigilance. Another reason for this practice is that for those destined to move into higher positions they thereby acquire knowledge of the whole company and its various functions. From the officers' point of view, this movement provides variety and exposes them to different types of risks.

Through this system of job rotation, all officers become multi-skilled across a range of areas. In addition to basic policing skills, the staff also acquire skills in handling travel documents, in guarding prisoners, in CCTV monitoring and surveillance, in the interpretation of x-ray images and in the ability to detect irregularities. The other area of central importance is computing, as computers become increasingly central to the running of the company. Information technology is therefore seen as one of the central skills.

Supporting performance

The introduction of these various practices required a steep change in the skills necessary for effective performance. The company therefore provides a range of support in the form of both formal courses and on-the-job training. Extensive use is made of formal courses, as many of the technical skills required by the police officers can be best transmitted in a formal classroom context. Eighty per cent attended at least one course in 1999. These included external courses on service quality, as well as outward-bound courses for developing group identification and identification with the company. SSS also uses CISCO, the commercial arm of the state police, to provide the basic training for the auxiliary police, which consists of a five-week course. This is supplemented by training tailored to the requirements of SSS. Management training is provided through the parent group, Singapore Airlines, and SSS's own police leadership courses. In addition to these general skills, there are courses in specific skills such as fraudulent protection investigation, x-ray screening, etc. For those identified as having leadership potential, there are leadership and team-building courses, corporal and sergeant development courses and an advanced leadership course.

In addition to formal courses, there is an extensive system of on-the-job training (OJT) associated with the practice of job rotation and the use of teams as focal points for continuous improvement. The company provides structured on-the-job training with the theory being tested through the use of community-based training (CBT). Every team leader is a trainer, having been trained in the skills required for the effective delivery of day-to-day working practices, company processes and communication.

For all staff, there is a wellness programme. This was introduced by SSS after it realized the full cost of sickness. It is a preventative scheme that is now a core part of the business requirement; keeping fit and well is now fully recognized as not just an individual but also a company concern. The company provides free medical screening, health awareness talks and fitness provision. A $20 screening test can save thousands of dollars on cancer treatment. This programme saves the company money.

Like the hotel group, the general manager of SSS has mapped out a system of continuous learning which is being externally certified. Working with colleges in Singapore and Australia, officers can now progress through a Certificate and Diploma in Police Studies or Security. It is anticipated that within six months all training programmes will provide credits which will lead first to the Certificate and later to the Diploma. All those in leadership positions (team leaders) will have a Diploma in either Police Studies or Security.

The provision of formal training starts with an annual manpower plan, which is used to identify staff, and associated training requirements for each year. This also incorporates any new demands which may be coming on stream in the medium term - for example, the staffing and training demands resulting from the new terminal which is currently being planned for Changi Airport.

SSS has developed a sophisticated system of tracking the development of individual members of staff. After initial training, the recruit then starts to move up the career ladder. His or her progress through training and job rotation is then systematically tracked at each stage in his/her career. If the recruit fails at any point in progressing through the system, he/she is then sent for retraining that is followed by a proficiency test and then re-entering the ladder, moving on to the next section.

Individual feedback on performance is provided to staff through the appraisal system. Each officer is subject to an annual appraisal. He or she is appraised every year for on-the-job performance and every two years for promotion potential. Leadership potential is also identified through the appraisal process. The company is not yet ready for 360-degree appraisal because of the problem of face. This is particularly true for Asian cultures, where individuals are hesitant to criticize those in superior positions.

The evaluation of training takes the form of a report on the employee's perception of the success of the course, together with a trainer's report on the motivation of trainees and the changes taking place over time in their motivation. The other form of evaluation consists of the supervisor counselling the trainees before they go on the course, then again immediately after training. There is also a measure of the success or failure of the course three months after its completion, when an assessment is made of the extent to which skills acquired on the course have been transferred to the workplace.

Rewarding performance

This extensive system of training is also linked explicitly to a system of performance-based rewards. These include salary increases following salary reviews, upgradings, promotions, and payments from the award scheme and other benefits; for example, the top five performers annually receive a trip to a conference overseas. Salaries are reviewed every two years against levels in the external market. Then there is a different pay scale for each level and within each level a series of steps for upgrading. A panel makes salary decisions.

In addition to the upgrading and promotions, financial benefits are also derived from performance in crisis situations as identified in an audit. There are also a number of other areas where awards are made, and these also carry a number of points. These awards include the Service Excellence Awards, Citation Awards, Merit Awards, Best Team, Best Employee and Long-service Awards. Those who receive a certain number of points can convert them into a cash award. These cash awards are small, representing only 5 per cent of the wage bill, but at the margins they provide powerful incentives for the staff. In addition to the cash awards, the company makes extensive use of other rewards to create a culture in which high levels of performance are seen to be praised. These include letters of appreciation, items in the newsletter and letters of commendation.

At the company level, one of the most important measures of performance is the annual survey of clients and the rating they provide on the company's performance in terms of service quality. This has revealed continuous improvements throughout the decade. This same success is also reflected in other measures such as the crime detection rates and the baggage and cargo pilferage reports. For example, in 1993-94 there were over 70 reports of cargo pilferage for just under 0.5 million tons of cargo handled, while in 1998-99 there were 20 reports for a total cargo of 1.2 million tons. The same applies to baggage pilferage.

Because SSS is a police force, it is essentially a hierarchically organized company. However, the introduction of HPWPs here is still based on the concept of teamworking allied to intensive and extensive training as well as to performance measurement and rewards linked to organizational objectives. This suggests that teamworking may not be inimical to hierarchy. In many ways, the reliance on training is similar to that in the United States government bureaucracy. Of course, these are only two case studies, but they do suggest that maybe in the configuration of HPWPs the bundles may be different in the public sector and that delayering may not be a prerequisite for enhanced performance in this area.

Conclusions – What have we learned?

If we now reflect on some of the questions we asked in the introduction, some interesting answers emerge. Clearly, the introduction of these HPWPs in a range of organizations in different countries over this last decade has revealed certain commonalties in their experience. One of the most significant has been the building of trust as a precondition for the effective implementation of these practices. This has been particularly important in organizations which previously had a large element of tension and conflict in the relations between management and employees. The process used to build this trust differed between companies with strong unions such as Thorn and SAB and those without unions, but the outcome was the same. Moreover, this is not a one-off process; in all the case studies, determined efforts have been made to ensure a steady flow of information from the centre about the current state of business and from the employees about changes necessary to sustain high levels of performance. The significance of this trust and the importance of shared values are difficult to capture through survey techniques, which is why they did not figure so prominently in the previous chapter. Nevertheless, it is clear that a shared culture forms one bedrock of successful performance. From the worker's perspective, the pay-off is employment security and opportunities to acquire further skills.

As for the specific dimensions we identified, work redesign and teamwork as ways of increasing employee involvement and performance have not been used in all the organizations. It was not used in the United States SSA, although that organization currently has a joint exercise with the union to explore its possible introduction in certain areas. At Thorn, SSS and increasingly SAB, teams provide one of the main foundations for the management system. As we saw at Comfort DC and the Laiki Bank, these can provide the context for a powerful learning experience and a means of linking behaviour to organizational objectives in a clear and transparent manner. In those two companies, they are an important means of achieving a competitive advantage in the market. Again, just how they are introduced differs from one organization to another, as does the extent of their use. However, in all these cases, the design of work provided the opportunity for employees to acquire new skills and knowledge and participate in the decision-making process.

Relating pay to performance is also a feature of all the organizations. However, the emphasis placed on this as a form of motivation differs substantially. At Thorn, the unions and employees are aware of the link during the annual pay negotiations. However, the company prefers to keep the link at that level so that the interest of the organization as a whole, rather than those of specific teams within it, is always seen to be the decisive factor. At SSS and Comfort DC, individual elements of performance are linked to pay. However, what comes across from all the organizations is the use of non-pay rewards, special mentions in the newsletter, trips to conferences and management taking time out to thank employees for their contributions. The consistency with which the organizations utilize these rewards suggests that they are a powerful form of motivation which the current preoccupation with performance-related pay in the literature leads us to neglect.

The third dimension, supporting performance, is crucial in all the organizations where extensive provision is made for both formal training and informal OJT. Taken as a whole, extensive provision is made for training and workplace learning in all these organizations, although not all of this would be captured by the formal training budget. In many cases, by focusing training around core competences, training is clearly linked to performance requirements. Feedback on performance is provided through the appraisal and mentoring provision in all organizations.

The fourth dimension, communicating information and values and providing feedback from employees to managers, is also important in all these organizations. In Thorn, a variety of techniques is used, ranging from regular union/management workshops, monthly team briefings to regular shift hand-over meetings between team leaders and frequent newsletters. In SAB, there are innovative "value-sharing" workshops, surveys and the regular sharing of information with unions. In SATS, the general manager uses his "skip-level-interviews" to obtain feedback from employees, as well as the annual SWOT analysis from each department, supplemented by newsletters and feedback from clients. What is crucial is that workers have access to this business information so they can process it and act on it to constantly improve performance.

While these practices are clearly applicable across all sectors, including the public sector, the dearth of evidence on their use in the public sector makes it difficult to produce conclusions on these matters with any degree of certainty. The experience of SSA raises doubts as to whether work redesign is essential, but the use of teams in a hierarchically organized company such as SSS suggests that there is no reason why teamworking could not be introduced into the public sector administration.

Do these practices apply equally to small and medium-sized organizations? The answers from Comfort and a series of other case studies recently completed in the United Kingdom, Thailand and China is a clear yes.[1] Where SMEs differ is that they do not have the formal procedures characteristic of the larger companies. Here they depend far more on the driving force of the head of the organization in using high performance working practices to structure day-to-day interaction in the company (Ashton and Sung, 2001; Keep and Coleman, 2001; Sung et al., 2000). It is this individual who leads, for example, in creating teams and leaving them to take decisions, in sharing information about the state of the company, in getting rid of quality control departments and showing individual employees and teams how to take responsibility for the delivery of quality and in using the workplace as a constant source of learning which is shared by all.

Notes

[1] These case studies are to be published on the ILO website.

CHAPTER 3

IMPLEMENTING HIGH PERFORMANCE WORKING PRACTICES

Introduction

In this chapter, we move on to examine what drives the introduction of high performance working practices. Our main question is why, if these new forms of work organization are so effective in enhancing performance, have not most organizations adopted them? In an attempt to answer this, we explore the main triggers which lead to the introduction of these practices. Are they driven by technological change or are there other forces at work? Why is it that some firms introduce them and not others? Perhaps one of the disincentives is that they are difficult to introduce. We ask what are the problems managers and workers face in implementing them. What do we know about the factors that lead to successful implementation? This is a broad range of questions which we seek to answer, using both quantitative and qualitative data.

What drives the introduction of these practices? What are the specific triggers?

In Chapter 1, we argued that, with the intensification of competition in world markets, these new forms of organization offer the prospect of providing a step change in the levels of productivity and crucially in the quality of the product or service they could deliver. In this sense, they represent new, more efficient ways of organizing human labour. In many respects, because these HPWOs have been able to make significant improvements in productivity and quality, they have changed the rules of the game, putting pressure on other organizations to adopt these practices to achieve the same levels of performance. However, these competitive pressures face all organizations; their mere existence does not explain why some adopt HPWPs at one point in time and others do not. Here our knowledge is thin and reliant largely on data from case studies, but we have sufficient knowledge to understand some of the main triggers.

Results of quantitative studies

Pil and MacDuffie (2000) used a longitudinal study of motor vehicle assembly plants to test a series of hypotheses concerning the factors that affect the introduction of what they term high involvement work practices (HIWPs) (e.g. job rotation, use of teams and suggestion schemes). They focus on high involvement working practices because they argue that such practices are more difficult to change than the complementary HR policies (e.g. new training, contingent compensation, status differentials and flexible automation) because the work practices are more intimately bound up with core business processes and coordination requirements of the organization.

The authors of the study found that plants are more likely to increase their use of high involvement work practices when they already have implemented complementary HR practices, supporting the notion that these practices are bundled. This is a finding in line with those presented from the research by the Centre for Labour Market Studies presented in Chapter 6. Pil and MacDuffie also found only weak support, in a statistical sense, for the hypothesis that the worst-performing plants would be more likely to introduce HIWPs. They did find that higher levels of managerial tenure have a positive and statistically significant association with greater increase in the use of HIWPs, suggesting that longer-term relationships provide a possible basis for greater trust. Company actions that reduce employee trust, such as management layoffs, production-worker layoffs and early retirement programmes, have no statistically significant association with the introduction of HIWPs, perhaps because on the one hand they can reduce the necessary "trust" but on the other they "unfreeze" resistance to change, with the two having the effect of cancelling each other out. There was some evidence that plants with traditional practices are more likely to undertake downsizing. The introduction of new automotive models was also associated with the introduction of HIWPs but not plant expansions.

Many plants in the United States and Canada retain traditional practices for the following reasons: management and unions are ambivalent about the value of work reform, and the competitive crisis is not necessarily viewed as requiring major change in the internal organization. Organizational learning both within and outside the organization is not always very effective. Most of the plants are focused on building single models at high volume and therefore are seen as having less to gain from the introduction of more flexible practices.

Pil and MacDuffie's qualitative findings

The quantitative field work which was also part of this study revealed other factors which were important in explaining why companies adopted HIWPs. Companies that moved rapidly toward adopting HIWPs in the period 1989-93-94 typically shared the following characteristics. They faced a serious competitive crisis in the period, and their senior personnel perceived the crisis as internal rather than external, in that it was perceived to be a result of problems with organizing production according to traditional mass-production principles. These perceptions were then validated by external benchmarking. Senior personnel reached the conclusion that lean production principles

---

should be introduced. The companies had little previous experience with work reform. Company and plan-level managers (and union officials) held neutral or positive views about the value of work reform as a means of improving performance. Companies found effective ways of cultivating organizational learning across functional boundaries within the organization. Companies had access to some learning models with other companies already using these principles.

In developing countries, Pil and MacDuffie found that companies use HIWPs but not automation. They found that plants in newly industrialized countries introduce new training, performance-based pay, elimination of status differences, and more selective recruitment and hiring practices rather than capital investments in robotics, as in these locations the volume of production is low as well as the wages. This would explain why in the statistical analysis they did not find a significant association between the use of HIWPs and flexible automation.

Results of qualitative evidence: Problems in the market

Case study evidence, including that presented here, suggests that the main trigger for the introduction of HPWPs in the private sector is a problem in the market. This problem often takes the form of a threat to the continued viability of the organization, but the precise form it takes differs from one company to another. Some of the pioneers of HPWPs, including companies such as Xerox, introduced these practices in response to the competition they faced from the Japanese in the 1980s. Like other leading US companies such as Ford in the motor industry, Xerox's competitive benchmarking noted significant improvements in customer satisfaction and productivity created by Japanese team-based organizations in their market for copiers. To remain competitive, Xerox had to increase significantly its responsiveness to customers while at the same time reducing costs. It did this by reorganizing the work of 13,000 US field-service employees around the world into empowered work teams. The result was a progressive reorganization of this aspect of the company over a 15-year period (Hackman et al., 2000).

Other researchers report that it is the pressures from the market which usually trigger the introduction of HPWPs such as teamworking. Mason (1999) found this to be the case among American and European manufacturing companies. Lloyd (2000:20) reports a similar finding in the case of one UK pharmaceutical company which introduced team working for production workers as a result of the need to cut costs and improve the poor state of industrial relations. She also noted that this had been a long slow process as the company went through "three years of structural and emotional change".

In the case studies reported in the previous chapter, SAB faced the problem of suddenly having to make itself competitive in a world market from which it had previously been insulated by the protectionist economic policies of the apartheid Government. If it was to survive in this new arena, let alone increase its share of the world market, the company had to learn very fast how to improve productivity and quality. Similarly, Thorn, Ltd. had to confront the challenge of a stagnant or declining market share if it was to survive. What is common here is the threat to the continued survival of the company.

When the survival of the organization is at stake, then fears about the consequences of disclosing information to trade unions and introducing radical change into working procedures become less significant when placed against the possible collapse of the company and subsequent loss of jobs. In these circumstances, awareness of the interdependence of all sections of the organization is increased, while the external threat provides the opportunity to mobilize resources in a way that is not often possible under more "normal" circumstances. However, not all our case studies faced the threat of closure. In the case of Comfort Driving Centre, the Mandarin Hotel and the Laiki Bank, the pressures were those to achieve or sustain a position as market leaders. However, what did characterize all our case study companies was an attempt to differentiate their products or services from those of their competitors on the basis of quality. This was part of a strong customer focus.

While these are factors evident in our own case studies, the literature suggests that they are not exhaustive. Sometimes the introduction of new technology provides the trigger for a more radical change in working practices. However, it is clear from our existing knowledge that there is no invariant relationship between the introduction of new technology and the introduction of HPWPs, as is evident from the case of Dutton Engineering, a small manufacturing enterprise in the United Kingdom. There, the opposite was the case. The introduction of HPWPs enabled that company to make major advances in both the quality of its products and the profitability of the enterprise with its old technology (Lewis and Lytton,1997). In other instances, the introduction of HPWPs is linked to the actions of the parent company; thus, the use of HPWPs in SSS was a result of the decision by the parent company to tackle problems of low morale and productivity by sending in a new manager.

Other research (OECD,1999) suggests that foreign ownership is also linked to the use of HPWPs, suggesting that these practices are sometimes introduced by MNCs. This is certainly the case in the automobile industry, as the research by Pil and MacDuffie discussed in Chapter 6 testifies.

In the public sector, the impetus, as one would expect, has to come from the politicians. In the absence of a threat or command from above, system inertia ensures that existing practice continues. In the case of the United States SSA, it was the pressure from President Clinton and Vice President Gore that initiated the change. In the United Kingdom, the attempts to introduce market principles into the delivery of public health services may be having the same effect by providing management with greater discretion over the running of its organizations. Our own research into SMEs (Sung et al., 2000) has uncovered instances of group medical practices in the UK health service which have introduced HPWPs in an attempt to improve the quality of client care.

Triggers in the developing economies

In the developing economies, there are two important triggers at work. One is the spread of MNCs. As these companies start to use HPWPs in the parent organization and the benefits are established, they then implement them in their subsidiaries in the developing world. This was the case with Proctor and Gamble in China, another one of our case studies.[1] There the company has introduced HPWPs into its plants which manufacture a variety of products, ranging from paper sanitary products to hair shampoos. Again, this company made considerable efforts to ensure that all the staff share the same company values. Job rotation, multi-skilling and teamworking are central organizing principles when it comes to work design, with each team being a focus for workplace learning centred around the continuous improvement of the product. Performance measures have been established across a range of areas which are closely linked to the reward system. While it has taken a little longer to introduce these into the Chinese plants because of the need to replace expatriates with Chinese managers, the company reports few other differences in the rate at which these practices are being introduced into the Chinese plants when compared with those in other countries.

The other trigger which is helping spread these practices in the developing world is the growing use of international standards such as the ISO 9000 series. These are increasingly being used by companies operating in world markets as a guarantee of quality from suppliers located in the developing world. A recent ILO study of SMEs in Thailand revealed that one of the major triggers for reform in working practices and the training which supports the new working practices is the demand by customers for ISO 9000 certification. While ISO 9000 is no guarantor of the quality of HRD practices, it does place demands on companies for improvements in quality control and in the documentation of their internal procedures which can then lead to the introduction of HPWPs.

HPWPs as "sensible management"

At this stage, it is worth reminding ourselves that the introduction of these practices is not necessarily seen by the management at the time as a conscious attempt to establish HPWPs. The label has been an invention of business academics and consultants trying to make sense of the new practices. For example, when they were introduced into the Nissan plant in Sunderland in the United Kingdom (now the most productive in Europe) the management responsible for them saw these as just good management practices (Wickens, 1999). Some of these practices had been learned from the parent company, but others were introduced and modified in response to the everyday problems facing the company. Similarly in SSS Singapore, when the general manager introduced these practices he did not see them as HPWPs but as a way of managing that would enable him to overcome the problems of low morale and productivity which the company faced in the early 1990s. Only now do we refer to them as HPWPs. However, those larger companies which have introduced them more recently are starting to refer to them as HPWPs, as was the case with Proctor and Gamble in China. However, for most SMEs the concept is still unknown. Where these practices have been introduced in SMEs, it is usually because the owner/manager has either introduced them as "sensible" practices which make the most of the workforce or as a result of knowledge of "effective" practices which he or she has discovered elsewhere, perhaps through a benchmarking exercise.

How extensive is the use of these practices within organizations? Are some workers always excluded?

There is little systematic evidence on which to base an answer to this question. In most of the case studies, the use of these practices is all encompassing; all employees are involved. However, there are also examples of companies which use HPWPs only for management and white-collar employees in the "core" labour force. Additional flexibility is then built in through the use of part-time workers, temporary workers and in some instances through the use of subcontractors. For these "peripheral" workers, work is organized on traditional Taylorist lines. This is the flexible labour force that can be hired and fired in accordance with fluctuations in demand. Just how widespread this practice is we do not know.

Another possibility is that these practices can be introduced only for certain departments or groups within the organization. This was the case in one of the companies visited as a possible case study in East Asia. The company had previously sold computers, telephones and copiers through different departments. However, in response to market pressures and in an attempt to differentiate itself from its competitors, it decided to offer its customers a "total office information solution". This meant multi-skilling the sales staff and organizing them as teams to provide the total solution. This in turn meant changing their own procedures. The whole process took many months to implement, and the company underestimated the time and resources needed to put the practices in place. As a result, it was having second thoughts on whether to multi-skill the maintenance engineers required to provide customer support and to apply the same working practices to them. At the time of the interview, the company was uncertain as to whether the benefits would outweigh the costs.

Results of research by Pil and MacDuffie (1999) in the automobile industry and by Mason (1999) in various types of industry also suggest that many companies make partial use of HPWPs. Thus, in some companies teamworking is not used for all workers; neither is job rotation or problem-solving groups. The results of their studies show many firms making some use of HPWPs, but particularly important is their observation that in many companies HPWPs are only used for groups at the centre of the production process. As Mason (1999) also notes, in cookie manufacture those doing the baking are organized along high performance lines while those doing the wrapping and packing have their work organized along Talylorist lines.

As with any set of management practices, they can clearly be applied to sections of the labour force. However, for the employees to gain the maximum benefit, it is important that they are applied to all employees, both full-time and part-time. However, it is more difficult to apply them in the case of temporary staff. This is because the practices require time to implement and a good knowledge of the organization on the part of the employees to enable them to contribute effectively to the problem-solving and decision-making activities of the work group. This can be done for part-time workers, provided they are in permanent jobs.

Why are more companies not using these practices ?

Other business strategies can deliver enhanced profits and productivity in the short term

From what little research evidence we have, the short answer would be that there are other strategies that can be used to deliver enhanced profits in the short term (Ashton and Green, 1996). Lloyd (2000), cited earlier, identifies four such strategies adopted by companies in the UK pharmaceutical and aerospace industries. The first is the ability of firms to produce substantial savings by reducing the terms and conditions of non-core workers or outsourcing production and service functions such as catering and cleaning. Second, new technology is used to reduce the number of employees and de-skill them, thereby reducing costs. This sometimes involves the use of "lean" manufacturing to standardize the work process, reduce the skills required and ensure faster throughput. A third strategy is to pay relatively high wages and benefits as the central mechanism for recruiting, motivating and training employees. For professional engineers, career prospects, pay, working on new projects and broad job experiences are seen as the means of keeping them, in the same way that they are for research and development staff in the pharmaceutical industry. For sales staff, performance-related pay on its own appears to do the trick. In the short term, all these three are cheaper solutions than introducing HPWPs. In the fourth case, mergers and acquisitions are used to maintain competitiveness. These enable companies to buy in new products, increase the economies of scale and enter new markets and crucially to cut staff costs.

HPWOs may be more suitable for some product markets than for others

Another reason for companies not adopting HPWPs is that these practices may not be suitable for all companies and organizations. The OECD (1999) suggests that their use may be linked to Porter's typical product market strategies for competitive advantage (Porter, 1985), being especially suitable for a strategy of quality enhancement and innovation. As we have seen, many of the case studies were pursuing a strategy of differentiating their products or service from competitors on the basis of quality and service (Stevens, 2000). Indeed, much of the current literature points in the same direction. Osterman (1994) found those employers most likely to adopt them are in sectors exposed to international competition, employing more advanced technology and pursuing strategies which blend quality and service. Weinstein and Kochan (1995) also found that innovative work practices are likely to be found in greenfield sites, larger firms and in high value-added industries.

Ichniowski et al. (2000) suggest that innovative work practices may not be appropriate in industries where labour turnover is high and the employers cannot recoup their investment in training or in industries where technology determines the output, leaving little in the way of value-added to be produced by problem-solving groups. Alternatively, it may be that where employers are operating in markets where the products are labour intensive and low value-added in nature and the determinant of sales is cost, then there may be little to be gained through the use of these practices. It may be that Taylorist forms of management are more appropriate for companies operating in those markets. This is an argument that Mason (1999) makes very strongly. On the basis of research in Europe and North America, he argues that HPWPs are not appropriate for companies operating in mass-production, low value-added markets, such as the cookie market in the United States. There, Taylorist forms of mass production are seen as reaping higher profits and productivity than the use of HPWPs. HPWPs are seen as more appropriate for the smaller more differentiated product markets which are more characteristic of many northern European countries

Surveying this literature, Boxall and Purcell (2000:191) conclude "overall, the US research suggests that high-commitment practices are most popular in those sectors where the firm competes through quality and service and can only remain viable through exploiting advanced technology (as in complex manufacturing) or through a highly skilled interaction with clients (as in professional services)". Of course, this does not mean that they are only to be found in those sectors, as our case studies have shown. In Singapore, Comfort DC and SSS are not in general using complex technology but are nevertheless delivering a high quality of service.

Betcherman's (1997) evidence from Canada also suggests that high-commitment practices can also be used to deliver better performance among companies in more traditional, stable product markets. Thus, while HPWPs may be more appropriate for certain types of product market, they are certainly capable of improving the performance of many companies with more traditional technologies, as Betcherman's work suggests. Clearly, the short answer is that our existing knowledge just does not provide a clear answer on this point. The relationship between the use of these practices and the product market is an area where further research is urgently needed.

System inertia

Another reason for not implementing HPWPs is what Ichniowski refers to as system inertia (Ichniowski et al., 2000). This refers to the fact that once organizations have become established they can develop a strong resistance to change. It is therefore a particularly difficult problem in organizations on "brownfield sites", those sites where the company is already established and where organizational practices and culture have become embedded, for example at Thorn, Ltd. and SSS. For those in "greenfield sites", where the company is setting up the establishment and where there was no prior organization such as Comfort DC in Singapore or the Nissan company plant in the United Kingdom (Wickens,1999), they start with a clean sheet and therefore the introduction of these practices is seen as easier. However, as both these examples illustrate, the establishment of HPWPs still requires substantial vision and effort from the leadership. However, the system inertia that Ichniowski refers to would help explain why many established organizations do not take up these new practices.

Ichniowski et al. cite three reasons for this inertia. First, research by Levinthal (1994: cited in Ichniowski et al., 2000:28) has shown that firms tend to get "locked into" their initial choice of practices. Once a company has settled on a set of practices, these generate their own vested interests. Change will then threaten the interest of one group or another, whether these are managers or workers or both. In these circumstances, it may take a threat to the survival of the whole organization before that resistance can be overcome. A second reason is that companies may experiment with individual workplace innovations and when they see no improvements then discard them as a failure and give up attempting further change (Ichniowsli et al., 2000:30). As we have seen, individual practices do not produce the results; what is required is the introduction of bundles of practices. Thus, many employee-participation and quality-circle initiatives are abandoned after a few years (Lawler and Mohrman, 1987; Drago, 1988).

A third reason cited by Ichniowski et al. is that for some firms the switch to new work practices may also mean adopting an entirely new set of production and distribution technologies if major improvements in productivity are to be achieved. For example, Dunlop and Weil (2000) show how, in the clothing industry, the adoption of a modular production system required that the companies also invest in information and order-tracking technologies to streamline distribution channels if they are to achieve significant improvements. This may mean that the costs involved extend well beyond those spent in introducing the new working practices, as a substantial investment in new technology may also be required. Some companies refuse to make that investment. However, as our case studies have shown (SSS and Mandarin), an investment in additional technology is not always required. The introduction of HPWPs is not invariably linked to the introduction of new technology.

Mistrust between management and employees prevents the introduction of HPWPs

What our case studies do illustrate is the difficulty of introducing HPWPs in organizations in which there is a high level of mistrust between management and employees. Ichniowski et al. cite examples from some of the traditional steel mills they studied in the United States where worker participation schemes were seen as management tricks by the employees. They report that US unions see one of the major barriers being the behaviour of employers who ostensibly seek cooperation and partnership in existing unionized facilities while at the same time engaging in union avoidance practices at other sites (AFL-CIO, 1994).

Pil and MacDuffie (1999) provide an interesting set of findings in this area. The quantitative analysis of their automobile company data revealed that downsizing and measures which might undermine employee trust does not have an adverse impact on the introduction of HPWPs. Yet their analysis of the resistance put up by the Canadian Auto Workers' Union on the basis of their mistrust of management suggests that this had a major impact in reducing the use of HPWPs in the Canadian auto industry. However, as our case studies illustrate, a number of companies introduced HPWPs on the back of substantial downsizing, but this did not necessarily result in heightened mistrust between the managers and workers, providing management put in place measures to sustain the development of trust. SAB provides a good example of how this was done.

The role of unions

In some instances, management has tried to introduce variants of HPWPs to marginalize unions by excluding them from the change and seeking instead to develop direct lines of communication with the workers. As Lloyd (2000) points out, individual appraisal, merit pay, team briefings, and individual forms of employee involvement can operate in competition with union forms of communication and representation. Moreover, unions are inevitably concerned when the introduction of new working practices is associated with downsizing and increased employee insecurity. Nevertheless, recent work has found that new working practices are more likely to be adopted in unionized plants in the United Kingdom (Sisson, 1993 and 1994). Bacon and Blyton (2000) also found that within the UK steel industry union attitudes do not provide an important obstacle to the introduction of teamworking, although union representatives are more critical where managers seek to introduce teamworking for narrow economic reasons. However, formal agreements protecting workers, involving job security and redundancy provisions, do encourage cross-functional working and teams adopting more responsibilities.

Within the United Kingdom, further analysis of the Chartered Institute of Personnel and Development (CIPD) Training and Development Survey for 2001 revealed a significant association between the use of certain HPWPs and union involvement in policy decisions and implementation. In short, where trade unions are involved in training policy at the level of the work establishment, there is greater likelihood that the company will make use of staff attitude surveys, workplace consultative committees, job rotation, mentoring, train-the-trainer programmes and quality circles. In terms of the bundles we identified earlier, union involvement in training policy at the level of the firm is associated with the use of the work-design/employee-involvement bundle, the support-for-performance bundle, and the communications bundle. However, here it is only involved with some practices and not others; for example, trade union participation in training policy at the level of the firm is not associated with the use of peer review/360 per cent appraisals, personal appraisals and personal development plans. These are the individual-based practices which may threaten union-based forms of representation. The only practices for which there is a negative association with union involvement in training policy are in the use of profit-sharing and share-ownership rewards. Where these practices are in place, unions are less likely to be involved in training policy matters at the level of the firm. In general, however, this shows a more extensive involvement of trade unions in the introduction of HPWPs in the United Kingdom than has been generally recognized.

At the European level, evidence from a survey of ten European countries revealed that Works' Councils and union representatives are in most cases "agents of change" rather than barriers to worker participation (Gill and Krieger, 1999:587). If the workers' representatives have a degree of trust in the management, then forms of representation such as Works' Councils can be a powerful agent of change.

Overcoming problems of implementation

Building trust

Once a decision has been made to introduce these practices, our case studies suggest that there is far more involved in establishing trust than just securing the acquiescence of the unions. Almost all the case studies above suggest that managers must actively engage in capturing the hearts and minds of all employees and gain their commitment to the core values and objectives of the organization. This is also one of the major findings of the New Forms of Work Organization in Ireland Programme, a programme designed to help companies introduce HPWPs. The evaluators of that Programme report that "...the Programme demonstrates convincingly that effective and sustainable change, including competitiveness improvement, can best be achieved through dialogue built on trust and cooperation" (Savage, 1999:11).

The building of trust and cooperation requires a fairly fundamental shift in the balance of power within the organization if it is to be effective. Unless employees are directly involved in the decision-making processes, the introduction of these practices is unlikely to achieve its objectives. Lowe (2000) provides a series of examples of companies which have introduced some HPWPs without securing effective worker participation, thus producing high levels of dissatisfaction among the employees. The following example is cited by Lowe.

The need to secure employee support: The case of CAMI in Canada

CAMI is a joint production venture, between General Motors and Suzuki, to produce small utility vehicles in Ontario, Canada. CAMI selected 2,300 recruits and trained them in the values of empowerment, open communications, continuous improvement and team work. Initially union-management relations were harmonious as the workers settled in. However, over time the workers lost their trust in management. "Flexible use of labour came to mean using the fewest workers possible; multi-skilling (acquiring a range of skills through training and performing a variety of tasks over time) became multi-tasking (doing several tasks at once). Job rotation became a way of having team members cover for absent or injured co-workers by doubling up on jobs. Repetitive strain injuries became a frequent symptom of work speed-ups in pursuit of reduced production costs. For CAMI workers, hopes of having a say in making their jobs more interesting evaporated. As one team leader put it, beyond the language of a new work philosophy, workers came to view CAMI as "just another auto plant" (Lowe, 2000:152). The result was the first workers' strike at a Japanese plant in Canada, endorsed by 98 per cent of the workers. After five weeks, the workers negotiated changes in team organization, work pace, health and safety provision and provision of relief workers.

Lowe cites two other Canadian examples of instances where HPWPs have been introduced and where employees have experienced work as repetitive and stressful. Getting the full involvement of workers in the decision-making process is not easy, and there is a real danger that HPWPs can lead to work intensification with little or no benefit to the employee.

Overcoming managerial resistance

The other major barrier to the introduction of HPWPs frequently mentioned in the literature is the resistance from managers. The shift from command and control organizations usually involves a major redistribution of authority in the organization, especially if self-managed teams are introduced. Inevitably, these latter changes remove authority from the manager. For managers who have been promoted into such jobs on the basis of seniority or technical skills and where they rely on privileged access to information and the authority invested in the position to maintain their control over the workforce, these new practices are very threatening. Not only are they seen as being deprived of their authority; they also have to relate to subordinates in a very different manner - they have to win their consent and support as a leader rather than a commander. In view of this, it is no surprise that managers can be one of the main sources of resistance to the implementation of HPWPs. Lloyd (2000) cites the concerns of a senior technical manager in one pharmaceutical company which had delayered the organization and then had difficulty in finding appropriate managers, having to move specialists from other departments such as quality control into first-line management (called supervisory positions in this firm).

> "Supervisors' level of skill is poor, the level of training is poor, the level we've trusted them is poor. Getting them involved in change is difficult… One big problem is incestuousness. A lot (of managers) have seen nothing else but this site. It is difficult to get empowerment and involvement, they have had no experience of that and there is an unwillingness to look outside. They believe we are at the leading edge" (Lloyd, 2000:22).

In some cases, those managers who are resistant are replaced. In others, the companies or organizations have to use extensive training to enable the managers to acquire the behaviours appropriate to their new role.

Upskilling the HR directors (and trainers)

Another major impediment to the introduction of these practices is the capabilities of HR managers (Becker et al., 1997; Beer, 1997). The effective implementation of these practices requires that the HR director acts with the head of the organization as a partner in strategic change. The problem is that many HR directors do not have the requisite business acumen and knowledge of strategy and change management. In the United States, the expertise of many HR managers is restricted to the delivery of traditional HRM activities; they are limited in terms of their abilities to translate the firm's strategy and operational goals into actionable HR goals and then to implement those goals. They are good administrators (Huselid, Jackson and Schuler, 1997; cited in Becker and Huselid, 1998). The same findings have emerged from research in the United Kingdom (Guest, 2000). There, Guest reports that many CEOs and managing directors see the link between business strategy and HRD as important but have not done anything about implementing it because they feel their senior HRD personnel do not have the requisite skills. In the absence of this knowledge and expertise residing in the HR manager, the CEO and managing directors are severely handicapped in attempts to introduce these practices.

Using benchmarking

Another problem to be overcome is the lack of knowledge about these new working practices and the impact they are capable of generating in terms of enhanced performance. This requires publicity, and here the professional HRD institutes and government departments can play a role, as well as the providers of continuing professional development. In the absence of this, companies are left to their own devices. In view of this, it is not surprising that many of the companies which were among the first to introduce HPWPs had links with Japanese companies, either as subsidiaries or direct competitors. Thus, in the case of Nissan UK, it had access to the parent company in Japan and knowledge of leading-edge developments among UK and US automobile manufacturers. In the case of the Laiki Bank, many of its practices were adapted from those of the HSBC which had an interest in the Laiki Bank.

Where these kinds of links are absent, companies use benchmarking exercises to identify best practices, as in the case of SAB and Xerox. In the auto industry, Pil and MacDuffie report that "lead plant" approaches perform a similar function. Efforts are concentrated in creating change in one plant with the lessons learned being used to implement change in other plants. The authors report that this works well when the two plants are in different parts of the world and not seen to be competing for resources. In other instances, plants are assigned by the parent company to a "sister plant" to learn HIWPs. At the level of the individual establishment, some plants bring in "champions", people with experience of introducing these practices, to advise on the introduction of HIWPs. However, the problem here is that the changes are far too complex for one individual to be able to provide all the requisite expertise.

Benchmarking enables the company to compare aspects of its systems and processes with best practice elsewhere and so identify the tasks to be undertaken. Benchmarking also has important motivational consequences, especially if employee representatives participate in benchmarking visits. There are numerous reports that once employees see what is possible and what the benefits are in terms of enhanced productivity, job satisfaction, potential income and job security, then the natural fear of change is overcome. These trips frequently result in the employees "buying in" on the project.

When Thorn Lighting became independent from Thorn-EMI in 1993, the senior management team set out to identify new strategies and operations for competing in world markets. A programme of "exploration" was activated to find and learn from best practices in world-leading companies and to compare those practices with the status quo inside Thorn. Project teams were set up to review the existing internal processes and challenge their effectiveness in contributing to business performance by comparing the internal situation with external, equivalent processes. Each project team was asked to focus upon an area of the business that asserts maximum leverage on overall performance. A major transition then began to take place for shifting the culture from relative "introversion" to "customer focused and outward looking". This process is common among organizations which have successfully implemented HPWPs.

Internal training

Hackman et al. (2000) conceptualize this process as an inversion of the traditional management triangle. The traditional concern of management is to coordinate workers in order to produce specific goods or services which are then delivered to the customer. In HPWOs, this is inverted: the customer is the focus of all activities, work teams are there to ensure customer satisfaction and the manager's role is to support work groups in the delivery of the product or service.

The significance here is that the introduction of new working practices such as those described above almost always involves fairly extensive training. The use of teamworking involves more extensive training in the German pump manufacturers, whether that is technical training for semi-skilled workers to make them multi-skilled or in communication and management skills for the skilled workers to make them effective members of self-managed work groups. The case studies introduced in Chapter 2 all involved a substantial investment in training in order for the new practices to become embedded. Once the new practices are established, the process of learning and training does not stop there. Skills constantly need upgrading, and new problems facing the employees in their everyday activities necessitate further learning. Any attempt to change the culture of an organization usually involves intensive training. In the case of SSS in Singapore, an organization which bridges the public and private sectors, we witness the extensive use of training to help change the company culture and to introduce and sustain new working practices.

In view of this, it is not surprising that the research findings from large-scale surveys show an association between the use of HPWPs and more extensive training within the organization (Osterman, 1995; Whitfield, 2000). Those organizations with HPWPs tend to exhibit higher levels of training. This is a feature of HPWOs that we discuss in more detail in Chapter 4. Here it is sufficient to point out that it is the introduction of the new practices that creates the demand for training. It is not that the firms start to increase their level of training and that produces the new practices; rather, the causal sequence is the other way round. In this sense, the demand for training is a derived demand.

Changing recruitment

Another area that frequently requires attention with the introduction of HPWPs is the selection process. Not only does it require a good grasp of basic skills but also the personality that will facilitate its "buying in" to the philosophy of the organization. The general manager of Comfort deliberately recruited young people because it is easier to mould them into the company's way of thinking, its values and behaviour patterns. Similarly, when Proctor and Gamble introduced HPWPs in its plants in China it also deliberately recruited young graduates for the same reason. The Laiki Bank also targeted young graduates. For other companies where this tactic may not be realistic, considerable resources are devoted to recruitment and selection in order to select only those with a personality and values appropriate to the demands of the organization. Pil and MacDuffie (1999:101) report that Japanese transplants in the United States selected only one in 25 of all applicants.

What do we know about the factors that lead to successful implementation?

Commitment from the leadership

Research from both the United States and the United Kingdom suggests that a strong and active commitment from senior management is essential for successful implementation of HPWPs (Guest, 2000; Patterson et al., 1997). This is understandable, as the use of HPWPs involves a substantial change from the command and control approach of traditional management, with its reliance on hierarchy, narrow job specifications and unquestioned acceptance of authority. This is evident in the case of all the private sector case studies we cited above where senior management is invariably committed to the introduction and use of HPWPs.

This kind of leadership is difficult to identify through the use of survey questionnaires. Nevertheless, Wood et al. (2001) have used the UK Workplace Employee Relations Survey (WERS) data set of 2,191 cases to investigate the possibility that senior management plays a crucial role in the introduction of what it terms high involvement management practices. Using a latent variable approach with the high involvement or high performance working practices as manifest indicators, they found evidence of a strong underlying "high involvement orientation".[2] This is defined as "an underlying managerial orientation towards the development of a particular role orientation on the part of employees so that they are flexible, are expansive in their perceptions and willingly contribute proactively to innovation. Its ultimate aim is for employees to behave (adapting a phrase from a practicing manager) as if they have two jobs: one to execute tasks, the other to think of better ways of doing them". This manifests itself in the use of core high involvement (performance) practices which the authors call task oriented (e.g. teamworking,[3] quality circles) and individual-level supports (e.g. training in human relations skills, team briefing). In short, the implementation of these practices is the manifestation of an underlying management philosophy. It is not just a question of aggregating individual practices over time.

Change in the basis of control

The successful introduction of HPWPs also requires a radical change in the basis of control within the organization, with less reliance on external pressures and more on the internal commitment of employees to organizational objectives. Rather than being told what to do, managers and workers have to determine their own behaviour in the light of their knowledge of the organization and its objectives and values. In the jargon of modern management textbooks, the workers become self-empowered. Peter Wickens (1999), the former director of Nissan

69

UK, attempts to capture this through the phrase "Energize your Enterprise", a phrase he uses to point out how ordinary employees feel good when everyone contributes towards the improvement of performance and where everyone is valued for helping make the enterprise a better place to work in. It is a phrase he uses to talk about the dramatic changes in the level of commitment which can be achieved on the part of workers when these practices are effectively introduced.

Continuous improvement

These changes are clearly not a one-off activity. Our case studies illustrate the fact that in many organizations it takes years to bring them about. Moreover, once they are introduced they require continuous refinement, as changes in areas such as the product market, company ownership and technology generate the need for constant change. In the case of Xerox, Hackman et al. (2000) speak of a journey over 15 years (which is still continuing) to introduce empowered work teams. They point out, on the basis of very thorough research, that teams require a vision of where they are going, responsibilities have to be structured, reward and communication systems have to be implemented and personnel have to be skilled in the process of coaching and team development.

What are the costs?

The introduction of these practices involves substantial costs, not least in the time and effort of those involved. It requires increased coordination, but Hackman et al. (2000) also point out that communicating goals and objectives is always fraught with difficulties, while market pressures can undermine team stability. Moreover, high quality team-based reward and recognition systems are difficult to design and implement. Even the acquisition of new skills takes time; the relevant knowledge has to be acquired and new skills have to be practiced before they are embedded in the workforce. Finally, teams need time to absorb the relevant business information and then learn how to use it to solve problems.

From the individual employee's point of view, such changes are also not without their costs. The emphasis on commitment to the organization's values and going beyond the immediate call of duty is not an attitude that everyone is comfortable with. Peer-group pressure can easily lead to the intensification of work. Work in HPWOs can be stressful if it is not managed carefully. Moreover, because of the emphasis on teamwork, workers who are uncomfortable with this can easily disrupt the morale of other employees. Therefore, while there is always considerable emphasis on the importance of incentives and workers "internal" motivation, managers usually move rapidly to deal with employees who do not "buy in" to the values of the organization and who do not work effectively in a group or team context. Although this problem is rarely confronted in the academic textbooks, "successful" managers' accounts of the process of implementation are replete with reference to the use of "the stick as well as the carrot" or to "terrorists" in the ranks. One way or another, these employees have either to buy into the change or leave.

The American Society for Training and Development (ASTD) critical success factors

The ASTD, using a combination of experienced practitioners and consultants, identified the following as critical success factors that can make or break a high performance work system (Gephart and Van Buren, 1998):

- a compelling case for change linked to the company's business strategy;
- change owned by senior and line managers;
- sufficient resources and support for the change effort;
- early and broad communication;
- teams implemented in a systematic context;
- adequate capability training;
- capacity for measuring the results of change;
- continuity of key leaders and champions.

Finally, it is important to note that once HPWPs are established this is merely the start of the process, because with continuous changes in the organization's environment and in its internal processes, there is always a constant need to realign practices. At any one point in time, it is easy for the team, functional and organizational goals to move out of alignment with each other. As we saw in the case of Thorn, Ltd., the company was reluctant to reward team performance lest the team members lose sight of the fact that it is the collective organizational performance that is crucial. There is always the fear that by placing teams in competition with each other, the teams' immediate goals may displace those of the organization as a whole. Each organization has to find its own solutions to these problems but the potential rewards, when they get it right, are substantial.

Conclusions

We started this chapter asking why more organizations have not adopted HPWPs. The answer is in part due to the fact that they are not easy to introduce. They tend to emerge as one response to crisis situations. They may be more appropriate in some industries and in some markets than in others. However, perhaps the most important factor is the sheer difficulty in implementing them when there are other routes that employers can adopt to increase profits and performance in the short term. Nevertheless, once implemented, there are substantial benefits for both employers and employees. One of the secrets is securing the effective collaboration and cooperation of the two parties.

As for the question as to whether there is a magic set of best practices which can then be implemented, it is clear that the answer is a resounding no. All work practices are embedded in a wider set of institutional structures which are shaped by the national history and politics. HPWPs are no exception; the way they are introduced is conditioned by the pre-existing organizational characteristics and the wider labour market and training infrastructure as we saw in Germany. It means that each senior management team or CEO has to feel his/her own way in how to introduce the practices. We have attempted in this chapter to provide some guidance as to the main pitfalls and how they may be avoided.

All this points to the fact that investment in HPWPs represents a long-term commitment on the part of both senior managers and workers. Therefore, broader institutional arrangements, such as the form taken by the financial infrastructure and the political framework, have a crucial role to play in determining whether the HPWOs is a viable option. If all the emphasis is on the push for short-term profits, this is not a fertile ground for the spread of HPWOs. Even if the practices are in place, changes in ownership bringing an owner concerned with increasing profits in the short term can threaten the continued viability of HPWOs, as in the case cited in the previous chapter. At the same time, as Heckscher and Schurman (1997) have pointed out, labour-management cooperation can easily run into problems because of pressures from outside the organization. As we have argued, implementing and sustaining HPWPs is not easy but the rewards for both parties are certainly worth it.

Notes

[1] These were case studies by the authors and the Centre for Labour Market Studies in conjunction with the ILO.

[2] This approach is used to reveal relationships which exist among the variables in the data set but which are not necessarily evident to the researchers.

[3] The assumption is that the teams are oriented toward and responsible for the execution of a range of tasks.

CHAPTER 4

WORKPLACE LEARNING AND HIGH PERFORMANCE WORKING

Introduction

In this chapter, we aim to show how the way in which we organize work determines the opportunities for learning in the workplace. Essentially, we argue that the traditional Taylorist forms of work organization minimize the skills required of most employees to perform the job. They also minimize the involvement of these employees with the organization. The assumption behind Taylorist management systems is that the most efficient ways of organizing the production of standardized goods for a mass market is for each task to be broken down into its most elementary components. This achieves economies of scale through an intensified division of labour. Management, as the repository of the requisite scientific and technical knowledge, is responsible for overseeing the process and ensuring maximum performance.

HPWPs, as we have seen, are totally different. There, the organization of production is based on the assumption that competition is based not just on the cost but also on incremental improvements in the quality of the goods or services produced. Here the division of labour is organized to ensure that all employees are in a position to contribute toward the overall performance of the organization and its improvement through time. Management is no longer the sole repository of knowledge; it is now its task to shape the production process in such a way as to maximize the contributions that the workers make to the improvement of the organization's performance. This means implementing the types of practices we have identified in the four bundles. For the workers, it means that work provides an opportunity for more involvement from them in the process of production. It also means that they must acquire the social and problem-solving skills required for the management of production, in addition to the technical skills required for their immediate work tasks. This generates the conditions not just for higher levels of learning and skill formation but for learning to become a continuous process. It also involves a radical transformation of the role of managers and trainers as they become responsible for managing this process of continuous learning.

Supporting workplace learning for high performance working

Understanding workplace learning

Workplace learning is a relatively new area of academic enquiry but, as our knowledge expands, it is evident that it must be seen as part of a more general process of skill formation. This is because learning is not a one-off activity like buying a pair of shoes. How we learn and the intellectual capacities we have developed to aid the process are dependent on our prior experiences in family, community and school, which in turn form part of the way we see ourselves, our self-image. Our successes and failures in these areas form the background against which we experience the workplace and the opportunities it offers for learning and the acquisition of skills. These experiences condition our attitudes toward learning and the basic skills we bring with us into the workplace. It is in this sense that workplace learning is part of a general process of skill formation, a process that is ongoing as we change jobs and raise children, a process which leads on into retirement and beyond.

Here we only examine two arenas, namely the school/college and workplace. The family and school provide the initial basic education, the grounding in numeracy, literacy and now computer literacy, the building blocks on which other skills are built later.[1] In the case of those entering traditional Taylorist forms of organization as low-level, white-collar, service or manual employees, work offers little more in the way of opportunities to further develop their capabilities. For others, destined for professional, managerial and technical jobs, basic schooling is followed by further general and technical education that provides the underpinning knowledge for the performance of specialized work roles. For those who enter HPWOs at all levels, the workplace offers the opportunity to continue to develop their skills throughout their working life. First, we turn to an examination of the process of learning in Taylorist organizations.

Learning, training and performance in traditional organizations

Taylorist organizations

These organizations emerged out of the success of pioneering industrialists, such as Bolton and Watt in the engineering industry in the United Kingdom and Ford in the automobile industry in the United States, in rationalizing the process of production. They combined new forms of organizing labour in factories, together with the new technology, to find new ways of increasing productivity. Over a number of decades, these replaced the older craft-based production of goods which had developed out of the medieval guild system. The old system was based on one craftsman or group of craftsmen producing one-off items. To increase production required more craftsmen.

The new pioneers devised ways of reorganizing the process of production. The work of each craftsman was broken down into its constituent elements or tasks, and these were often further broken down into fragments of tasks. The performance of these tasks was then coordinated by supervisors, superintendents or managers. The managers had knowledge of the overall system of production. They were often assisted in this by technical experts who provided the technical knowledge. Workers required little or no knowledge of anything other than their immediate tasks. Whereas in the past craftsmen had required a period of several years' training, the new form of industrial production could now use unskilled workers, sometimes barely literate, and train them within days, if not hours, to become efficient operatives. Workers became more or less interchangeable "hands" or units of production. Of course, not all craftsmen were replaced; some remained to maintain the equipment, as the new workers had no knowledge of the machinery with which they were working, but the skills of the craftsmen no longer formed the basis on which production was organized.

This new system achieved major improvements in performance. The intensified division of labour on which it was based enabled dramatic improvements to be made in labour productivity. The same number of workers could now produce far more units of production, whether these were stationary engines, bars of soap, motor cars or bread loaves. The costs of production fell dramatically, thereby enabling what were previously often luxury items to be made available to a mass market. However, for the system of mass production to be economically viable, it did require a massive market. Only then could the economies of scale on which it was based be realized. This was one of the reasons large-scale mass production was so extensively developed in the United States.

This had a number of consequences for the process of learning and performance within organizations. We now take each group and examine what these were. First, the managers: under a craft-based system of production, managers were primarily responsible for the sale of the goods and determining the payment and conditions of the craft workers. The craft workers had a knowledge of the production system, and it was they who organized the ways in which goods were produced. With the advent of mass production, workers lost control over the organization of production and of their work. In many respects, this was a zero-sum struggle: the workers' loss was the managers' gain.

Management

In the system of mass production, managers became the repository of all knowledge about the production process and how it was to be organized.[2] There are a number of dimensions to this change. The knowledge and skills required by managers increased substantially. Managers now required knowledge of the technical details of production or alternatively ready access to those who have such specialized knowledge. They also required new skills in organizing work and in designing jobs and tasks that could be split into their basic components. They required knowledge of how to coordinate large numbers of employees performing routine tasks, all this in addition to their previous knowledge of selling and determining the conditions of work.

Knowledge of how to coordinate the work of numbers of employees was available from the armed forces. There, over the generations, experience had been accumulated on how best to discipline and organize the activities of many hundreds and thousands of people. The basis on which this was done was through a command and control hierarchy. Many of these "principles of management" were readily transferable to the problems of coordinating hundreds and thousands of workers involved in the routine fragmented tasks associated with mass production or the coordination of the thousands involved in areas such as rail transport.[3] Strict hierarchies of command with their associated span of control were as effective in the new industrial arena as they were in the armed forces. The authority of the new managers was vested in their position within the hierarchy, giving them powers of command over subordinates.

The solution to the problems generated by the rapid increase in the knowledge required of managers was to differentiate their functions. Selling became a separate function as it was transformed into marketing for mass-produced goods; finance became a separate function, as did personnel and production and so on. To operate effectively in these new organizations, managers required higher levels of knowledge and new skills. In the Anglo-Saxon countries, the technical expertise was provided through technical experts such as engineers who had an advisory function to management, a staff position, as in the armed forces. In Germany, managers were predominantly recruited from the ranks of engineers who already had command of much of the technical information.

In the United States, this growth in the knowledge required of managers resulted in the emergence of specialized provision in higher education – what later became the ubiquitous Master's in Business Administration. In some areas such as finance and personnel, specialized professional qualifications emerged. Managers had to undergo intensive education and training in the skills required for the various specializations. The new knowledge they required became codified knowledge, part of a systematized body of knowledge based on theory, often formalized in terms of laws. This abstract knowledge was, and still is, transmitted in an academic context either in the university lecture theatre, through books or in a formal training course. The time taken to acquire and master this knowledge is measured in years, and success in the learning process is usually assessed through some type of formal examination. Given the fact that the mass markets and the new technologies were initially fairly stable, once the requisite knowledge had been acquired and the learner certified as competent in its use, it provided the basis for a lifetime of practice, albeit with the need for occasional professional updating. For managers, work came to require a lengthy period of initial education.

However, formal education could not provide knowledge of the organizational structure within which the managers operated. This required a different form of knowledge of how the production process operates or the service is delivered, how the various component parts of the organization fit together, how the financial controls operate in terms of specific procedures, how the company strategy operates and how relationships with superiors, subordinates and colleagues are handled. This knowledge about the procedures and personnel within the organization as well of the informal relationships through which a great deal of information flowed and which could be crucial in ensuring that the requisite actions were initiated cannot readily be codified. This is tacit knowledge, knowledge acquired through everyday interaction with colleagues and personal experience. When it comes to problem solving, managers have to draw on all this together with the technical knowledge they have acquired over the years. The range and depth of the tacit knowledge required is not something that can be acquired overnight; in some cases, it takes years. However, because this knowledge is not codified and formalized, it is difficult to transmit in a formalized context.[4] To acquire this knowledge as well as the additional technical skills, managers required "developing".

In large organizations, this process could not be left to chance, and therefore elaborate programmes of management development were developed. These systematically expose trainees to the various functions within the organization, providing access to a range of different learning experiences within each function or section, thereby providing both breadth and depth of knowledge. The breadth is required in order that the managers are aware of the overall structure of the company or organization and their position in it. Depth of knowledge is required in order that they have the technical knowledge to perform their specific duties effectively. The management development programmes ensure that for managers and professional/technical workers the process of skill formation in the workplace is relatively highly structured. It also means that for many managers the workplace is a source of continual learning and development.

This concentration of knowledge of the scientific basis of the technology and production process, together with the formal and tacit knowledge of the organization required for effective management, explains why management training has traditionally taken the lion's share of company resources devoted to training. The other employees, especially the operatives, did not need to know so much. Indeed, they were only required to have a fraction of the knowledge acquired by managers in order to perform their routine tasks.

Production workers

In mass production organizations, the organization of work is determined by managers. Tasks are broken down into their constituent elements, with each worker performing one limited set of operations, whether that is placing one component on a car as it moves down the assembly line or stitching the collar onto a garment or sweeping up peas as they fall off a belt conveying them to the freezing process. These tasks can often be learned in minutes, although it may take hours to learn to coordinate the motor operations involved to get the execution of the task up to the speed required by the line or to make a minimum level of pay if paid by the piece. The knowledge requirements are minimal. There may be a literacy requirement to enable the worker to read safety instructions. The organization of work is not the concern of the worker. The speed of work is often determined by the line or the work study engineer. Discipline is required in order to turn up regularly for work and to accept the commands issued by the supervisor. Beyond that, the company makes no demands on the worker.

In these organizations, the line managers or supervisors decide what the workers need to know. That small fraction of knowledge and information is then transmitted from the expert "trainer" to the novice or trainee. Training is highly structured and task specific and usually occurs in a classroom situation or, if the task is very basic, on the job. Workers are given information on a "need-to-know" basis providing them with just enough information or knowledge to perform their clearly defined task.[5]

Krogt and Warmerdam (1997:92) describe the delivery of knowledge in two such food-processing organizations in the Netherlands as follows:

> "The work process is broken down into individual, short-cycle jobs (conveyor belt work) in a profoundly hierarchical staff-line organization. Work in the production

departments is to a great extent standardized, with planning and preparation taken care of by lower management staff, which normally leaves operators on the line little or no room for independent decisions about work tempo, order or method. Only in non-routine situations are operators expected - within certain limits - to take decisions themselves."

In these organizations, the researchers report that it is the managers who determine the training content and who participate in it. Training is primarily seen as an instrument for providing the skills and attitudes required for the proper functioning of the production process: it is pre-designed by experts, with the subject matter supplied in the small portions required for specific tasks, planned beforehand and monitored during the training process. Having had the need for training identified by the departmental manager, the trainer draws up the training plan and implements the programme. Normally, in the organizations studied by Krogt and Warmerdam, this involves a needs assessment exercise, the definition of training goals, the design of curriculum, implementation of the course and sometimes an evaluation at the end. In this entire process, the workers tend to play what the authors term "a consuming role", with short courses being delivered to them in a somewhat coercive manner.

These examples are of course from companies that would normally be regarded as having good training provision. In the majority of companies in countries such as the United States, the United Kingdom, Australia and Canada, such training would be less systematic both in terms of the identification of the training need and in the delivery of information and knowledge required by the worker. Very often training is ad hoc and the requisite "skills" required to perform the tasks are transmitted by fellow workers. Moreover, because the tasks are so limited in nature, the knowledge and information required for their mastery, together with the practice required to achieve satisfactory performance, can be acquired in a matter of days at the start of the person's time with the company. Further "skills" are only then required when there are changes to the work routines (Smith and Hayton, 1999). However, even for these companies, the basic point made by Krogt and Warmerdam still holds, namely that training is delivered to workers by experts, and such training is only sufficient to enable the workers to perform clearly delineated, often fragmented, tasks. That is all workers are expected to know.

From the trainees' perspective in such organizations, they are receiving an important message from their superiors. The fact that their job is broken down into fragmented tasks that require only a limited amount of skill to perform directs their attention to the immediate job. Knowledge of anything outside those narrow tasks is off limits, for they should only be concerned with, and will only be rewarded for, performance of their immediate job (Darrah, 1996). The narrowly defined work role means that they are not expected to know anything beyond the immediate work tasks; the operation of the wider production process is of no concern. Moreover, given the narrow definition of their tasks, they have few if any opportunities to develop broader skills. The feedback they receive on their performance concerns only those fragmented tasks. Indeed, the overall performance of the company is seen as management's responsibility; the worker's responsibility is merely to turn up regularly and perform his or her tasks as determined by management.

Of course, not all industrial work is as restricted as that portrayed here. Where a different technology such as batch production is used, the opportunities for learning are slightly broader. Using ethnographic techniques, Darrah (1996) provides valuable insights into the process of learning in these conditions. He studied the experience of operatives in a US wire and cable company producing batches of cables. There recruits are provided with a short period of formal classroom instruction (usually one week) in the training centre before leaving for the shop floor under the guidance of a trainer or experienced operative; then they are left on their own to handle the machines. He pointed out that while the basic description of the job sounds simple - verifying paperwork, stringing up the wire or cable, and monitoring - the reality is far more complex. He noted that workers need to acquire the tacit knowledge to diagnose problems with the machine and the materials with which they are working. This results in each operator developing his or her own style. In addition to this knowledge, each worker has to acquire (informally) knowledge of how to operate effectively in the department: for example, knowledge of whom to approach for help when things go wrong, how to approach colleagues and knowledge of what is going on in the shop and what is expected of them. This is the same informal learning that we observed with the managers, but because the world of the operative is more circumscribed the learning opportunities are fewer. Their "careers" are restricted to that section of the enterprise which contains their "shop" or department. Because they are working in batches, they need to know how to adjust the machines on which they are working and how their operations fit in with others within the department. This is more than the operator on the line, but the opportunities it provides for learning are still minimal.

From the perspective of the worker, what is crucial is that the range of learning opportunities and the access to knowledge and information provided by the company are extremely limited. In addition, the expectations of the company about the level of performance are restricted to the one set of tasks. This is especially the case in mass-production companies. In this context, the employee has few opportunities to exercise discretion and develop more complex skills, which as Kohn and his associates (1983, 1990) have shown can limit the potential of the person to develop both his/her self-confidence and their intellectual skills.

Not all employees, even in mass-production companies, have such limited learning opportunities. Even in Anglo-Saxon countries, craft workers are still required to maintain the equipment and machinery. In Germany, craft workers play a more central role in the production process. For these workers, there is still the requirement that they undergo a prolonged period of training after leaving the education system. This involves off-the-job, classroom-based learning of the theory underpinning their practical work, as well as extensive practical experience in the workplace. Together, this means several years of further training culminating in certification. Traditionally this training has been seen as providing sufficient knowledge and skills for a lifetime, although modern forms of ICT and new working practices are starting to change that. Nevertheless, this depth of training as part of an occupational community means that these trade occupations form an important part of the young person's identity, especially in the Germanic countries where the quality of the training is high.

The picture we have drawn of the ways in which mass, process and batch production shapes opportunities for learning has been confined to the manufacturing and food-processing industries where these ways of organizing production were primarily developed. In recent decades, these have declined in importance as sources of employment, especially in the older industrial countries, to be replaced by the service industries. In view of this, can we make the same claims in these latter industries there for the impact of Taylorist forms of management on the learning process? Here the answer has to be a resounding yes. The growth and deregulation of financial services, the introduction of new technology, and the growth of the communications and computer industries have created the opportunities for radical changes. In banking, the major UK companies have long relied on an extensive division of labour to deal with the processing of cheques. In the early 1990s, O'Reilly found that "in the Central London Offices, an entire floor was given over to the work of tray agreers (a specialized clerical job) and VDU operators. On another floor, the large sorting machines were operated by shifts of full- and part-time staff". Of the workers she interviewed, 36 per cent described their work as "very routine and repetitive" and a further 39 per cent described it as "routine, occasionally do new things" (O'Reilly, 1992).

Baldry et al. (1998:171) also report employees in the UK financial sector solely engaged in routine data entry, while others are engaged in oscillation between repetitive screen tasks and telephone work. They report that in many offices the inherently uninteresting repetitive manual clerical work has become more monotonous through the widespread use of IT systems, even where the basic unit of work organization is a multi-functional team. These same authors also report that the introduction of teams, far from leading to enhanced collective effort, increased job satisfaction and worker autonomy, often produces the opposite: individual output devoid of conceptual content, job dissatisfaction and tight physical and technological surveillance, referred to as "Team Taylorism". As we noted in Chapter 3, without the active consent and involvement of the employees, teamworking and other forms of HPWPs can readily lead to exploitation.

In the US banking industry, Hunter (1999) reports the use of two "ideal types" of employment system: the inclusive model, referred to here as high performance working, and the segmented model. In the inclusive model, tellers' jobs are enriched to include sales responsibilities as well as basic account opening and the communication of product information, and all employees are responsible for initiating and maintaining customer contact. In the segmented model, employees are matched to different roles. The specialized and "personal bankers" deal with elite customers and clients. Ordinary customers are dealt with by relatively low-paid, part-time employees. Cross training is scant. Technology is used to deskill jobs and to script and monitor the routinized performance of employees. However, while most banks are introducing some elements of high performance working, Hunter found that few had moved unambiguously in the direction of one model or the other. Clearly Taylorism is far from dead in the US service sector. If the analysis offered by Hunter is correct, then it appears that the banking sector is still something of a battleground between the two contrasting ways of organizing production. The future quality of working life for a substantial sector of the population is still undecided.

Skill formation in HPWOs

Translating learning into performance at the individual level

In this section, we continue to illustrate how the organization of production determines learning opportunities for employees, but in the case of HPWOs these opportunities are designed to maximize the contribution of all employees to company objectives. This enables us to highlight the contrast with Taylorist ways of organizing work activities and to explain how the organization of the learning process in HPWOs creates higher levels of performance.

As we have seen in Taylorist organizations, it is the job of managers to achieve company goals; they are the sole repository of knowledge about the production process, and they are responsible for organizational performance. In HPWOs, production - whether of goods or services - is organized in a very different way. The organization is structured in such a way that through their work activities all employees are actively involved in achieving organizational goals; they are continually learning and linking their behaviour to the achievement of those goals.

Just how HPWOs are able to link the behaviour of their employees to collective goals of performance improvement is a matter of some debate. However, we believe that we have made sufficient progress to be able to identify the main mechanisms involved. We have therefore separated our discussion of the theory of high performance working into a separate chapter to enable us to do justice to that topic. Here we are more concerned to use existing research findings to show how HPWOs operate to enhance employee learning and link the outcomes from that learning to performance improvement.

We start by showing the importance of trust and commitment within the organization. From there, we move on to show how work design creates opportunities to acquire the requisite skills, and then we move on to show how that learning is linked to organizational performance, first at the individual level and then at the group level.[6]

Trust

Perhaps the most fundamental point about HPWOs is that all employees are involved in learning. Unlike their Taylorist counterparts, managers and technical workers are no longer seen as the sole repository of knowledge. The organization achieves its enhanced performance through the explicit commitment of all employees to the company's or organization's goals.[7] This means that all employees share the same values and objectives; they have to "buy into" the organizational goals. This is aided by the abolition of much of the hierarchy associated with Taylorist organizational structures but is predicated on the building of trust between management and workers.

A background of trust is also essential if learning is to become continuous. We know from case study evidence as well as the studies on workplace learning in Japanese companies by Koike (1990) and others that if workers are to develop high-level skills then the learning involved has to be underpinned by a sense of trust with the immediate colleagues. Trust is necessary in order that the supervisor or manager feels free to convey information and knowledge to the employees. (As we shall see below, this free flow of information is absolutely crucial for the development of intellectual and problem-solving skills.) Managers must feel that in conveying such information to other employees they are not threatening their own position in the organization. Trust is also required on the part of the learners in the person who is coaching them. Feedback on performance is an integral part of the learning process; therefore, the learners have to feel free to make mistakes from which they can learn, secure in the knowledge that they will not be penalized as a result of such events.

As we saw in the case studies, the building of this trust is crucial. At Thorn, the company's finances were opened to the union. At SSS, the general manager made himself available to listen to the complaints and suggestions of all employees with guarantees of anonymity and at SAB, they worked with the unions as well as throwing open the company culture to re-evaluation by the workforce. What those case studies and other empirical evidence suggest is that it takes time to break down old attitudes and generate new ones. Such trust also appears to be a precondition if the workplace is to be used as a source of learning for high levels of skill development.

Commitment

Once trust has been established, the leadership has to secure the commitment of the employees to the organization's objectives. As we saw in Taylorist organizations, where employees are requested to routinely perform a limited range of tasks, their commitment to the goals of the organization is almost irrelevant; it is certainly not necessary for the effective performance of their tasks. If, however, the tasks are not clearly delineated but involve working with others in the pursuit of broad organizational objectives, then working arrangements have to be negotiated and determined on a daily basis. In these circumstances, a high level of commitment to organizational objectives is essential. In these high performance organizations, as the case studies demonstrated, the company or organization is asking its employees to take on the organization's objectives as their own. In addition, they are asked to monitor their own behaviour in order to maximize the achievement of those objectives. This requires the employees to internalize controls and use them to direct their own behaviour.

Values

Both these factors, trust and commitment to organizational goals, are often embedded in the organization's values, hence the frequent reference in the mission statements to the need to treat all employees with respect and to portray organizational objectives as contributing toward the greater public good. For example, this is evident in SAB's mission statement "To be a world-class manufacturer and marketer of fine-quality beers whilst behaving in a progressive and socially responsible manner" and that of the United States SSA "To promote the economic security of the nation's people through compassionate and vigilant leadership in shaping and managing America's social security programme". The importance of success in "selling" these values to employees is that, once this has been done, they are motivated to participate in the process of learning and collective achievement. Once employees are committed, then it is possible to draw on all their tacit knowledge and intellectual capital in pursuit of performance improvement. This is what Patterson et al.(1997) are referring to when they point to the importance of organizational culture in producing higher levels of productivity. From a theoretical perspective, it suggests that the requisite levels of employee motivation are to be found not just through the design of jobs but through the commitment of the individual to the group and to the broader values of the organization.

Work design

The importance of work design is that it provides the opportunity for employees to acquire skills in breadth and depth.[8] In most - if not all - high performance organizations, this is demanded by virtue of the way in which work activities are organized. In this sense, the skills required of employers are derived from the way in which work is organized. In the jargon of the economists, skills are a derived demand. We can illustrate this by reference to the work of Onstenk (1997) in the Netherlands and Koike (1995) in Japan. Onstenk argues on the basis of his research in Dutch firms that the following are important features of job design that produce high levels of learning and skills:

- broadening the set of tasks undertaken by the team to provide scope for performing more tasks, e.g. job rotation;
- enriching the job through integrating maintenance, repair and quality controls into the job;
- giving the group responsibility for problem solving, as well as extending their domain of authority to make decisions;
- organizing team meetings and discussion opportunities which allow team/cross-team members to learn from one another;
- structuring the groups to ensure that they contain members with different levels of skills;
- including coaching of colleagues as an explicit part of the job description.

The work design that gives rise to these skills is precisely that which we have outlined earlier as characteristic of HPWOs: namely, the use of self-managed work teams, multi-skilling, job rotation and cross training and the devolution of decision-making. These are almost identical to the work systems we encountered at Thorn, SAB, and SSS.

Designing work in this way inevitably demands higher levels of skills from employees. By requiring workers to become multi-skilled or to rotate between jobs, the organization gains flexibility but this can only work if employees acquire technical skills additional to those they would normally acquire in a traditional organization. In requiring the workers to be able to conduct simple maintenance, rather than wait for a specialized engineer in the event of machinery breakdown, also requires them to acquire additional knowledge and skills. Similarly, if the worker is responsible for quality which is no longer vested in a separate quality control department, this also requires additional skills of monitoring and attention to detail.

Perhaps of even greater significance when it comes to skill formation is the organization of work in groups or teams, with the team having authority to organize its own work and resolve problems. This has quite a radical impact on the skills required of employees. First, if the outcome of problem-solving decisions is to enhance the performance of the organization as a whole, then the group must have access to all the requisite business and financial information for it to be aware of the consequences of its decision. This in turn means that the organization must have in place the kind of communication systems we witnessed in the case studies; for example, regular briefings which provide the workers with a good knowledge of the business plan and how their specific function relates to the work of others within the organization. Thorn in particular devoted considerable resources to ensuring that employees are aware of the ways in which all activities in the enterprise are interdependent.

A second requirement for effective group problem solving is that workers must have a full understanding of the way in which the production system operates, whether it is producing goods or services, if they are to ensure its smooth operation at high levels of efficiency. Third, if the group or team is to function effectively in producing decisions, the people within it must learn communication and teamworking skills.

Finally, if they are to make effective decisions, they must also acquire intellectual skills. This means learning how to think critically, developing a capacity for independent and collective problem solving and moving from the level of objects and actions to the level of meaning. Schuck (1996) argues that this requires an environment where enquiry and questioning of procedures and ideas is part of everyday activities, where managers and workers become partners in learning, and where people engage in dialogue in situations in which roles are not predetermined and where the person with the best idea takes the lead, irrespective of his/her status within the group. He argues that it is only through the application of this intellectual skill that people can perceive the meaning of data in an information-rich environment and thereby make intelligent choices when solving problems and identifying more efficient ways to achieve business objectives. These are precisely the kind of conditions created by the use of HPWPs.

In devolving authority for decision-making to self-managed teams, the organization is creating the conditions for a much higher level of skill formation among its employees. This is one that demands continuous learning on the part of all employees. In view of this, it is not surprising that the remaining two items cited by Onstenk should relate to the process through which this knowledge is spread throughout the team, namely that the team has members with different levels of expertise and that coaching is part of the team members' job description. Different levels of knowledge are essential for learning to take place among those who are new to the team or have lower levels of proficiency. Ensuring that the members of the team are effective in supporting the learning process for others ensures that knowledge is delivered to other team members as effectively as possible.

While Onstenk's work enables us to see how the redesign of jobs could lead to the development of higher levels of skills among employees, we still need evidence of a causal link. In fact, there is considerable research evidence to support the existence of such a link between work design and higher-level skills, although none is conclusive in terms of identifying the exact nature of the causality involved.

Work design and skill levels: Establishing the link

First we have the evidence from case studies which suggests that these new working practices actually generate the new skills. Certainly there is a large number of case studies, stretching back two decades, which have examined the implication of these new working practices for the development of skills. These have all reported that where the new practices have been introduced workers have developed the type of intellectual, problem-solving, communication and teamworking skills we discussed above.

Case study evidence on the link between skill level and work design

In 1984 Hirschhorn, in his study of operators in continuous process plants, argued that the integrated nature of the production process required that operators develop what he called "synthetic reasoning", that is the ability to determine the kind of problem one faces and the information that is relevant (ibid.:90). A decade later, MacDuffie (1995) reported that new forms of organizing production in the automobile industry had generated a demand for similar skills. In an international study of the automobile industry, Thompson et al. (1995) reported that the new forms of production utilized in commercial vehicle manufacture are creating demands for "new skills":

...One of the things most researchers agree on is that, due to automation in advanced manufacturing, skill requirements shift from dexterity and other manual competencies toward cognitive abilities and from skills related to a particular material or substance to skills related to machinery and production processes. ...On the one hand, this means the "system skills", including organizational and technological knowledge and abilities, are required; on the other hand, workers have to be able to work in teams, with an emphasis on behavioural or "extra-functional" skills (ibid.:738).

Outside the automobile industry, reports of such changes in skills have been found in the service sector. Bertrand and Noyelle (1988) identified common emerging competencies in the banks and insurance companies they studied in five countries – Japan, France, Germany, Sweden and the United States. The new skills they reported were: an ability to operate in an ill-defined and ever-changing environment; the capacity to deal with non-routine and abstract work processes; an ability to handle decisions and responsibilities; and a capability for interactive group work and system-wide understanding, that is, an ability to operate within expanding geographical and time horizons. Kelley (1989) in a separate study of US insurance companies reported that where new technology was introduced in a manner which upskilled the workers, they reported an increase in their "contextual knowledge". This consists of a substantial knowledge of the firm's products, customers, processes and procedures, together with the authority to make decisions and resolve problems. This enabled workers to operate with a minimum of supervision and to integrate properly with other related tasks. In addition to contextual knowledge, sales, clerical and administrative jobs in robustly organized firms required mastery of skills not previously associated with such work. The list is as follows: social and communication skills required to meet and integrate the needs of customers, clients, marketing staff and product designers; managerial skills related to planning, organizing time effectively, thinking more comprehensively about the enterprise and acting in a strategic manner; and general skills related to computer technology such as the ability to access larger networks, store and retrieve data, turn data into useful information and use standards software packages. here there are numerous examples of new forms of work organization being associated with the new skills.

A second set of evidence comes from the results of survey research on employees' skills. Using survey data, Felstead and Ashton (2000) report a strong association between the use of modern management (HPWPs) practices and the level of problem solving, communication and teamworking skills. As we would expect, these skills are more highly developed in organizations which use at least some of what we have termed HPWPs. While this evidence does not in itself "prove" that these organizational characteristics create the new skills, when taken together with case study evidence it certainly suggests that such a causal link is highly probable.

Survey evidence on the link between skill levels and work design

This research based on a representative sample of almost 2,500 employed people in the UK labour force was designed to identify the skills of the labour. The survey used a list of 35 skills including three soft skills; communication, problem solving and teamworking. Using a multivariate analysis which controlled for personal and other social characteristics, the authors report a strong association between the presence of what they call "modern" organizational characteristics and the level of problem solving, communication and teamworking skills. They use any five of the following characteristics as indicators of a "modern" organization, namely the use of appraisal systems, quality circles, suggestion schemes, meetings to inform employees, meetings to consult with employees about company policies, and registering with Investors in People. Taken together, these characteristics approximate the definition we have adopted here of a high performance work organization. The results suggest that the organizational context in which the respondents work is a powerful and significant predictor of individuals' scores on all these three skills. This finding is reinforced by the fact that the growth of these skills is greatest among employees who had spent the last five years employed in such organizations. Certainly we can conclude that those employed in these types of organizations have higher levels of problem solving, communication and teamworking skills (Felstead and Ashton, 2000).

In view of all this evidence, we can be fairly certain that the work design characteristic of high performance work organizations does provide the opportunity to develop additional technical skills as well as to enhance the level of the new skills. The next question is: How does the higher level of skills among the labour force translate into higher levels of individual performance? After all, just because we have higher levels of skills, this will not necessarily improve the performance of individual employees. The graduate working as a cleaner in the office will not necessarily produce higher levels of performance than the unqualified person working alongside. One needs the opportunity to create and introduce improvements to enhance performance. Skills alone will not create that opportunity. Theory suggests that it is the organization of work that leads to workers exercising more discretionary effort and creativity and that in turn leads to higher levels of productivity and profitability. The problem now is just how that is achieved. Here we are fortunate in having the work of Koike in Japan to suggest possible answers.

Koike (1990; 1995) conducted a programme of research with companies in Japan and South East Asia using direct observation in the workplace to seek answers to these questions. He argues that when work is structured in the way described above, it produces high levels of skills because of the opportunity it provides for what he terms the acquisition of skills in breadth and depth. By breadth, he means that the workers have the opportunity to acquire knowledge about the organization as a whole outside the confines of their immediate task. This is usually achieved by moving into other related jobs either within a person's own department/team or adjacent departments/teams. This enables workers to see their immediate tasks in the broader context of the organization as a whole. Knowledge in depth is acquired by persons developing a deeper knowledge of the production process, the technology and the finer details of how it operates in practice and over time. For this to be achieved, the workers require a period of off-the-job reflection or study combined with extensive on-the-job learning. The off-the-job training provides access to the theoretical, codified knowledge which provides a greater depth of understanding of the technical issues. Together these two components provide the workers with a detailed knowledge of the organization, the production system and their role within it.

When it comes to the transformation of these skills into higher levels of productivity, in both manual and white-collar work the key factor is the employees' breadth and depth of understanding which enables them to identify problems in the production process before they manifest themselves as breakdowns or disruption (Koike, 2000). Having identified possible disruption, then the employee has the authority to intervene and rectify the situation before it does become a problem which disrupts the work process. For example, an assembly line in Japan rarely stops, because the employees have prevented possible problems materializing. By contrast, in plants with the same technology in Thailand where workers are only skilled in one task, they have neither the knowledge to spot potential problems nor the authority to rectify them.

Koike found the same in the service sector where a highly skilled employee can identify potential problems in, say, an administrative system and rectify them before they create disruption and generate inefficiencies in the system. The key for Koike lays in the ability of the worker to deal with unusual situations and therefore to prevent them from becoming problems. It is these abilities which he sees as crucial in explaining the threefold difference in productivity which he observed between Japanese companies operating in Japan and those with the same technology operating in Thailand and Malaysia (Koike and Inoki, 1990).

The work of Koike provides an example of one of the ways in which enhanced individual skills can increase productivity. However, there are other factors at work in the contemporary HPWOs that would also help explain the way in which these skills impact on productivity and performance. Indeed, our case studies provide some examples of this, especially of the ways in which the use of these intellectual/diagnostic skills have been used to ensure continuous improvements in performance over time. For example, Motorola has used the services of Motorola University to generate substantial improvements in productivity. The company set a goal to reduce product-development cycle time. The University developed a course that brought marketing, product development and manufacturing personnel together to sort out the problem. The result was a reduction in design time from anywhere between three and seven years to 18 months. Here we can see how by generating high levels of skills - especially the creation of these intellectual skills - the application of this knowledge can produce significant improvements in performance. What is crucial is that the learning is geared to business objectives.

While our focus has been on demonstrating ways in which higher skill levels can lead directly to higher levels of performance we must also be aware that the type of behaviour observed by Koike will not be sustained through time unless workers are rewarded for their efforts. Similarly, workers will not make the requisite problem-solving decisions unless they have access to the information required to inform the decision as well as the authority to implement it.

Translating learning into performance at the group level

So far, our examination of performance improvements has focused on the actions of particular individuals. This is just one way in which the use of HPWPs can enhance performance. A second is through the use of group-based or collective actions, often referred to as organizational learning.[9]

As we pointed out above, one of the consequences of a sense of trust and a commitment to shared values on the part of the labour force is that individuals are more willing to share information with each other, whether they are fellow workers or managers and workers. Once this has been achieved, the conditions are established for use to be made of that shared information and knowledge to enhance the performance of the organization as a whole.

This sharing of information throughout the labour force is likely to be more crucial in some circumstances than others: for example, when the company is operating in a turbulent market or a niche market where customer requirements are crucial to ensuring success. We saw this in the case of Thorn, WH Smith,[10] SAB, Comfort DC and SATS. In the case of WH Smith which manufactures a range of plastic-related items, the use of self-managed cellular-based teams means that the team leader for each product, for example the manufacture of the plastic casing for hand-held electric drills, is in constant touch with the customer on a day-to-day basis to ascertain customer requirements. This means that the company can respond immediately to any changes required by the customer, such as changes in the numbers to be made or adjustments to the design. There is no delay while information is processed through a sales department and less chance of misinformation being transmitted. When this is repeated across the company for all its customers, it makes for a much greater flexibility in response.

The same holds true in the service sector where the Comfort driving instructors were seeking to make the learning process for trainees a more pleasurable and less stressful experience. Through the instructors' experience, direct feedback was obtained from clients on the impact of various measures they had adopted to relieve the stress of learning and to speed up the process of learning. Because this information was immediately shared, the company as a whole "learned" how better to adapt its service. This sharing of information and knowledge is a central feature of all the HPWO case studies.

Concern with sharing information is also a product of working practices such as teamwork and multi-skilling. Central to the use of effective self-managed work teams is the sharing of values, a common framework for communicating work-related issues and shared objectives. The use of "learning islands" in Germany is an attempt to facilitate this process among trainees. It is through this same process that the project team at Comfort DC was able to design and introduce a computer-based system for theory instruction, despite the team's limited initial knowledge of ICT . Once established on a basis of mutual trust, self-managed teams are perhaps the most effective means of creating a climate of continuous learning and improvement. Learning becomes a continuous process as team members work together to resolve problems that emerge in the course of their day-to-day work activities.

Other examples of more formal procedures to encourage mutual learning are cited by Stern and Summerlad (1999) in the form of "action sets" and "study circles". The action sets are groups of employees who work together for a period of time each week on work-based problems brought by each individual. Study circles were developed by the Swedes and consist of representatives of management and unions and/or different functions within the organization. They take a problem and ask for help from external researchers and consultants to help them find the new knowledge they require; then they proceed through problem formulation to problem solving and finally to implementation.

Individual improvements in performance, if embedded in organizational procedures, can result in each one building on the achievements of others. This is the underlying rationale behind much of the continuous improvement philosophy. One employee introduces an improvement in the efficiency of one procedure, while another may link the improved procedure to other procedures in a way that enhances the operation of the system as a whole. The results of such continual improvement can be dramatic. Thus, Dutton Engineering, an SME in the United Kingdom, was able to achieve dramatic improvements in the use of its existing technology as a result of such incremental gains. In these circumstances, the whole is greater than the sum of the individual parts.

At the level of the organization, there are also a number of more formal mechanisms that can be used to facilitate performance improvement through "organizational learning". One of the most commonly used is benchmarking, a practice we touched on briefly in the last chapter. This enables organizations to study best practice elsewhere in their industry. Benchmarking enabled Ford to become aware in the 1980s of the ability of Japanese motor companies to outperform their western competitors in terms of productivity. It was used by Comfort DC in Singapore to learn from its Japanese partners of the latest developments in driver techniques as well as the contribution new technologies could make in enhancing driver performance. It was also used by the management of Thorn UK to acquire knowledge of the latest management techniques, and so the list goes on. Some of this type of knowledge can often be acquired through conferences. In the field of training and development, for example, the major exhibitions and annual conferences organized by the US American Society for Training and Development (ASTD) and the UK CIPD provide important means whereby professionals can update themselves on best practice and recent developments. However, there is no substitute for observing the practices in action, which is what benchmarking offers.

Other effective techniques are the use of customer satisfaction surveys and employee satisfaction surveys. We saw this in the case of the SATS where customer satisfaction surveys are organized by an external agency to provide data on the performance of the company as a whole. However, SATS had also initiated "skip-level" interviews when it was introducing HPWPs in order to discover any internal failings of the company as well as to establish trust. At SSS, the annual Strengths/Weaknesses/Opportunities/Threats (SWOT) exercise performs the same function. The Mandarin Hotel uses employee surveys in a similar manner to acquire regular feedback on the impact of measures the company is taking to improve employee morale. Using information from these "tools" senior management is then able to adjust procedures or institute action as appropriate.

Another tool used by companies to acquire information and knowledge is the personal appraisal. This can be used in a number of ways to provide feedback on the operation of procedures and to acquire new ideas on improving performance as well as for providing employees with feedback on their performance. However, this is not an easy vehicle, as much depends on the skill of the appraiser and the general level of trust in the organization if it is to be effective. More obvious techniques are team meetings and quality assurance or continuous improvement meetings where employees sit together to identify possible ways of improving performance. These were common among the case studies and are frequently referred to in the literature as techniques for organizational learning (Huseman and Goodman, 1999).

In organizations where work is based on modern scientific knowledge, for example R&D departments, the exchange and sharing of knowledge are often facilitated by the use of seminars. These enable staff who have been to a scientific conference to share the knowledge they have gained with colleagues in the workplace. This type of knowledge sharing has been facilitated more recently by developments in IT, especially the use of software such as Lotus Notes. These and similar products enable the organization to build a central bank of information which can then be accessed and modified by individual members of the company in the light of their experiences. It forms a collective memory and reservoir of knowledge for the company as a whole. In banking, for example, it enables companies to store knowledge acquired by specialist managers, such as that required to approve loans to old-people's homes or nursing homes which tend to be geographically concentrated in one part of the country, and to make that knowledge available to managers elsewhere. These managers may only have the odd nursing home as a client, and therefore the local manager would not have the opportunity to build up a store of knowledge on the specific requirements and characteristics of this type of client. However, through the IT system he/she would have immediate access to the experience of those colleagues who do possess that knowledge.

In many HPWOs the new technology has facilitated the decentralization of authority that is one of their hallmarks. It enables information on the business and production system to be instantly available to all members of the work teams. This has undoubtedly made it feasible for the work groups to make decisions about the production process or the delivery of the service in the context of the overall business needs. Similarly, the use of the Intranet has enabled customers and suppliers to "talk" to those immediately involved in the process of production.

The increasing use of ICT to store and utilize knowledge as an organizational asset has provided the impetus for much recent discussion of knowledge management. However, there is a danger that we start to lose sight of the reality of modern technology, which simply facilitates the storage and use of knowledge. If we begin to reify the technology, as many writers are prone to do, we start to assume that the use of IT on its own can create a knowledge company or learning organization. It is important to remember that the effectiveness of technology depends primarily on the ability and willingness of personnel to use it. Here again, we come back to the issue of trust: if managers or workers have no trust in the organization and its leaders, they will tend to keep possession of their knowledge to protect their position in the organization.

The other area where companies have sought to enhance learning within the organization is through developing their own corporate universities. These may be no more than the sum total of the training courses they already provide brought together under the name of a university. All this does is to enhance the role of the HRD professionals within the organization. Others, such as Motorola University used in the case study, are attempts to add value within the organization. Here, by bringing together members of different departments in one project, they are able to achieve significant savings for the company.

A different way of stimulating learning within the enterprise is through linking the learning process within the organization to universities and colleges. This enables staff to access external certification for their learning. This occurs both in the Mandarin Hotel and in SATS where the use of external accreditation is being used to enhance the generation of a learning culture within the organization. The problem here is how to keep the balance between the need to satisfy the external accreditation agency while ensuring that the learning taking place at work is focused on performance improvement. There can be a tension here which requires managing.

Finally, we would point out that at the level of the organization there are a number of other ways in which HPWPs can be used to improve performance. Perhaps the most basic is to use them to reduce the total number of employees, which improves productivity by reducing labour costs. However, this can be counter-productive in the long run as employees lose their trust and become disillusioned by the associated insecurity and work intensification. Applebaum et al. (2000) found that HPWPs could reduce costs in other ways, for example by reducing inventories of raw materials or work-in-progress or the amount of space required to produce items. Another way is by increasing revenue through improvements in response time. "The gains from horizontal coordination of production by front-line workers show up in performance improvements that increase the company's sales and profits without necessarily increasing productivity and reducing costs" (ibid.:105). Thus, team sewing in the garment industry enables plants to respond rapidly to unexpected changes in customer demand. This means that the companies can develop long-term relationships with retailers and achieve increases in profitability over the long term. The processing and communication of information by sewing operators working in teams create the added value. The important point with these examples is that HPWPs can generate a range of options for enhancing performance. However, these only become available when the other mechanisms are in place to encourage learning behaviour and when the results of that learning are able to flow relatively freely within the organization and become focused on improving performance, what Kessels refers to as "knowledge productivity" (Kessels, 1996).[11]

Training in HPWOs

The use of formal courses

In view of the amount of learning taking place in HPWOs, it should come as no surprise that these are "training-intensive" organizations. There are a number of studies which have established a statistical link between the amount of training undertaken by an organization and the use of HPWPs; for example, Osterman (1995) in the United States found that higher levels of training are required for the introduction of HPWPs, but thereafter such practices do not require extra training. Also in the United States, Frazis et al. (1997) found a relationship between the use of HPWPs and formal training, as did Lynch and Black (1997). In the United Kingdom, Whitfield (2000) found a strong correlation between the adoption of bundles of HPWPs and training, suggesting the main impact of HPWPs is to increase the intensity of training given to a distinct group of workers.

However, this is only part of the story when we look at the process of skill formation more generally. In order to measure training, researchers require an index, for example the number of days spent on training courses or the amount of money a company spends on training. This may seem reasonable at first sight, but the need to obtain an "objective" index in order for statistical tests to be carried out means that all the informal training tends to be ignored. What the researchers are measuring is the amount of formal training that takes place. Yet, as we have seen, HPWOs are characterized by a large amount of informal learning at the workplace, especially for the newer skills of problem solving, communication and teamwork which are all acquired primarily through informal workplace learning. This makes the findings that HPWOs train more even more interesting. Indeed, if we could measure informal workplace learning, it is likely that HPWOs would stand out well above more traditional organizations in terms of the amount of skill formation that takes place.

The extensive use of formal courses by HPWOs suggests that they are also responsible for transmitting a significant amount of formal codified knowledge to their employees. This may be linked to their requirements for extensive multi-skilling, cross training and a high level of technical skills among their employees. These skills require the acquisition of theoretical and conceptual knowledge, such as that required for craft and technician work, which is more cost-effectively transmitted through the lecture theatre or classroom.

However, it does appear, at least in the United States, that some of the skills which have been traditionally delivered in the classroom are now being delivered through the use of ICT. For example, computer-based programmes permit the individuals to train themselves outside the classroom context but still use the same or similar instructional programme, this time transmitted through the computer rather than in the classroom. Thus, the ASTD report points to a growth in the use of technology to deliver training which it sees as associated with a small decline in the use of the classroom. However, the ASTD surveys of training practice show that both in the United States and in other countries, classroom training still dominates the delivery of training, with over 78 per cent of training time being devoted to classroom instruction (Van Buren and King, 2000). However, the proportion of classroom time is smaller for those US companies that invest most heavily in training (ASTD, 2000a:16) where the figure is closer to 70 per cent. Other surveys such as that cited by Huseman and Goodman (1999:82) put the figure of classroom training lower, at 56 per cent of all training hours. However, to put our discussion in perspective, it is important to realize that formal off-the-job training is still the dominant mode of training, even in HPWOs.

Given the extensive use of formal training courses in some of our case study organizations, these findings should not come as a surprise. For companies such as Motorola, this has led to the growth of the corporate university designed to deliver formal courses to all employees. There, factory workers study all types of business-related topics from the fundamentals of computer design to robotics and from communication skills to customized manufacturing. They learn by attending lectures, reading manuals and action learning. In the service sector, we see the extensive use of formal courses in SSS to improve the general skills of the labour force, while there, and at the Mandarin Hotel the company is using formal external courses to build a culture of learning.

The extensive use of formal training would also require relatively high levels of literacy, numeracy and other basic skills among employees. In general, employers expect the state to provide this training in basic skills as an output from the education system. Without these basic skills, it would be difficult for employees to participate in either the formal training courses or the more informal workplace learning, all of which require an active contribution from the employee.

The growing use of informal learning

The soft skills, which are acquired through more informal learning, are more difficult to transmit. The work of Green et al. (2001) on the UK Skills Survey found that while education and training programmes are effective in generating most types of skills, for example computing skills, work-based learning in the form of on-the-job training is more effective in delivering problem solving, teamworking and some communication skills. Formal education is found to play only a small role in the production of these skills - the workplace is far more important.

Stasz et al. (1996) using participant observation in the United States came to a similar conclusion. She examined the use of these new skills in four firms in different industries and found that teamworking, problem-solving and communication skills are readily identifiable across different jobs. However, while these skills are identifiable in all jobs, their specific characteristics and importance varies amongst them. "The characteristics of problem solving, teamworking and communication requirements are related to job demands, which in turn depend on the purpose of the work, the tasks that comprise the job, the organization of the work, and other aspects of the work context" (ibid.:218). For example, with regard to problem solving, the technicians she studied face troubleshooting problems, the health-care workers face situation-assessment problems and the construction inspectors are confronted with quality-assurance and control problems. Similarly, teamworking takes different forms in the various sites; test technicians work in autonomous, self-managed teams with the authority to manage their own work, while home health workers are members of larger managed care teams which include doctors, health specialists and nurses. These findings suggest that while there may well be generic components to such skills, it is evident that other aspects are specific to the work context. Indeed, Stasz documents the different ways in which they are learned, which in all cases involves on-the-job learning. In some instances, learning is supported by formal courses, in others by structured on-the-job training provided through the union, while in others it is by systematic informal training from dedicated workers with managerial support.

In view of this, it should come as no surprise that the surveys of employers' use of training methods, both in the United States by the ASTD (2000) and in the United Kingdom by the CIPD (2001), have revealed that HPWOs tend to make more use of e-learning at the workplace, structured on-the-job training and coaching and mentoring, all of which are designed to support the acquisition of new skills. Thus, even though the HPWOs make more use of formal training for their employees, these courses are declining in importance relative to the use of more work-based techniques designed to support the learning or skill formation process in the workplace (Raper et al., 1997).

At the moment, we have few studies showing how companies are tackling this problem of enhancing workplace learning. One exception is that by Dybowski (1998) who cites the examples of German employers such as Carl Schenk AG, a machinery manufacturer, and Mercedes Benz AG, both of which were obliged to radically reorganize their approach to training on introducing higher levels of teamworking into their organizations. In the case of Carl Schenk, internal reorganization involving the introduction of teamworking led to the subsequent reorganization of training and the introduction of "learning and working islands" through which to transmit the new skills. In the case of Mercedes Benz, systematic benchmarking revealed that the skills required for modern work processes (teamworking, problem solving and communication) cannot be acquired through simulated working and learning processes in the classroom and training centre. They too introduced "learning islands".

Essentially, learning islands involve decentralizing the learning away from the training centre to the point of production. This ensures that training is directly integrated into the production process but can still take place within a sheltered environment. Real production job orders are processed, but sufficient time is allocated so that the team can, step by step, autonomously plan, execute and evaluate or improve its work. "The intention is to enable not only the individual but the team as a whole to autonomously organize its work processes and jointly reflect learning progress so that experience and skills can be acquired" (Dybowski, 1998:129). The fact that the German curriculum authority (BIBB) is examining ways of integrating the use of learning islands into the curriculum suggests that these are not just isolated examples but represent part of a wider movement in Germany to integrate the learning of these new skills into the process of production.

Transforming the delivery of learning in the workplace

The introduction of such extensive learning within the organization has equally dramatic consequences for the delivery of training. Managers in this context have to acquire a whole new set of skills. Similarly, the role of the trainer is also transformed.

Managers

For the managers, one of the major changes is the end of their role as "commanders", people who coordinate the actions of subordinates by telling them what to do. Their supervisory role is dramatically diminished. In a situation of devolved authority, their task is to facilitate the actions and solutions of relatively autonomous work groups or self-managed teams. Crucial here are skills of leadership. Using HPWPs, the managers derive authority less from their position in the hierarchy and more from their ability to lead.

For some managers, the transitions involved are very difficult to handle. They are no longer the guardians of knowledge; it is now their responsibility to ensure that knowledge and information are disseminated throughout the organization. As we have seen, it is crucial that information about the business, its internal processes and the problems it faces, the opportunities available in the market and the threats from competitors is made available to all employees. In addition to this downward flow of information, managers have to ensure that the employees' knowledge of what works and what does not work and of how improvements can be achieved and new opportunities created flows back to inform the main decisions being taken about the organization and its functioning. This is a major change in their role.

As part of their role as facilitators, managers play a crucial role in the training of subordinates. Training is no longer something that can be left to the training department in the form of formal courses. As more and more skills are acquired in the workplace, the manager plays an ever more important role as coach and mentor, developing the skills of subordinates. Much of this involves acquiring new skills in supporting the learning process. They need to know how to convey information in a form comprehensible to subordinates and colleagues, how to identify areas of weakness in the employees' skills, how to support the process of learning through the provision of feedback and how to reward the acquisition of the new knowledge. Finally, they must be capable of linking that process of knowledge and skill acquisition to the organization's objectives. This is crucial if collective goals are to be achieved.

The trainer

A similar process of change impacts on the trainer. As we saw in the traditional organization, training - apart from some management development - is largely confined to short courses that are delivered in bite-sized pieces to workers by professional trainers. A system of formal training needs analysis is used to identify just how much knowledge needs to be delivered. The appropriate training course is designed and then presented in a highly structured manner through "instruction" in the classroom or training centre. As we stated above, some of this continues. The delivery of technical skills in this manner may even become more important. However, in an HPWO the trainer requires additional skills to deal with a fundamental transformation in the generation and use of knowledge in the organization.

Knowledge is no longer just handed down in small amounts in the form of short training courses. Much of the knowledge that is of value to the organization in furthering its objectives is embedded in the tacit knowledge of the workers. They are the ones with the detailed knowledge of the production process or of the customer to whom they deliver the service. That knowledge has to be accessed and passed back to the centre. As we have seen, in the workplace much of this learning takes place through interaction with others and through the individual or group discovering a problem and actively seeking the solution, which may mean accessing information from books or reports as well as through discussions with other colleagues. For others, it means developing a meaningful relationship with the customer to ensure a better fit between the service on offer and the requirements of the customer. The worker is no longer the "consumer" of training as Krogt and Warmerdam (1997) put it, but he/she becomes an active agent in the process of learning. Learning is no longer clearly bounded and contained within the classroom to be transferred later to the workplace; rather, it becomes embedded in the work organization and production process.

The growing importance of the workplace as a source of learning in this context means that the trainer becomes a consultant, a person who helps identify performance requirements. These may be different from department to department, and solutions have to be tailor-made for each. Trainers now have to be able to work with line managers in developing appropriate courses of action that meet the precise needs of each department. Research in the United Kingdom (IPD, 1998) revealed that one of the main areas trainers identified as a change in their role was an increase in the emphasis on the role of the line manager in development and the support required from trainers for them to take on these responsibilities together with an increase in consultancy and advisory activities.

In this new context, much of the trainer's role is therefore transformed into supporting the learning process. The workers, perhaps in discussion with colleagues and supervisors, identify their own learning needs and take it upon themselves to acquire the relevant information, for example in the case of the Comfort project team designing the new CBT learning system for its trainee drivers. Here the support takes the form of advice, help and feedback on their performance from the "expert", whether that is an external consultant, a more experienced worker or a supervisor. The trainer becomes the expert in the field of supporting informal learning and linking that to business objectives (Robinson and Robinson,1995; Pepitone, 1995).

In this context, the role of the trainer is also transformed into that of a facilitator, a person who provides advice and guidance to the learner and the line manager on how to support and facilitate the learning process. In some instances, this may involve delivering an appropriate technical input through a formal course, but it primarily takes the form of helping identify the performance problem in relation to business needs or organizational goals and facilitating the subsequent learning process within the workplace. Little wonder then that many trainers are transforming themselves into "learning consultants" or "performance consultants" (Robinson and Robinson, 1995).

For the more senior training or people managers, there are also new demands. If the human resources department is to play an effective part in introducing and supporting HPWPs, then the senior staff have to be knowledgeable in business finance, business planning and strategy. This is essential if they are to advise top management on where and how the HR department can support the learning involved and where the gains in performance can be made. As we saw in Chapter 3, it is the failure of top HR managers to develop these skills that many managing directors and CEOs blame for their failure to introduce HPWPs.

Conclusions

In demonstrating the ways in which the organization of production shapes the process of skill formation, there has been an almost inevitable tendency to create ideal types of the two contrasting systems, the Taylorist and the HPWO. This was necessary in order to draw out the main points of comparison. In reality, most organizations sit somewhere between the two contrasting types we have portrayed. Only a minority of organizations have fully implemented HPWPs throughout their organization, while only a minority of organizations still operate exclusively on Taylorist principles. The majority of organizations use a combination of both forms of work design.

The majority of organizations contacted in the various surveys we have cited will have some HPWPs, thereby introducing modifications into the Taylorist principles of management. In other organizations, HPWPs may have only been implemented for the core of the labour force, leaving large parts of the labour force still learning under Taylorist conditions. The reality is "messier" than the one we have portrayed here. This can sometimes lead to confusion over the use of basic terminology. For example, surveys in the United Kingdom have revealed that the majority of employers require communication skills from their employees (Dench et al., 1998). Here we have used the term communication skills to identify the social skills required to participate effectively in self-managed teams, to address fellow workers and to receive and send effective, sometimes detailed, memos and reports to managers and others in the organization. However, the same term "communication skills" is also used in Taylorist systems in the service sector. There employers use the term communication skills to refer to the employee's ability to be pleasant during the 30 seconds or so that it takes to take an order for a burger and medium fries or to route a call to another person in the call centre. Unfortunately, this confusion is likely to persist until our language starts to approximate more closely to differences in the level of skills required in the two types of organization.

Another danger associated with the use of these ideal types is that we have underplayed the degree of learning and skill formation that occurred in more traditional organizations. Many companies that we would call traditional did require extensive technical skills on the part of their technicians and skilled trade workers. Here, in the electronics, engineering and other established industries, the introduction of HPWOs does not eradicate those skills but builds on them. The technical and scientific knowledge is still required as are the skills of the trades person; it is just that in HPWOs they are no longer sufficient and now form the basis on which the new skills are built.

In other industries, especially in the service sector, the whole process of skill formation is being drastically changed. For example, many of the old skills of the bank manager are being re-engineered and in some cases form the basis for a more highly skilled labour force organized along HPWO principles, while in other cases only a small group has the professional skills, with the majority of the remaining employees being organized along Taylorist principles. Here again, our attempt to contrast the two types of organization has meant that we have had to suspend consideration of processes of change currently transforming labour markets across the world.

Finally, although our understanding of the process of learning at work and its links to performance is lamentably weak, we do have powerful evidence that the growth of HPWOs is posing serious challenges to the way in which we have traditionally organized training. In the past, technical skills have frequently been delivered through the apprenticeship system based on the assumption that there is an organized body of knowledge that can be handed down to the next generation from master to apprentice at the start of the career. In the world of HPWOs, these technical skills are still important, but there are at least two reasons why the apprenticeship model may require some modification. First, some of the technical skills and the body of knowledge in which they are based may be changing so fast that the "master's" knowledge base may be rapidly outdated. We can observe this in the field of ICT where many older workers are being taught by younger employees. Secondly, the growing importance of the workplace as a source of individual and "group" learning may mean that we have to devise new ways of supporting the process of learning throughout a person's career and not just in the initial phase of the working career, as is the case with the existing apprenticeship. Here we are already starting to see the elements of a new approach taking place in HPWOs with the growing use of mentors, coaches and work-based tutors and with support for the learning process being delivered through a new type of trainer or learning consultant. However, even where a system of continuous learning is in place, the same combination of short spells of off-the-job theoretical reflection combined with ongoing on-the-job experience is still required.

Notes

[1] There is a voluminous literature on the transition from school to work; see Furlong and Cartmel (1997) and Crysdale (1998).

[2] Braverman (1974) provided the classical account of the process whereby this knowledge of the production system is appropriated by the owners/managers.

[3] See S. Pollard (1965) for a discussion of this within the UK context.

[4] This is one of the reasons why the process of informal learning has not been studied in any depth by academics until very recently. For an overview of current work, see Stern and Sommerlad (1999).

[5] It is no accident that this approach to training was associated with the growing influence of behaviourist psychology. The assumption required to organize training for these types of jobs, the clearly specific objectives in terms of motor activities and the inputs of training required to produce these outputs closely match the assumptions the early behaviourists make about the process of learning.

[6] In terms of our earlier discussion of bundles, we are showing how these generate the conditions for linking learning to performance.

[7] This had led some writers to equate HPWOs to learning organizations. We have avoided that temptation because HPWOs are geared to constant improvements in performance; learning is the means by which that is achieved; commercial organizations do not exist just to promote learning.

[8] This is the term Koike and Inoki (1990) use to describe the different components of the learning processes required to achieve high skill levels in Japanese organizations.

[9] Here we must introduce an initial word of caution. All too often, we see this type of focus referred to as group learning or organizational learning. This way of addressing the problem is useful in directing our attention to the group level of analysis but all too readily lends itself to the temptation to move beyond that and talk of group or organizational learning as though an organization can perceive and learn independently of the people who comprise it; it reifies the concept of organizations, giving the group or organization an existence independent of those people who comprise it at any one time. For this reason, we seek to avoid concepts such as the learning organization.

[10] This case study, while not included in the text of this publication, is available on the ILO website.

[11] For a good account of these issues, see Harrison (2000).

CHAPTER 5

THE DISTRIBUTION OF HIGH PERFORMANCE WORKING PRACTICES

Introduction

In this chapter, we explore how far these HPWOs are embedded in different countries. Because they emerged as a consequence of the reaction of Anglo-Saxon companies to Japanese competition, there is an inevitable question about how far these practices have spread to other countries. Are they just a product of Anglo-Saxon capitalism or are they in some respects "culture free" and capable of being adopted in any country? To answer these questions is not an easy task, not least because our knowledge is fragmented and there are few comparable international data sources.

As our knowledge grows, we are increasingly becoming aware of the different forms taken by HPWPs in national contexts. Unfortunately, studies are few but these fragments illustrate the impact which national structures of various kinds, ranging from training systems to product markets, have on the form taken by HPWPs as they become embedded in different national contexts.

The distribution of HPWPs across countries

The United States

One of the pioneers in collecting data in this field has been the American Society for Training and Development (ASTD) which has been exploring the use of HPWPs in the United States for some time. In 1996, its publication Training trends (ASTD,1996) reported that the use of team-based work structures and alternative compensation systems rose dramatically between 1990 and 1993 among the Fortune 1000 companies. The use of self-managed work teams rose from 47 per cent to 68 per cent and the use of team or group compensation from 59 per cent to 70 per cent. In 1997, the ASTD joined forces with other partners and the US Department of Labor to launch the Human Performances Practices Survey of 542 organizations. This was a postal questionnaire sent to 9,815 companies which achieved a response rate of 3.5 per cent. Of these, the ASTD identified 32 companies as "leading edge" in that they make extensive use of HPWPs, namely self-directed work teams, employee involvement and employee access to key business information. There are no significant differences across industries in the use of HPWPs as defined by the ASTD. However, these 32 "leading edge" companies also make more use of other innovative HR practices such as innovative compensation schemes, quality initiatives and competence-based training which we have included under our broader definition of HPWPs.

More recent data on the United States is available from the MIT Task Force on Reconstructing America's Labor Market Institutions (reported in the Financial Times, 19.10.00). This study found that the use of quality circles/problem-solving groups rose from just under 30 per cent of establishments in 1992 to just under 60 per cent in 1997; a similar increase is reported for the use of job rotation. The use of self-managed work teams has remained relatively stable at just under 40 per cent while total quality management (TQM) rose from about 25 per cent to just under 60 per cent. Seventy per cent of establishments now report the use of two or more practices, while 40 per cent report the use of three or more. However, here we are only talking of work practices and, as we have seen, the full-blown HPWOs will also be using group compensation schemes and innovative training practices. Nevertheless, this does suggest that HPWPs are now becoming embedded in US organizations.

Europe

At the European level, the results of the EPOC (Employee Direct Participation in Organizational Change) survey enable us to start to identify how many organizations have moved in the direction of HPWOs. This was a nationally representative questionnaire survey conducted in ten European countries including the United Kingdom. The results of further analysis, together with other comparable data, are reported in the 1999 OECD Employment Outlook. The authors of that analysis found that, on average, 15 per cent of European managers report initiatives undertaken in the last three years in favour of the introduction or extension of job rotation, 27 per cent report the introduction or extension of teamworking, 33 per cent report greater involvement of lower-level staff and 29 per cent the flattening of management structures. However, there are substantial variations between countries. These are illustrated in table 5.1.

In general, the incidence of job rotation is higher in the Nordic countries, Japan and Germany than in the United States, the United Kingdom or France. This may well reflect the impact of different national institutional structures on the ways in which work is organized, a question we examine in the next chapter. Considerable variations have also been found in the use of teamwork. This is more prevalent in Sweden, the United Kingdom, France and the Netherlands and less so in Ireland, Germany, Italy and Denmark. On the delegation of responsibility, there seems to be a distinct Southern European pattern, with the incidence of individual and group delegation low in Southern European countries but higher in Northern Europe.

*Table 5.1: Percentage of workplaces in 1996 reporting the use of HPWPs
in the last three years*

Country	Job Rotation	Team-based work	Employee involvement	Flat hierarchy
Sweden	38	29	60	46
Denmark	28	40	10	42
Germany	7	20	19	30
France	6	30	44	21
Ireland	10	27	32	23
Spain	14	34	33	-
Portugal	9	22	9	3

Adapted from Table 4/4, p. 188, OECD (1999).

Unfortunately, the OECD (1999) does not provide a detailed breakdown by country of the combination of the four practices of job rotation, teamworking, devolved decision-making and flattened management structures. In view of this, we are not in a position to say what proportion of companies in specific countries have taken all four initiatives. However, what the results do reveal is that for the ten European countries as a whole, only 1.9 per cent reported taking all four initiatives and only 8.5 per cent reported three. The adoption of more than three of these practices therefore appears to be somewhat limited. Similarly, there are no reliable data sets which enable us to compare Europe with the United States. However, when comparing the results of different surveys in European countries and the United States, the authors of the OECD report conclude that "... there is a group of large firms in Europe which use flexible (HPWP) working practices to a roughly similar extent to large firms in North America" (p. 187).

The United Kingdom

In the United Kingdom, we do have additional evidence which enables us to make detailed observations. First, the EPOC data reveal that 13 per cent of managers report initiatives on job rotation, 33 per cent on teamworking, 48 per cent on greater involvement of lower-level employees in decision-making and 45 per cent report a flattening of management structures. Overall, these findings suggest that the United Kingdom is on a par with other European countries in terms of the development of high performance work organizations.

The results of the 1999 Chartered Institute of Personnel and Development (CIPD) Training and Development Survey, a telephone survey of a representative sample of 800 establishments in the United Kingdom - provides further evidence of the distribution of HPWOs (IPD, 1999). This survey contained information on 13 high performance working practices, ranging from the use of self-managed work teams to performance appraisal and multi-skilling. Further analysis revealed that these were to be found in five main combinations or clusters (Ashton et al., 2000). Approximately one-third of UK establishments do not make any use of these management practices; just under 50 per cent have mentoring and coaching practices linked to performance appraisal and focused on the fine-tuning of individual skills; just under one-quarter have practices such as TQM and quality circles and hence a focus on quality enhancement; almost 20 per cent have forms of multi-skilling and job rotation focused on the broadening of skills; and just over 10 per cent have introduced teamworking and self-managed work groups. However, relatively few have all these combinations, suggesting that some of the practices may be more appropriate in some industries than in others.

The fact that few organizations use all these practices has led some to argue that HPWOs are very much the exception rather than the rule (Coleman and Keep, 2001; Payne and Lloyd, 2001) being restricted to less than 5 per cent of organizations. However, reviewing the UK evidence, Felstead and Ashton (2000) argue that something in the region of 20 per cent of UK organizations can be meaningfully labelled HPWOs. This is very much in line with the recent analysis by Wood et al. (2001) of the UK Workforce Employee Relations Survey data set, the largest available, which suggests that 24.2 per cent can be meaningfully labelled as HPWOs or in the words of the authors as having full, high involvement practices,[1] while 49.4 per cent have partial high involvement practices and 26.3 per cent have minimal high involvement management practices.

When we combine the teamworking and self-managed work group initiatives with TQM and quality circles, only 4.8 per cent report this combination, while if we include the multi-skilling/job rotation and the coaching and mentoring practices, then only 1 per cent of organizations report all four combinations.

Taken together with the results of the EPOC survey, all this suggests that while the use of specific practices associated with high performance work organizations may be extensive among UK organizations, the kind of combinations which are likely to produce continuous learning in the workplace are still relatively rare. Thus, the picture we are left with is one of a very small proportion of organizations which are implementing clusters of HPWO practices, perhaps in the order of 5 per cent, and a larger group of companies (which includes this 5 per cent) which have implemented what may be recognizable as modern forms of HRM. Collectively, this group represents something in the order of 20 per cent of organizations. A further 40 per cent of organizations have some form of training practice such as employee development plans, while for the remaining 40 per cent there is little or nothing in the form of modern or systematic training and development provision. Of course, these are only approximations based on the evidence of the WERS, EPOC and CIPD surveys, but they do provide some measure of the distribution of the different approaches UK employers adopt toward training and development.

Other national studies

There are a number of other studies of aspects of HPWPs in different countries. In Taiwan, China, Tung-Chan Huang (1997) reports the result of a survey of 308 enterprises which found that HPWPs associated with participative forms of management have an impact on employees' performance in terms of labour turnover and absenteeism rates, while quality control (QC) circles and profit sharing are found to be related to profit and revenue growth. In New Zealand, Guthrie (2001) reports the results of a survey of 190 firms which revealed a positive association between the use of high involvement practices and employee retention and firm productivity. In Singapore, Barnard and Rogers (2000) in a survey of 105 firms found that the use of employee development practices such as extensive training, performance appraisals and a strong corporate culture are positively related to high performance work systems (e.g. team-based systems, quality control circles, self-direction at work, employee involvement and the free flow of communication between levels within the organization). While these surveys cannot provide data on the precise proportions of companies which have adopted HPWPs, they nevertheless provide evidence of the existence of these practices within these countries.

International comparisons of HPWPs

In an attempt to establish international comparisons that extend across continents, the ASTD received responses from over 400 organizations in 47 countries concerning their training and related activities in 1998. To this, the ASTD added responses from over 500 companies in the United States. While there is no pretence that these organizations are in any way representative, they do provide the opportunity to explore the spread of HPWPs across countries, especially Canada, Europe, Japan and Asia and Australia/New Zealand. Equally, while not all these organizations can be termed HPWOs, the data set does provide some evidence about the distribution of HPWPs.

The report (Van Buren and King, 2000) found little cross-country variation in the use of six practices; thus 76 to 95 per cent of organizations in all regions use task forces/problem-solving teams/quality circles. A substantial majority also reported the use of job rotation/cross training, total quality management, employee access to key business information and employee involvement in business decisions. Self-directed work teams show more variation, ranging from 37 per cent in Canada to 72 per cent in Asia. However, they did find substantial regional variations in the use of compensation practices. Profit-sharing/gain-sharing and employee stock ownership plans are much more prevalent among Japanese respondents. Incentive compensation is much less widely used in Japan than in the other regions, while respondents in Europe are more likely than those elsewhere to use group- or team-based compensation. As for performance management practices, annual performance reviews and personal development plans are almost universal, at least for some employees. About two-thirds of organizations in all regions use formal skill certification, computerized training information systems and formal documentation of individual competencies. Least common is the use of peer review and 360-degree feedback.

Within the auto industry, Pil and Macduffie have developed a work systems index which cites Japanese plants in Japan as having the highest use of HP, followed by Japanese plants in North America. Below them come the Koreans, followed by the Europeans and Australians, with the United States and South Africa at the bottom. Table 5.2 based on Pil and Macduffie's work provides details of the use of different HPWPs in auto plants in the various countries covered by their study.

Table 5.2: The use of HPWPs in the automobile industry in different regions

Plant ownership/location	North America	Japan/ Japan*	Japan/ North America**	Europe	Korea	Australia	South Africa
HPWPs % in teams (if teams present)	46	70	70	64	70	65	57
No. of plants with teams	10/25	12/12	8/8	20/20	4/6	3/4	4/5
% in EI or QC groups	26	81	27	47	92	51	29
% suggestions implemented	41	84	70	40	44	23	15
Extent of job rotation (1 = none; 5 = frequent)	2.0	3.9	4.0	3.6	3.0	4.0	3.8

*   Japan/Japan: Japanese companies in Japan.
**   Japan/North America: Japanese companies in North America.
Adapted from Pil and Macduffie (1999), table 3.5, p. 99.

There are a number of interesting features in the above table. First, in spite of the fact that most of the literature on HPWPs comes from the United States, American-owned US auto plants are generally speaking the laggards when it comes to implementing HPWPs. In general, it is Japanese-owned companies in Japan together with Korean companies which have gone furthest in implementing HPWPs. In Japan, Japanese-owned companies have 81 per cent of their employees in employee involvement or QC groups, while the Koreans register over 90 per cent, compared with 26 per cent in American-owned plants in the United States. Europe and Australia sit comfortably in the middle with 47 and 51 per cent respectively. It is the same story when we look at the percentage of the workforce in teams, if use is made of teamworking. Both Japanese and Korean companies register 70 per cent compared with 46 per cent in American-owned companies and 64 per cent in European companies.

Another data set which has enabled us to examine the global uptake of HPWPs is that created by the Centre for Labour Market Studies (CLMS) (University of Leicester, United Kingdom) in association with the CIPD (United Kingdom) and the International Federation of Training and Development Organizations (IFTDO). This is an international project which uses the same base questionnaire to examine the use of training and development in establishments. The survey also contains information on the use of HPWPs. Those responsible for the training and development function within an establishment were asked either by telephone interview in some countries or postal questionnaires in others to state whether they were using any of 13 HPWPs. The full list of the practices is given below.

HPWPs used in the CLMS International HRD Survey	
Annual performance reviews	Profit sharing
Peer review or 360o feedback	Multi-skilling
Personal development plan	Quality circles
Job/rotation/cross training	Total quality managemen
Mentoring or coaching programmes	Teamworking
Training for trainers	Self-directed teams
Group or team-based compensation	

The research sought to use nationally representative samples of employers by size of establishment and industry, although this was not always possible, especially in those countries where the survey was carried out by non-governmental agencies. The samples from Singapore and to a lesser extent the United Kingdom, Cyprus and Barbados are the most representative and those from Greece and Thailand the least representative. For this reason, we have not attempted to rank countries, because those with representative samples such as Singapore include a much higher proportion of SMEs than those from Thailand which has relatively few SMEs and where the sample was biased toward larger companies which are more likely to use HPWPs. For this reason, we have separated the more representative samples from the less representative samples.

The results illustrate without any shadow of doubt that HPWPs are used fairly extensively in both western and non-western societies. Table 5.3 illustrates the frequency in the use of these HPWPs in a range of countries. However, as in the United Kingdom and the United States, relatively few establishments have all these practices in place. There is a significant proportion in some countries, such as Bahrain, which have few if any of these practices, but the majority of establishments cluster at the lower end with between two and six practices in place. Similarly, at the top end there are only a few countries in which we find a sizeable proportion with all the practices in place. High performance working practices are used but not necessarily systematically across the range of areas we identified in the discussion of the case studies. We can be certain, however, that these practices are not just found in Anglo-Saxon countries.

Table 5.3: Frequency of adoption of individual HPWPs

Country	Less then 2	2-6	7-9	More than 9
Bahrain* N= 121	31	42	27	1
Greece N=298	24.5	61.7	11.1	2.7
Thailand N=86	5.8	34.9	38.4	20.9
UK N=502	0	7.4	18.7	63.9
Barbados N=142	6.3	52.8	26.8	14.1
Singapore N=1209	27.5	54.1	11.8	6.6
Cyprus+ N=386	13	60	21	6

*   In Bahrain, only 11 of the items of HPWPs were used.

\+   In Cyprus, 12 of the items of HPWPs were used.

Note: The United Kingdom and Singapore have 18 items; others have 13 items.

The use of "bundles" of practices in different countries

Using some of their national data sets, researchers at the CLMS in the United Kingdom were able to explore the extent to which the same bundles of practices are used across countries. Do employers in different countries use the same bundles of practices we identified earlier? Are these bundles only characteristic of western countries? Are some bundles being used in some countries but not in others? Answers to these questions should also help us to identify where national adjustments are taking place in the implementation of these practices.

We used the data from four countries, the United Kingdom, Singapore, Cyprus and Barbados, to test these ideas. Each provided a different set of institutional and cultural factors which we might expect to impact on the use of the bundles. Singapore has extensive institutional supports for training and workforce development which the others do not; Cyprus has a reliance on SMEs, while Barbados - like the United Kingdom - has few national institutional supports for workplace learning and development. These are just some of the differences.

Following the model first discussed in Chapter 1, we identified four bundles of practices: work design/employee involvement; support for performance; rewarding performance; and communication/information sharing bundles (see box below). Unfortunately, not all the practices which make up each of the bundles were included in all the country surveys, but there was sufficient commonality to make a meaningful analysis possible. Management practices in the work design/employee involvement bundle provide opportunities for employees to increase and broaden their skills, the learning opportunities we discussed earlier in Chapter 4. The performance bundle provides the support required to acquire the necessary skills to enhance performance in this new work context. The rewarding performance practices provide the rewards to reinforce the new behaviours, while the communication/information sharing practices provide the means whereby employees acquire the necessary knowledge about the organization and its operation.

The four bundles of HPWPs

Work design/employee involvement
Multi-skilling, quality circles, TQM, teamworking, self-directed teams

Support for performance/training
Annual performance reviews, peer review/360o appraisal, personal development plan, job rotation/cross training, mentoring, training for trainers

Rewarding performance
Group-based compensation, profit sharing, employee share ownership

Communication and information sharing
Regular meetings of the entire workforce, consultative committees, staff attitude surveys

---

The practices which are included in each bundle are not exhaustive; for example, there is no reference to rewards directed at individual performance. Nevertheless, they do provide the basis for an initial exploratory analysis. We used a multivariate statistical technique to identify what factors affect whether or not an organization uses these practices, either as bundles or as individual practices.[2]

The findings revealed that two bundles are closely linked in establishments in all four countries. In all these countries, the adoption of the performance support bundle is closely related to the use of the individual practices in the work design/employee involvement bundle and vice versa. These are very strong statistical relationships at a high level (0.001) of significance. There are some minor national variations, but it does appear from this that these relationships are fairly fundamental and hold across the four countries.

These cross-national findings establish a clear statistical link between what we observed in the case studies, namely the use of work design in providing workers with autonomy and responsibility for decision-making and the use of support mechanisms such as personal development plans, cross training, mentors and formal training to provide the appropriate skills. These findings suggest that once management introduces one set of practices, then it will also introduce another, part of what Wood et al. (2001) call the "underlying high involvement orientation" or what we would call a high performance orientation. It appears that the use of these new working practices pushes establishments into developing better and more varied ways of supporting learning, as evident in the case studies at SATS in Singapore and Thorn in the United Kingdom, to name but two, and this results in higher levels of training. This also helps explain the relationships that Osterman (1995) and Whitfield (2000) have found between the use of HPWPs and higher levels of training.[3]

The links between the use of these two bundles and individual practices in the other two bundles, rewarding performance and communications, are more variable. This may be in part a result of a failure to include all the relevant practices in our questionnaire or reflect genuine national differences in the use of these practices. For example, there is a weak statistical link between the use of self-directed work teams and the performance reward bundle in Cyprus, the United Kingdom and Singapore but not in Barbados. There is also a weaker and more variable link between the use of the communications bundle and work design practices such as TQM in Singapore and quality circles in the United Kingdom.

Performance improvements in different countries

When it came to the performance of these organizations, the results revealed fairly consistent links between the use of these practices and performance improvements across a range of areas in the two countries for which performance data were available, namely the United Kingdom and Singapore. For example, in the United Kingdom there is a link between the use of the work design/employee involvement bundle and employee satisfaction, better product service quality, customer satisfaction, productivity and meeting organizational targets. In Singapore, the use of the support-for-performance bundle has a similar impact across the board on performance. Again we have the same basic finding, namely that the use of these practices and the bundles they comprise are linked to performance improvements in both countries, although there appear to be differences in the ways in which they operate between countries. In view of this, we now turn to an examination of how these practices operate in different countries.

The impact of national culture and institutional structures on the use of HPWPs

For some time, we have been accumulating knowledge on how work is structured differently across nations. The work of Whitley (1999) has done much to demonstrate the range of variance we observe across the globe, leading him to speak of different capitalisms. However, when it comes to examining the impact of national culture and institutional structures on the use of HPWPs, we have only fragments of knowledge, but these do demonstrate the range of ways in which these practices are modified as they are adapted to national conditions, as well as some indication of the costs involved. We first examine the ways in which the original

Japanese practices have been modified in the American context and then how they have been adapted by the British and the continental Europeans.

Modifying Japanese practices

Given that many of the current HPWPs originated from the Japanese, there has been considerable interest in examining how the Japanese modified these practices in their European and American transplants. In North America, Pil and MacDuffie show how Japanese automobile manufacturers have sought to modify their practices to accommodate differences in national institutional structures. In their US plants, the Japanese owners sought to introduce a variant of their lifelong employment system for core employees and, even though US employment law does not permit enterprise unionism, they have sought to introduce a variant of that in the form of the consultation mechanisms. In the United Kingdom, they have established single union agreements. Where they have accommodated to the US institutional structure is in abandoning the Japanese seniority wage system. However, in both the United States and the United Kingdom, Japanese transplants spend considerable resources on selection and the subsequent socializing of recruits into the philosophy of high performance working. Pil and MacDuffie also report that the other area where the US transplants differ from their Japanese counterparts is in the use of quality circles, which are not so extensive in North America as they are in Japan.

However, while some Japanese practices continue to be used in US and European companies, the very fact that they are transplanted means that they are usually modified in the process. Pil and MacDuffie (1999) use the example of on-line teams to demonstrate the way in which the use of these teams differs from those in Japan. In the US plants, management generally appoints team leaders, whereas in Japan the team members have some say in the selection process. In Japan, teams report more influence over performance evaluations and settling grievances and complaints, whereas in the transplants the teams have less influence in these areas.

This point has been developed further by researchers such as Sisson (1999). He makes a distinction between the Scandinavian model of work groups and the Toyota/lean-production model. The Scandinavian model is characterized by voluntary membership, selection of members and leaders by the group, a large degree of autonomy, complex skills and rewards linked to skills. These were the types of work groups used by Volvo in its experimentation with group working. The US/Toyota model is characterized by management selection of the membership and leadership of groups, more uniform skills and simpler tasks, with the group exercising a relatively low level of autonomy (Sisson, 1999). This, as the name implies, is the type of group organization developed by Toyota and used more extensively in North America.

The impact of national product markets and skill levels

The work of Mason (1999) enables us to take the analysis further. He identifies differences in national product markets and initial training as also having a significant impact on the adoption of HPWPs. He uses the method of matched samples of manufacturing companies in a number of different countries first pioneered by the National Institute of Economic and Social Research in the United Kingdom. The first point his work illustrates is that some HPWPs, such as flexible multi-skilling and teamworking, have a much longer history in some countries than in others, in part because of the different product markets employers have adopted.

He studied the introduction of workforce flexibility and teamworking in a number of cookie (biscuit) manufacturing plants in the United States, the United Kingdom, the Netherlands, Germany and France. First, he noted that these new working practices were only introduced in the "process" departments. The wrapping and packing departments are all organized along Taylorist lines with low-skilled, highly repetitive tasks being the norm. In Germany, France and the Netherlands, nearly all the process workers are able to switch flexibly between the main areas of work, mixing, cookie-forming and oven control. These countries had already gone some way along the HPWP route, facilitated by the high levels of skills the systems of vocational training had delivered to their employees. However, these teams are not self-directed but are managed by a supervisor. Here there is still some way to go. In US and British factories, all work is organized along Taylorist lines. All employees are given limited training linked to the performance of specific tasks. This applies just as much to the "process" workers as to other employees.

Mason (1999) links these differences in the use of work practices to differences in the product market in the various countries. The continental Europeans are producing small and medium-sized batches for a highly differentiated product market. The British and Americans are producing low-cost, standardized products for a mass market, with the sheer size of the US market leading to higher levels of worker productivity. Mason also notes that US and British managers are more likely to be implementing ways of increasing their control over the behaviour of their workers, whereas the continental Europeans are more likely to support the multi-skilling of employees to support their involvement in the management of the production process.

In the precision engineering industry in the United States, the United Kingdom and the Netherlands, Mason also found that HPWPs are being introduced. Again, differences in the product market and the prior training of employees are important factors in explaining the differences he found. In response to the intensified international competition occurring in the late 1980s and early 1990s, companies in all three countries were attempting to introduce more self-inspection by shop-floor workers and eradicate separate inspection departments. Another response was to reconfigure shop-floor layouts, often to introduce cellular production. The latter led to the introduction of more multi-skilling and self-directed teamworking.

Again, he finds that US companies are making far more use of semi-skilled and low-skilled labour than the continental Europeans, the Dutch. This meant that the introduction of self-inspection and cellular production in the United States required a much more intensive programme of retraining and upskilling for the workers than in the Netherlands. The US workers had to be trained in quality-related areas such as statistical process control, as well as blueprint reading, shop maths and the use of computer numerically controlled machine operation. In the Netherlands, the use of more highly trained employees meant that there was less retraining to be done with the introduction of these new practices.[4] The costs of introducing these practices in the United States was therefore much higher.

In the high-speed machinery and vehicle components industries, Mason was able to observe the more full-blown introduction of HPWPs in three countries, the United Kingdom, the United States and Germany. Under intense international pressure in all three countries, companies are attempting to involve production workers in more day-to-day decision-making and problem-solving activities. In many plants, supervisors are expected to take broader responsibility for supporting and coordinating the activities of production teams. In the United States, this has led to the abolition of some grades such as general foreman, but there is no big increase in the ratio of supervisors to those supervised. This has left the supervisors with more opportunities to engage in medium-term strategic planning, liaison with management and participation in cross-functional product development teams. The production teams then assumed responsibility for daily decisions on production management, for example, machine loading, absenteeism, monitoring of quality. There are similar changes in UK establishments.

In Germany, there are some differences. There is less immediate need for cellular reorganizations, as there had been years of incremental improvements in the layout of plants as a result of the activities of the highly (apprenticeship) trained employees. However, the recent intensification of international competition which took place in the early 1990s has meant that there was a sudden increase of interest in the use of self-managed work teams as a means of improving productivity further. Many of the responsibilities of supervisors (Meisters), such as materials and production scheduling and quality control, were taken over by teams. The new role of the Meister is one of coordination and motivation, focusing on product improvements as well as recruitment and training. In Germany, the existence of highly trained, skilled workers has enabled supervisors to expand further their span of control.

The national costs of introducing HPWPs

All this led Mason to conclude that the costs of introducing HPWPs will be higher in the United States than in continental Europe. This is because the skill levels of much of the US labour force are relatively low, and therefore they have a steeper learning curve. In the United States, he also reports more variation in the use of HPWPs because of the sheer size of the market. There, US companies have more opportunities to make the most of economies of scale from the use of Taylorist forms of mass production. In Germany and the Netherlands, the existence of a highly trained labour force has enabled companies to implement high involvement working practices relatively quickly. While this makes good sense, other research has revealed that there may be hidden costs in Germany to the introduction of HPWPs, namely the resistance of some skilled workers to the introduction of these practices.

Work by other scholars has shown that German skilled workers have often seen the attempt to introduce multi-skilling as a threat to their trade and therefore resisted it. The long period of socialization into a trade creates a strong sense of occupational identity (Heinz, 1999; Evans and Heinz, 1991). Through their long period of training, German apprentices learn to identify strongly with their trade, in which membership becomes an important part of their identity. This is reinforced by the relatively high level of pay they receive as skilled workers and which they are keen to defend. One response to the problem of skilled-worker resistance has been for companies to modify the form taken by self-managed work groups to accommodate these issues. The work by Finegold and Wagner (1998) is illustrative in this respect. They studied the impact of new production systems on firms in the German pump industry. Specifically, they were interested in attempts by manufacturers in this industry to introduce multifunctional teams which would enable broadly skilled employees to move easily between different tasks. They found considerable resistance on the part of the highly skilled, apprenticeship-trained workers to the introduction of multifunctional teams. Those plants with a higher proportion of semi-skilled workers are more likely to implement multifunctional teams than those with a high proportion of skilled workers. This has not been the case in the United States where skilled workers are more likely to have accepted these changes. The technical director of one plant where the German skilled workers had shown resistance explained it as follows:

> "They view it as a reduction in skill because they focus solely on the technical skills and not the responsibilities that would come from the move toward cellular production. For them it means producing one range of parts on a few CNC machines, whereas in the past they could produce any part on any machine in the plant. What they fail to take into account is the other skills that the team requires – production scheduling, ordering, managing supplier relations, programming and the communication required to make a team work effectively across several shifts. This is the mindset we're trying to bring about" (Finegold and Wagner, 1998:477).

Some employers have succeeded in overcoming this type of resistance by introducing mini-business units which include engineers and other support personnel together with skilled workers. Collectively, this group is responsible for taking a product line from raw materials to the customer. The front-line workers are now given the responsibility for scheduling and quality. The skilled workers retain their technical skills but are given further training in organizational competencies, team dynamics and project management. This enabled one plant to boost productivity by 40 per cent in three years. In terms of our discussion, it illustrates the ways in which the German manufacturer was able to introduce ideas of self-managed work teams in different ways which accommodated the strengths of the German apprenticeship system. This highlights how each country is adopting the principles of high performance working to its own specific institutional conditions.

National responses to the spread of HPWPs

In addition to having to accommodate different national institutional provisions, especially in the form of training systems, the introduction of HPWPs is not being universally welcomed at the national level by employers and trade union organizations. Here we encounter the impact of a range of different suspicions and resistance based on historical conditions in each country.

We illustrate this by the national responses to an initiative taken by the European Union in a Green Paper Partnership for new organization of work (April, 1997). This Green Paper was an attempt to encourage debate on the new high performance forms of work organization. While it was broadly welcomed at the European level by both employers' organizations and unions, at the national level there were considerable variations in response.

In Finland and the United Kingdom, the response from employers and unions has been positive. In Germany and Austria, the response from both unions and employers was more sceptical. The German employers' organization (BDA) was sceptical of any shift away from Tayloristic forms of organization towards more flexible, team-based forms of work organization. They argued that developments in work organization depend on specific national, company and market conditions. For the BDA, questions of employee security are paramount, and this is related less to the organization of work than to labour costs and the national tax and labour law regulations. They wanted change in these areas, not in the organization of work. Indeed, given the importance of the legal framework in Germany in enhancing working security, this is an understandable response.

The trade union responses were equally interesting and varied. The radical French union CGT-FO pointed out that the concept of partnership runs counter to its own idea of independence, leading it to conclude that new forms of work organization are just tools for obtaining flexibility with all the negative implications that has for them. The German DGB was more sympathetic but pointed out that the implementation of HPWPs could differ between companies, a point we also stress in this book. The union was also concerned with ensuring a balance between flexibility and employee security. The Irish and Spanish unions were more positive.

Conclusions

There can now be little doubt that HPWPs are spreading rapidly in many countries and across the globe. Nowhere do they appear in the majority of organizations, and in many countries their presence is still confined to "leading-edge" organizations. In others, HPWOs have a substantial presence.

This chapter has shown, however, that there is no single "blueprint". There is some evidence that when they are implemented, the work design/employee involvement practices are accompanied by other HR practices which provide support for the performance of individuals and groups. Even within these core practices, the actual form they take when implemented is strongly conditioned by prior forms of national culture and training provision. Even basic team structures are shown to be influenced by national culture. So too is the organization of self-managed work. In Germany, the prior existence of highly skilled workers moulded by the apprenticeship system is seen to impact on the form taken by these groups.

Outside these core practices or bundles, reward structures and communications systems are also strongly influenced by national institutions. In Japan, seniority-based payment systems still pervade the reward system. In continental Europe, unions still play an important part in shaping reward systems independently of the existence of HPWOs. The implementation of HPWPs appears to bend those pre-existing systems in a specific direction. In view of the power of these national institutional structures, we are unlikely to see the introduction of HPWPs bring about any universal convergence.

The importance of these national institutional structures is also seen in the impact they have on the cost of introducing HPWPs. While a strong apprenticeship system will produce a high level of skills among the labour force, thereby reducing the immediate costs of upgrading the labour force, those same institutional structures can act as a barrier to the introduction of HPWPs. This is because of the threat the use of HPWP practices can make to the skilled workers' trade monopoly and their identity.

Beyond these national institutional structures, we have the major players in the economy to contend with if we are to make more use of HPWPs as a means of enhancing the quality of working life, namely the employers' organizations and the unions. Here we encountered vested interests created by existing structures, for example the preoccupation of German employers with reducing employees' job security at the expense of a concern with the organization of work and the ambivalent attitude of some national unions toward the use of HPWPs. It is not for us to either applaud or condone these positions; we are merely using them to show how national politics may influence the adoption of HPWPs. In the next chapter, we move on to take a closer look at the role of governments, how they are supporting the implementation of HPWPs and some of the equity issues raised by their spread.

Notes

[1] Wood et al. (2001) use nine practices: organizations which they label as full HIM had between seven to nine; partial HIM had between three to seven and minimal HIM had between one to five.

[2] Details of the analysis can be found in Ashton and Sung (2001) "The use of HPWP and 'bundles': a cross-national comparison", CLMS Working Paper series, forthcoming.

[3] Details of the analysis can be found in Ashton and Sung (2001) "The use of HPWP and 'bundles': a cross-national comparison", CLMS Working Paper series, forthcoming.

[4] Mason also notes that Dutch firms have not gone as far as US firms in introducing these reforms.

CHAPTER 6

EQUITY AND HIGH PERFORMANCE WORKING: THE ROLE OF PUBLIC POLICY

Introduction

The case we have made out for the spread of HPWOs is that they represent a new way of organizing the production of goods and services that makes more effective and productive use of human labour than has been the case hitherto. This is especially so when these practices are combined with the use of the new information and computer technology (ICT). From the point of view of the national economy, that would be sufficient reason on its own to encourage their growth - they offer the possibility of higher levels of economic growth. However, the growth of these organizations is even more important for the citizens of the twenty-first century, for these organizations are creating jobs which are more demanding on the skills of human beings than has traditionally been the case. Whereas earlier "Taylorist" forms of production created jobs and an income that took many out of poverty, the nature of those jobs was such that they offered no prospect of facilitating the further development of human capabilities. Indeed in some respects, as we have shown, they may have impaired the development of many workers. In contrast, the jobs created by HPWOs offer the prospect of developing the practical and intellectual skills of all those employed in them, not just the management and selected groups of white-collar workers. These organizations offer the prospect of making the workplace a source of lifelong learning for all those employed within them. For these reasons, we move on in this chapter to examine the ways in which public policy can be used to encourage their development and to explore some of the equity issues which arise from their introduction.

In exploring these public policy issues, we face two main problems. The first is that as there is no one best way to support the growth of HPWOs we cannot provide one set of prescriptions. Moreover, public policy in the field of human resource development in each country is already influenced by a range of factors, including the existing educational and training institutions. In some respects, each country is unique. However, this does not mean that we have to examine every country in detail to identify new possibilities for policy. Earlier work (ILO, 1998; Ashton et al., 2000) has identified strong similarities in VET systems across countries and common ways in which their systems are adapting to the requirements of HPWOs. For this reason, we explore the impact of some of these different institutional frameworks on the measures that may be used to support HPWOs.

The second problem we face is that some countries have progressed more in supporting HPWOs than others. For this reason, we delve a little more deeply into public policy in countries such as Singapore which have gone further down this road.

Adapting institutional frameworks

In Anglo-Saxon countries, governments tend to have their range of policy measures limited to "voluntary" measures aimed at encouraging employers and individuals to "invest" in training. The belief in the primacy of the market to deliver workforce development, especially training, means that government policies are restricted to programmes which employers and individuals can either opt into or out of as they desire. All governments can do is to provide opportunities and encourage. Only in the case of market failures, such as unemployment, can they "interfere" in the market.

In the Asian Tiger economies, governments have developed a much broader range of policy measures. There, governments are far more pragmatic in their approach and therefore have devised a much broader range of measures to push employers into developing their workforces, often based on taxation in the form of levies or prescribed training. This does not mean that the market is ignored, rather that the government seeks to shape the way in which the market operates instead of waiting to respond to market failures.[1] The implications of these different approaches for the support of HPWPs is discussed in the main body of this chapter.

In this introductory section, all we are concerned to highlight is that these different "philosophical" approaches are sometimes embedded in national legal regulations and customs which also place limits on the extent to which HPWPs can be implemented. This may mean that attempts to introduce HPWPs may require modifications to national institutional structures. We illustrate this with reference to the problems facing governments in two contrasting systems, the Anglo-Saxon and the Germanic.

Adapting the Anglo-Saxon system

In the Anglo-Saxon countries, there has been more of a history of governments refusing to intervene in the market or place "constraints" on employers in the form of legal obligations either to consult or train workers. There, employers have more autonomy in terms of both the range of working practices that can be introduced and the ways in which they are introduced. The introduction of new practices such as teamworking, performance-based pay, appraisals, etc. is usually seen as part of the managerial prerogative. However, even here there are always some limits on managerial discretion. These may stem from the influence of trade unions which, in those organizations that are unionized, often have the power to be consulted over the introduction of new practices.

118

Sometimes the legal framework that underpins management/worker relations may act as an impediment to the introduction of new practices. Thus in the United States, Ichniowski et al. (2000) point out that there are certain legal impediments to the spread of HPWOs. For example, considerable uncertainty exists over the legality of some forms of employee participation in non-union settings. According to the Commission on the Future of Worker-Management Relations (1994), systemic workplace innovations run the risk of violating the National Labor Relations Act's ban on company-dominated unions. This has left many managers cautious about broadening existing participation programmes or instituting new ones (Ichniowski, 2000:33).

While the Anglo-Saxon framework provides more freedom for managers to determine the introduction of new working practices, it also generates counter-pressures against the introduction of HPWPs. These are most evident in the operation of the financial markets. This is especially the case in the United States and the United Kingdom where the markets generate pressure on companies to maximize immediate returns, a point we initially raised in Chapter 2. As Ichniowski points out, the short-term costs involved in developing and maintaining HPWPs may be rejected by management strategies that are aimed at boosting profitability through short-term cost reductions. Indeed, this very strategy has threatened one of our case studies, Thorn Lighting in the United Kingdom, which was bought out by a company intent on maximizing short-term returns.[2] In this kind of financial environment, HPWOs will always be subject to this type of threat, where new owners, unaware of the relationship between the use of HPWPs and profit/productivity, may see the prospect of dismantling such practices as a means of achieving higher profits in the short term. These pressures, which stem from the growth of shareholder capitalism, are less evident in the Germanic countries where the financial markets have less power in influencing company strategy (Dore, 2000).

One of the Anglo-Saxon countries which has done most to incorporate employers into the policy process is Australia. There, the Government has established a clear national VET policy which has emerged after extensive consultations with employers and unions, VET providers, students and trainees. One distinguishing feature of this policy is that the key issues for education are separated from those for VET so that the work-related nature of VET maintains its prominence. As we shall see, this is important in relation to the distinctive challenges posed by HPWOs. Finally, the policy includes national objectives for VET which are capable of being measured and monitored so that progress can be reviewed.

Adapting the Germanic system

In the Germanic countries, for example Germany, Denmark, Austria and Switzerland, there is a long history of the government providing a legal framework for industrial relations and training, especially in the form of apprenticeship. This in turn has provided a much more institutionally dense environment. Government "intervention" is part of the taken-for-granted world. The problem facing governments there is how to modify those institutions to accommodate to the demands of HPWOs.

It has long been argued that the national frameworks, based on more comprehensive agreements amongst the state, employers and unions on the regulation of the workplace, have been responsible for the high level of skills which characterize German workers (Crouch et al., 1999; Brown et al., 2001). Streeck (1989), among others, has shown how the legal framework and regulations which unions, employers and chambers of commerce have agreed upon to structure the apprenticeship system create a high level of training. Dore (2000) has shown how the system of Works' Councils and co-determination together with the legal framework have been instrumental in generating trust between employers and workers by placing constraints on managers which lead them to be as concerned with the welfare of their employees as they are with their duties to shareholders. The Works' Councils provide a forum for the discussion of human resource practices including training. As we have seen earlier, this trust is a crucial precondition for the introduction of high performance working practices. In this sense, the German system could be seen as more accommodating to the introduction of HPWPs than the more confrontational relations between management and workers which have often characterized companies in Anglo-Saxon countries in the past.

However, this institutionally dense environment also creates problems for attempts to introduce HPWPs. The very fact that it is institutionally dense means that it is slow in bringing about change in the framework to accommodate to some of the other requirements of HPWOs. For example, it has taken some time to develop training for the new ICT trades and incorporate these into the apprenticeship system (Crouch et al., 1999; Brown et al., 2001; ILO, 2001). Creating such change involves the government, unions and the other partners reaching agreement. Similarly, it has taken some time for the new skills of teamworking, problem-solving and communication skills to be introduced into the curriculum. These have been difficult changes which, as we shall see, require time and goodwill on the part of all those involved.

Public policy: Encouraging the spread of HPWOs

It is against this background of the different challenges which their institutional frameworks create that we move on to consider the range of ways in which governments have sought to facilitate the introduction of HPWPs in their economies. In its role as a facilitator for the development of HPWOs, the government can act on both the demand and supply side. On the demand side, it can encourage the adoption of HPWPs in public organizations. For companies in the private sector, it can influence employers by putting in place schemes which provide incentives for them to adopt HPWPs as well as help in providing the appropriate advice and guidance on how to do it. On the supply side, it can operate on the labour market to ensure a flow of skills appropriate for HPWOs. It can do this either by acting directly in introducing the transmission of such skills through the school and college curriculum or indirectly by ensuring that the national qualifications framework supports the certification of such skills.

Demand side: Public sector

On the demand side, the most direct way in which the government can introduce HPWPs is to do what the Clinton administration did in the United States, namely to set up a system that ensures public sector organizations adopt HPWPs. We have seen how this was done in the United States through the President's Management Council (PMC) which is committed to improving the performance of the federal Government. In this case, the PMC then asked the government-wide Human Resource Development Council for action to improve the performance of the federal Government. In the US Social Security Administration (SSA) case study, this was done by using the HR department to spearhead the introduction of these changes. While the SSA did not introduce job redesign and teamworking on a large scale, there is no inherent reason why this could not be done using this same approach. We do not yet know with any certainty how effective the HR department is as a catalyst for change in the public sector. Nevertheless, in this one sphere of policy administration, the use of selected public sector organizations to spearhead the introduction of HPWPs appears to have worked.

There is no reason why this same strategy should not work with other governments, including those outside the Anglo-Saxon world, providing that public sector HR departments have the appropriate skills to implement HPWPs. Even if these are absent, it should not be difficult for governments to provide the requisite training for HR leaders through their own facilities or to create incentives for the market to deliver such training.

Demand side: Private sector

In the private sector, the government can influence employers in at least two separate ways. First, it can provide incentives for them to rethink the ways in which they organize labour, with a view to improving performance through the use of HPWPs. Second, it can develop national standards for best HRD practice which would provide an incentive for employers to upgrade their HRD practices. These may take the form of national awards for Total Quality Awards, as with the Malcolm Baldrige Awards in the United States or the Investors in People (IiP) Programme in the United Kingdom, or they can take the form of standards for measuring intellectual capital. We deal with each in turn.

Providing incentives for employers: European approaches

There are numerous ways in which governments have attempted to provide employers with incentives to rethink ways in which they utilize labour. Business Decisions Limited (2000) examined the range of ways in which 11 European governments encourage the adoption of organizational change. They examined a total of 18 targeted programmes that support the introduction of new forms of work organization.

These programmes tended to support change in three main areas: the introduction of new organizational structures such as semi-autonomous work teams and fewer layers of management; new working practices such as multi-skilling; and new corporate cultures such as greater trust and employee participation. One example of such schemes is the New Work Organization in Ireland Programme described in the following box.

The New Work Organization in Ireland Programme

The Programme started in 1995 with funding from the European Social Fund and the Irish Government. It was implemented by the Irish Productivity Centre (IPC) in partnership with the Irish Business and Employers' Confederation (IBEC) and the Irish Congress of Trade Unions (ICTU). It started with a joint exercise between the interested parties to find ways of improving companies' competitiveness. Then a trained partnership forum was formed within each participating company to act as the driving force in planning and implementing the competitiveness improvement programme. The companies' achievements ranged from process re-engineering and implementing team-based production work cells to the development of new reward and recognition systems. The Programme sought to develop a new capability to address change through cooperation between employers and unions in partnership and to help end adversarial industrial relations. It developed practical models for introducing new working practices in both public and private sector organizations. It also developed a national network of experienced social partner practitioners, offering expert support in developing a long-term framework for modernizing work organization. The essence of the Programme was to help enterprises in enhancing people and organizational competence and encouraging the development of innovative solutions to organizational deficiencies based on principles of mutual trust and mutual gains.

Source: Business Decisions Limited, 2000.

The other programmes examined in the 11 countries varied considerably on a number of dimensions. The first was on the amount of resources devoted to them, with the German Work and Technology Programme having a budget of 330 million EURO and the Belgium Working Conditions Programme with a budget of only 0.2 million EURO. They also varied in terms of their duration and the number of projects they supported, with the French Reduction in Working Time Programme supporting around 13,000 projects and the Finnish National Productivity Campaign supporting 20 projects in ten companies.

The programmes were heterogeneous in purpose, but all supported the introduction of new ways of working. In general, the majority of them were focused on research, education, demonstration and awareness raising, such as the Man Technology and Organization Research Programme in Sweden. Over half the programmes funded research into new forms of work organization, while over one-third promoted the development of inter-firm networks to educate companies and trade unions and to pass on best practice, such as the New Work Organization in Ireland Programme cited above. Just under one-third financed educational and awareness-raising projects to provide information to companies and unions and support demonstration projects, such as the German Work and Technology Programme.

In general, the programmes offered indirect support to companies and their workers, with approximately one-half directed at SMEs and just under one-half directed at manufacturing organizations, with the majority not discriminating between high- or low-tech companies. However, other organizations were also beneficiaries, such as public sector organizations and educational and research institutions, together with unions and employers' federations.

The most common form of support for these programmes was through the use of grants rather than tax incentives or loans. Most programmes provided grants or advice from consultants or trainers. The Irish World-Class Manufacturing Programme provided both grants and advice from consultants. Most financial support was focused on revenue costs, and all required expenditure to be directly related to the project supporting up to 40-50 per cent of the project costs.

The programmes were primarily implemented through the government, with relatively little use being made of private sector providers. The majority required the involvement of both management and staff, with one-third specifying that the project included trade unions. These projects had to involve management and staff and focus on specified areas of change. They also had to be evaluated.

One of the few government-sponsored programmes which has been directly designed to support the introduction of high performance work practices is the Finnish National Workplace Development Programme. Set up for four years in 1996 and renewed in 2000, it aims to improve organizational performance and the quality of working life by promoting the knowledge of workers and the use of innovative work organizations. It supports workplace-initiated projects, creates and maintains networks to disseminate knowledge and promotes research into improving working life.

Unlike other Nordic countries, the Finnish Government has no tradition of public policy involvement in employers' activities. This programme was therefore designed after research and examining the experiences of other (mainly Nordic) countries in their attempt to improve economic performance. They established an agreement with the employers and trade unions to promote changes in the organization of work and improve Finland's productivity.

The Finnish Workplace Development Programme

The Programme provides resources to use external advisers to bring about changes in work organization and productivity. Priority is given to projects that create a fundamental change in the organization of work, including the use of technology, work organization, management strategies, staff skills, working conditions and occupational health. In the first phase, projects received a grant of 50 per cent of eligible costs with SMEs receiving a grant of 70 per cent. To qualify for support, the projects must involve managers and workers and focus on target areas such as promoting new forms of work organization and promoting equality. There is an extensive post-project evaluation attached as a condition of the grant.

Between 1996 and 1999, 65 per cent of participants in the Programme were from the private sector and in general these organizations tended to be small and medium-sized enterprises of between 50 and 250 employees.

Source: Business Decisions Limited (2000).

The extensive system of evaluation attached to the Finnish projects revealed a number of lessons. First, the various stakeholders - Government, managers, employees and employee representatives - had to have a common view about the need for the change. Second, the workplace had to have the flexibility to determine their own goals. Third, all the parties - managers, staff and employee representatives - had to be actively involved in the implementation of high performance working practices. Finally, the Government had an important role to play in helping implement new work systems and in providing an institutional base at regional and central levels.

Providing incentives from employers: Lessons from the European experience

The authors of the report suggest that there are a number of lessons to be learned from their review of programmes. They argue that governments can help enhance "innovative capacity" and raise productivity; they can also help raise awareness of the benefits of these changes (especially in the service and low-tech areas where these practices are less evident) and help companies learn from each other. As these are European projects, they emphasize the importance of a partnership approach to change, involving both managers and employees/unions. As for the design of the programmes, they stress the importance of securing a genuine "buy-in" from all the stakeholders, that change is a slow process and that new forms of work organization cannot be divorced from other aspects of the organization. On a more critical note, what is noticeable in their relative absence are programmes which support TQM and continuous improvement or the introduction of new performance measurement and reward systems. These are serious omissions in view of our knowledge of the importance of bundles of practices and the significance of measurement and reward systems in ensuring the success of HPWPs. Nevertheless, these are innovative programmes which at least are starting to explore ways in which governments can assist the introduction of new working practices.

In addition to this type of programme, the OECD (1996) suggests that governments can foster the adoption of innovative practices by supporting the development of benchmarking services. These spread best practice and enable companies to highlight weaknesses and strengths. They also promote the development of inter-firm networks to educate companies and inter-union networks to influence trade unions.

Providing incentives for employers: Asian holistic approaches

In many respects, these European programmes represent a piecemeal approach to the task of encouraging the spread of HPWPs. They are one-off attempts to introduce what is in effect a major change in the way in which we organize our working lives. For a more holistic approach, we need to turn to South East Asia in general and Singapore and Malaysia in particular. In the Tiger economies of Singapore, the Republic of Korea and Taiwan, China, there has been more of a concerted attempt by governments to coordinate the demand and supply of skills and to use labour market and training policy to push the economy in the direction of higher value-added goods and services (Ashton et al., 1999). Toward this end, the Singapore

Government introduced the Skills Development Fund, a levy on the use of low-paid labour, the proceeds of which are used to fund increases in labour productivity and the upgrading of the skills of the labour force. In this way, the Government is transferring the cost of introducing new working practices and the employee skills required to make effective use of them onto those employers who persist in employing low-paid unskilled labour. Over the years, this has led to the creation of a number of programmes targeted at the training needs of specific groups. More recently, these programmes have been coordinated into what is now called an Integrated Workforce Development Plan.[3]

Through the Integrated Workforce Development Plan, the introduction of modern organizational forms is tackled in two ways. First and central to this plan is the attempt to develop the workforce to meet the needs of the new knowledge economy. This is achieved through a series of programmes aimed at developing workers' skills; for example, the On-the-Job Training Programme provides guidance to employers on how to introduce effective on-the-job training (OJT) through the development of OJT blueprints. These are initially developed with companies which are widely considered to be leaders in their field to identify model (best-practice) approaches to OJT. This ensures that the OJT blueprint is tailor-made for key personnel in that particular industry. Once developed and having been tested and found effective in leading-edge companies, they are then cascaded throughout the industry. The new soft skills required for the new economy and HPWOs are delivered through the Critical Enabling Skills Programme.

The Critical Enabling Skills Training (CREST) Programme was introduced in 1998 with the objective of establishing a system of core skills to tackle future skill needs among Singaporean workers. It moves away from emphasizing technical content in training and instead aims at building a foundation in the "critical skills" that will enable workers to constantly acquire and apply new knowledge and skills. It is designed to deliver seven critical skills: "learning-to-learn", literacy (reading, writing and computation), listening and oral communication skills, problem solving and creativity, personal effectiveness (self-esteem, goal-setting and motivation, personal and career development), group effectiveness (interpersonal, teamwork and negotiation) and organizational effectiveness and leadership. Many of these are known as "key skills" or "core skills" in other countries.

The Programme is delivered through a public/private partnership. The Government, through the Productivity and Standards Board (PSB), sets the standards and defines the outcomes, while a network of private providers deliver the programme.

Once the skills have been acquired on the courses, the companies have to commit to applying those skills in the workplace. In this way, the skills empower the worker and the company provides the opportunity to apply them in order to increase productivity. The Programme has been very successful. By the end of the year 2000, 1,569 employers of the country's 1.8 million workers had provided CREST training to their employees.

The second strategy of the Integrated Workforce Development Plan is to encourage employers to re-think their work practices. The Industry Capability Upgrading Programme encourages companies to develop collaborative schemes to meet common needs, for example for the travel industry to confront the new demands of e-commerce. Further help for employers to re-think their working practices is available through the Work Redesign Programme. The objective of the Work Redesign Programme is to encourage employers to continuously review their work processes and adopt what is called a total approach to work redesign, with the aim of improving long-term productivity. The Government's target is to develop 50 work redesign blueprints for companies to emulate in the 20 industry clusters identified by the Government as crucial to Singapore's future development.

Delivering critical enabling in Singapore: A public/private partnership

Here we describe how two of the modules in the Singapore CREST Programme were developed through the use of private sector expertise.

The first is the "problem-solving and creativity" module (called Intelligence), created by the British Council in Singapore. The module is designed to help participants break out of mindsets that discourage creative thinking and effective problem solving. Twenty-five organizations participated in the scheme's pilot stage, and it is now expected to become a major component within Singaporean company training plans.

The second example is collaboration with Motorola University. The "success through oral communication" module covers all the essential skills required in the communication process – interacting with different communication styles, active listening, establishing rapport and concluding. The fundamental concepts were derived from the "multi-channel communication" approach developed by US psychometric experts and Motorola itself. By integrating three channels of learning - figural, symbolic and semantic - the module aims at enhancing learning and retention in all learners, irrespective of their learning styles. Within a span of three months during the pilot stage, over 300 people from some 40 organizations participated in the module.

The Programme aims to help companies identify work redesign opportunities and solutions, to identify the competences required for the new jobs and to implement change. Consultation and communication are seen as integral to the process. The Programme provides the services of a series of consultants to help companies through the process. The level of financial support provided by the Skills Development Fund (SDF) is much higher than is the case in the typical European scheme. The SDF provides up to 90 per cent support for the costs of work redesign consultancy and up to 80 per cent for the training of managers and supervisors to implement the process in their own companies. Once implemented, these work practices then generate the demand for the new soft skills which can be delivered and certified through other programmes such as CREST or the National Skills Recognition System. The National Skills Recognition System provides a framework for establishing work-performance standards, job competences and certifying skills. However, as this strategy is still in its infancy, evaluation will have to wait until it has been in operation for a number of years.

Malaysia has adopted a similar approach. Fleming and Soborg (2001) make a distinction between what they term the reactive phase in Malaysia's approach to human resource development and the proactive phase. The reactive phase lasted until the 1980s and was characterized by political initiatives taken by the Government, often in partnership with business organizations and other interest groups, with the aim of realizing a political agenda set by business that was largely reacting to the demands of industry. However, education policy during this period was influenced by the political requirement to enhance the achievement levels of the Malays and other indigenous ethnic groups, the "Bumiputra".

After the mid-1980s, Fleming and Soborg argue that national human resource development policy became more proactive in that the Government while still acting through partnerships with different interest groups, including business, was now setting its own political agenda. The aim of the strategy was to change Malaysia's economy from labour-intensive to higher value-added forms of production. Fleming and Soborg argue that there were two main components to this strategy, namely to forge an alliance with foreign MNCs in higher value-added forms of production and to transform state-owned companies through privatization to become national "drivers" (as model companies) in the transformation process. These new drivers now act in association with the Economic Action Committee, previously the Economic Planning Unit, and the Malaysian Industrial Development Authority to lead HRD developments. Through these agencies, the Government is supporting leading companies in setting up private science parks and universities.

This shift in policy reflected very real changes in the occupational structure during the 1990s. Professional, scientific, administrative and managerial workers increased from 11.2 per cent to 14.2 per cent during that period, while production and related workers increased from 27.6 per cent to 32.8 per cent (Fleming and Soborg, 2001). The Government now had to ensure that it was supplying higher-level technical and managerial skills as well as the new soft skills required for the new high performance companies. It established advanced training centres in collaboration with the Japanese, German, British and French Governments, for example the Japan-Malaysia Technical Institute, to provide the high-level technical and engineering skills required for leading-edge companies. At the state level, joint public/private initiatives in the form of Skill Development Centres were established to deliver intermediate- and lower-level skills upgrading.

To encourage a higher level of training within companies, the Government established the Human Resource Development Fund in 1992, which eventually required almost all employers to contribute a levy representing 1 per cent of payroll (Wan Seman Bin Wan Ahmad, 1999). The income from this levy is used to fund training in enterprises which meet the criteria set down by the Ministry. This enables the Government to focus private sector training on those areas where it perceives the national need is greatest by only providing significant rebates for certain types of training. In the 1990s, this was for technical training. The HRD Fund provides a powerful tool to help the Government build up the requisite skills of the labour force. In 2000, a total of 2.6 million training places was approved, with most support going toward support for in-house training provided by external trainers.

During this second phase, the Human Resource Development Council which oversees the administration of the HRD Fund has sought to emphasize the country's medium-term skill requirements to counter industry's concern with short-term interests. This partnership approach has been reflected in the way in which the Government has sought to involve leading MNCs in setting up its IT hub, the Multimedia Super Corridor. In addition, the national champions, the "drivers" of the transformation such as Petronas, Telekom and Tenaga Nasional, have been encouraged to set up their own universities.

In addition to collaborating with leading-edge companies, the Government has also been proactive in developing the country's skills infrastructure. On the supply side, the system of accreditation was overhauled in 1993 with the introduction of the accreditation system to replace the old trade testing system. Now accredited centres deliver the Malaysian Skill Certificates at five levels. In an attempt to deliver the IT and soft skills required for leading-edge companies, the Government set up "Smart Schools" in 1999. Initially, 90 primary and secondary schools were selected to provide IT teaching with an emphasis on thinking skills and language tuition together with a more learner-centred approach to delivering the curriculum. Although only 90 schools were initially designated as Smart Schools, by the year 2010 it is envisaged that all the 7,000 primary schools and 1,500 secondary schools will be Smart Schools.

Like Singapore, not all the reforms have been directed at establishing HPWOs. However, the lessons for public policy appear to be similar. On the supply side, the intention is to build a public skills infrastructure that can supply the technical and soft skills required for HPWOs and knowledge-intensive forms of production. Meanwhile, the demand side is tackled through attempts to bring employers on board and encourage them to adopt a longer-term view when identifying skill needs. Finally, there is the same use of tax incentives and inducements to encourage higher levels of investment in training and development within organizations.

The use of national standards: HRD standards

The second way of encouraging the spread of HPWPs is through the use of national standards. These were pioneered in the United States and the United Kingdom, both societies where the Governments are very wary of "interfering" in the operations of market mechanisms. Awards, such as the US Malcolm Baldrige Award, the UK Investors in People Award and the Singapore People Developer (PD) Award, signify the achievement of national standards of HR practice amongst employers. To achieve these awards, organizations have to demonstrate to independent assessors that their HR practices meet certain national standards. In the case of all these awards, it can take a company two or three years to prepare for assessment.

At the moment, these standards are not explicitly modelled on those characteristic of HPWOs. Indeed, Applebaum and Batt (1994) argue that the criteria adopted for the Malcolm Baldrige Award reflect a version of total quality management that emphasizes the strategic role of top management and quality management systems in improving competitiveness. "Consistent with the TQM adage that 85 per cent of problems reside with management and 15 per cent with employees, 85 per cent of the points in the Baldrige Award application are for improvements in management methods and processes" (Applebaum and Batt, p. 130). They see the Baldrige Award as emphasizing the combination of TQM and more traditional hierarchical organization and employment policies based on careful selection, training and performance evaluation. There is little emphasis placed on worker empowerment and teamworking, although Applebaum and Batt emphasize that these are also characteristics of many companies which have been successful in achieving the award.

Similar points can also be made about the UK Investors in People Award, at least in its first manifestation.[4] Although it incorporates a requirement for effective communication throughout the organization, effective evaluation of performance and a comprehensive and systematic approach to training, all of which we would expect to find in an HPWO, it is perfectly compatible with traditional hierarchically organized structures. However, we must not be too critical on this point, as we have already seen through our case studies that some organizations, especially those in the public sector, have implemented many of the characteristics of HPWOs in hierarchically organized companies. Indeed, SATS Security Services in Singapore, like many Japanese companies, was able to incorporate the use of teams into such a hierarchical structure.

It must also be remembered that these standards, and the models they implicitly contain, are social constructs. Given that they were developed before the spread of HPWOs, we would not necessarily expect that particular model to inform them. However, because they are social constructs, they can be changed. Indeed, the UK standards have recently changed and are now more concerned with issues such as ensuring equality of opportunity and ensuring that the outcomes of training and development are clearly linked to performance objectives, thereby facilitating continuous improvement. The latest standards (2000) also incorporate a role for teams. Thus, if a government wished to push organizations further in the use of HPWPs, there is no reason why criteria relating to these practices could not inform the standards more fully.

The advantage of using these awards as a public policy measure is that they do not require government intervention in the operation of the organization, but they are capable of having a powerful influence on organizational practices and performance. In the United States, the prestigious Baldrige has only been awarded to relatively few companies, but it has had a powerful impact on other employers. Thus, Applebaum and Batt argue that in addition to the total number of companies which actually achieve the Award, many more are influenced by the criteria it has established. They point out that it has spurred networking and benchmarking among firms by requiring winners to respond to requests for information. Baldrige winners have given countless lectures to other companies interested in submitting for the Award. More than 1 million copies of the award criteria have been distributed (Levine, 1998). In the United Kingdom, the CIPD's Training and Development Survey (2001) found that in 38.3 per cent of organizations which had implemented Investors in People the programme had "a lot" of influence on organizational culture, while a further 51.6 per cent report some impact on organizational culture (CIPD, 2001:12).

These awards work by making firms and organizations introduce systematic procedures for HRD. In the case of IiP and PD, they ensure clear linkages between training and development and business strategy. They encourage a systematic approach to communication within the organization and make sure that all employees are aware of business objectives and their role within the organization and that they receive feedback on their performance. In addition, they ensure that all employees receive training appropriate to their needs. In this way, they facilitate the introduction of some of the work and organizational practices associated with high performance working. In the United States, studies have demonstrated a relationship between success on the Baldrige Quality Award criteria and organizational performance, with those companies implementing the Baldrige criteria outperforming others (Easton and Jarrell, 2000; Hendricks and Singhal, 2000).

Evaluations of IiP, while they have not been able to produce such hard evidence of the link to performance, have demonstrated a significant impact of the achievement of this Award on training within the organization (Spilsbury et al., 1995). In addition, evidence from the UK Skills Survey has shown that skill levels are higher in those organizations that have IiP (Felstead et al., 2000a). The success of the UK IiP can be measured by the fact that in 1997 approximately one-third of the labour force was employed in organizations involved in IiP (Felstead and Ashton, 2000). On the negative side, there were complaints by some employers that it is too bureaucratic in the sense that it is too prescriptive in terms of the type of practices that have to be in place, for example annual formal appraisals, too paper driven and jargon ridden as well as having too many indicators. Attempts to rectify these deficiencies have been made through the introduction of revised standards.

One of the more general criticisms of these standards is that some companies have been able to gain accreditation without introducing much change. However, this may be precisely because they have many of the procedures already in place beforehand. A further criticism of IiP is that it is just a matter of ticking boxes, a paper exercise. For some organizations, this may be the case, but this is offset by the fact that there are also a large number of organizations in the United Kingdom which fail in their attempts to reach the standards or give up in the process. This often occurs when the management realizes the extent of change required.

From the perspective of the organizations that are successful in achieving these awards, they are seen as performing important functions. One of these is to provide management with a clear set of guidelines for what may be taken as best practice in the field of HRD. They are an effective means of disseminating best practice. Moreover, the process of change which may be necessary to meet the standards can be an important learning exercise in organizational change for both management and employees. The fact that it takes UK organizations on average almost two years to reach the standard suggests that it often requires fairly substantial change (http://www.iipuk.co.uk/). Moreover, we know from survey evidence in the United Kingdom (Felstead et al., 2000a) that the achievement of IiP status is associated with higher levels of skills among the labour force of these companies and especially in the level of the new "soft" skills. Taken together, the evidence does suggest that the use of these awards has a powerful impact on organizational structure and employees' skills.

The use of national standards: Standards for measuring human capital

One further way in which organizations could be encouraged to introduce elements of HPW is through the introduction of standards for measuring human capital. As high levels of human capital are seen as integral to HPWOs, any attempt to measure it is seen as an inducement for companies to make more effective use of their people's skills. Developments in this area have been led by professional organizations such as the American Society for Training and

Development (ASTD). In association with leading-edge companies such as Motorola, Dow Chemicals and Price-Waterhouse, the ASTD has pioneered attempts to measure what it refers to as "intellectual" capital (Van Buren,1999). This includes a range of measures such as the retention of key personnel, IT literacy, training expenditures as a percentage of payroll, and employee satisfaction.

Governments can certainly help in this process through restructuring the accounting rules to place investment in people and quality on a more even footing with investment in plants and equipment. This would enable investors to identify those companies which are investing in the future through the use of measures which are comparable across time and companies.

The rationale for measuring human capital is to provide an alternative measure of performance to conventional financial measures which only address short-term performance. "Intellectual" capital measures direct the attention of managers to those other areas of performance which research has shown to be better indicators of companies' long-term performance and are more within the ambit of their own control (Van Buren, 1999). A company's financial performance is usually beyond the influence of individual managers, but customer satisfaction, employee retention and employee satisfaction are factors which are more directly under the control of the individual manager. Moreover, the fact that human capital is measured results in managers paying more attention to the management of it, reflecting the age-old adage that what cannot be measured is not managed. Managers are encouraged to share knowledge and best practice throughout the company, to define human capital, for example in the form of core competences, and to create human capital through training and mentoring. At the moment, the attempt to introduce standards in this area is still in its infancy but if this can be measured effectively it promises to be a useful technique in spreading the use of HPWPs.

The supply side: Supplying the new skills - changing the curriculum

On the supply side, there is a range of actions governments can and do take to increase the supply of appropriate skills. Just as on the demand side the focus was on embedding the organizational and work practices associated with HPWOs in private and public sector companies, so on the supply side government actions have been directed at increasing the supply of the "new" skills. These are the skills that we saw in Chapter 4 were required for effective participation in HPWOs. There are a number of areas where governments can act. They can enhance the skills of managers and others to support workplace learning through their influence over the curriculum. They can make the knowledge and techniques required for the support of learning at work an integral part of vocational qualifications at all levels. Also, they can forge new qualifications or amend existing ones to recognize the "new" skills required for HPWPs.

One of the most obvious ways whereby governments can increase the supply of these new skills in IT, communication, problem solving and teamworking is through changes in the school curriculum. Here governments across the developed world have been active in introducing computers into the schools and IT into the curriculum. Problem-solving and creativity skills have been specifically targeted in the Asian societies where the traditional reliance on rote learning has been seen to be inhibiting the development of more creative problem-solving skills among young people. Countries such as Singapore and Hong Kong, China have also attempted to tackle the problem at the top end of the educational ladder. In Singapore, there have been attempts to link their universities with leading institutions in the West to create a tradition of more critical thinking among undergraduates. Hong Kong, China has been encouraging university staff to become more involved in the worldwide research community and to make research a more significant part of the university teacher's job.

In the United Kingdom, the Government has attempted to introduce core/key skills into the curriculum. These include communication, application of numbers, problem solving, IT and improving own performance. Evaluation of the pilot exercise revealed a certain ambiguity over the meaning of key skills, but perhaps more importantly the researchers revealed that IT and application of numbers are more easily delivered through the school than problem solving which is more effectively delivered through the workplace (Unwin, 2000). In the United States, Stasz (1998) found that to introduce teamworking and problem solving into the curriculum would require radical changes to the delivery of education. Educators would have to make the classroom more like the workplace. In this respect, it is worth noting that Singapore delivers its "key skills" through employers. This reinforces the suggestion we made earlier that skills such as problem solving and teamwork may be best acquired in the workplace. Nevertheless, it is significant that many other countries (for example France, Germany, Sweden, Norway and Denmark) are exploring ways in which these new skills can be delivered to their workforce (Ashton et al., 2001).

The supply side: Changing national qualifications frameworks

The other major initiative aimed at delivering the requisite skills for high performance working is through the national qualifications framework. Here governments across the globe face different problems, depending on how the process of skill formation is organized. For the Anglo-Saxon nations with their traditional qualifications provided by both public sector and private providers, based on academic assessment, the problem has been how to introduce a more rational comprehensive system which can certify the new work-based skills. For those countries which have developed comprehensive systems of occupational certification, such as the German apprenticeship system, the problem has been how to incorporate demand for the new skills into existing provisions. For those countries such as Japan and the Republic of Korea with highly developed internal labour markets, there is less of a problem as companies already have control over the delivery of skills through their systems of on-the-job training. For developing countries with a relatively short history of vocational training and qualifications, there is an opportunity to incorporate demand for the new skills into their existing system and to mould new development around that demand.

The Germanic countries already have a comprehensive system of qualifications in place through the apprenticeship system, which covers almost all occupations. The problem they face is how to amend that framework to satisfy the need for training in the new skills. In

Germany, this is being done in two ways: first, new apprenticeships are being developed for the IT professions; second, modifications are being made to the apprenticeship curriculum to incorporate the new skills (Brown et al., 2001). IT skills are being incorporated into theory teaching which takes place in the classroom or training centre off the job, while the delivery of communication, problem-solving and teamworking skills has been tackled in more radical ways (see the earlier discussion of "learning islands") (Dehnbostel and Molzberger, 2001).

For those countries with an Anglo-Saxon approach, the problem they faced was in developing a comprehensive system of vocational qualifications. Given their tradition of voluntarism, qualifications were delivered through the market. In effect, this meant that educational institutions were responsible for the assessment of many skills, while private professional and qualifications authorities delivered others. The result was patchwork provision built up over the years, with many different qualifications available and some areas not covered by any provision. In the United States, approximately 400 professional societies and industry-based associations were involved in the promotion of skills-based certification in addition to that provided through the education system (Ashton and Sung, 2000). In general, the provision of qualifications tended to reflect the needs of Government and the older industries. Moreover, as Levine (1998) has pointed out, in the United States many States are creating separate standards to measure skills in problem solving and teamworking, creating confusion in the labour market and discouraging mobility. If standards are developed, they must be uniformly applied if they are to be effective.

The spread of ICT and the introduction of new HPWOs have revealed large gaps in the provision of vocational qualifications in these societies. This together with the lack of coherence in the existing patchwork of provision signalled the need for a rationalization of the system. Such a reform also created the opportunity to revise the nature of vocational qualifications and to replace academic qualifications with qualifications based on the demands on the workplace, that is on the competence required to perform the job effectively. The result has been the development of national competence-based qualifications systems in Australia, the United States, the United Kingdom, New Zealand and a host of other countries. Because these qualifications are founded on work-based competences, they should in theory be able to accommodate the need to certify the new skills. However, the results have so far been mixed in this respect.

The US system is still in the process of development. Part of the problem in the United States is that of developing a nationwide system when the central (federal) authority has limited jurisdiction over the individual States, which jealously guard their autonomy. Nevertheless, attempts have been made to develop a national system by the National Skills Standards Board, working through a network of "voluntary partnership" - coalitions of business, unions, employees, education, community and civil rights organizations - in 15 industrial sectors. However, given the voluntary nature of the exercise, progress has been slow and the uptake variable.[5] By the year 2001, only two partnerships were expected to complete their initial standards development (Ashton et al., 20001).

The UK system is now comprehensive in its coverage but has not been universally accepted by employers and has been criticized for failing to incorporate fully the new skills

(Keep, 2000). Standards have been produced for most industries and occupations, covering 86 per cent of the labour force in 1995. Although employers were involved in the development of the standards and their implementation, collectively they have not demonstrated high levels of enthusiasm for the system. Individual employers and groups in some industries have used the system, but Matlay (1999) reports that the new national vocational qualifications (NVQs) were implemented in only 26 per cent of larger firms, 15 per cent of firms employing 50-250 persons and 3 per cent of firms employing 11-49. This is not the level of success that was originally anticipated.

The take-up has been very uneven, both in terms of levels and industry coverage. The vast majority of NVQs are awarded at lower levels for what is generally regarded as semi-skilled and unskilled work. Indeed, many are achieved by those on government programmes for the unemployed, and it is argued that the present (low) level of take-up is only sustained through government insistence that NVQs are used in all their programmes (P. Robinson, 1996).

The Australian system has been more successful. There, each State/Territory has a high-level industry-based training board, and there has been a full incorporation of a wide array of industry boards into the process of developing industry standards for the competences required for each industry at each level of training. VET programmes have been modularized to make the delivery of them more flexible. This encourages people to take shorter bouts of training to meet a particular skill need without requiring them to enrol on a full VET course leading to a qualification. In addition, each set of standards is associated with a system of national training packages for each industry. These identify the relevant qualifications, competences and assessment guidelines for use in assessing the performance of trainees. By March 2000, there were 51 formally endorsed national training packages, comprising 47 industry packages and four enterprise packages covering about 85 per cent of Australian industry (C. Robinson, 2000:25).

One of the major achievements of the Australian system has been its ability to enhance the delivery of VET at the higher levels of skill development, e.g. diploma and advanced-diploma levels, which account for over one-third of total training hours delivered, as well as at the intermediate level, where a majority of apprentices and trainees undertake programmes at level 3 or higher of the Australian Qualifications Framework (AQF). By 1996, just over one-quarter of all enrolments in VET courses were for full qualifications under the AQF (C. Robinson, 2000: 32). Many other countries are in the process of implementing new systems.

For newly industrialized societies, the situation is similar in some respects to that faced by Anglo-Saxon countries, in that they have not yet had time to develop fully comprehensive systems of qualifications. In countries such as the Republic of Korea, where the "Chaebols" have traditionally provided something approaching lifetime employment, the Government could rely on them to deliver the new skills. However, the situation is very different for SMEs which cannot afford the cost of re-skilling their workers. If workers in these organizations are not to miss out, the Government must provide access to the new skills (Lauder, 1999). In Hong Kong, China, Singapore and Taiwan, China, employers cannot be relied upon to deliver the new skills, and therefore attempts are being made by governments to ensure their delivery

(Ashton et al., 1999). For example, Singapore has recently introduced a competence-based national skills recognition system informed by the UK system. However, this is only used for intermediate-level skills and below. South Africa is also in the process of implementing a similar competence-based system, this time based on the Australian experience. Through these reforms, governments are hoping to achieve a number of objectives, namely to plug the gaps in existing provision, to help deliver the new skills and to recognize everyone's skills irrespective of where they were obtained.

The extent to which these new competence-based systems will succeed in delivering new skills remains to be seen. In Australia, the adoption of competence-based training has varied across sectors; some employers complained that the system is overly complex and bureaucratic and too focused on the short-term needs of employers. Similar criticisms were made of the system in the United Kingdom. The result is that some employers prefer to rely on their own competence-based frameworks for the delivery of training. In the United Kingdom, doubts were also raised over whether the system tends to be reducing performance to the "average" level, although the US system of competence overcomes this through using the performance of exemplary or high-performing employees as the model on which standards are based. Clearly, we are still in the early stages of developing these new qualifications, with countries developing a number of variants and each attempting to build on past experience to produce a system appropriate to its own circumstances.

In developing countries, the main priority has to be the establishment of a basic national training infrastructure rather than amending an existing one. However, even here, as we would expect from the spread of HPWPs as depicted in Chapter 5, governments are already responding to the demands for new skills. In transition countries such as China, the main priority has been to establish a system of vocational education and training, namely to put in place an occupational classification, vocational training provision, skill testing, assessment and certification. Nevertheless, the Chinese Government has included a system of occupational standards in its provision (Wang Xiaojun, 2000). In Sri Lanka, the Government is reforming the current system of state-run development programmes to one which is demand driven in cooperation with the private sector. There will be a Skills Development Fund to promote training by private sector establishments as well as more involvement by employers in the design and implementation of training policy. However, the Sri Lankan Government is also experimenting with a scheme to introduce competence-based forms of assessment (Leelaratne, 2000). When we add to this the competence-based reforms in South Africa, we can see many developing nations starting to respond to the skills emanating from the new ways of organizing production. The advantage for the developing nations is that, as their national systems are still in the early stages of formation, they may be better able to adapt to the demand for the new skills precisely because they do not first have to amend existing institutionally entrenched systems.

This brief foray into various national VET systems illustrates that high performance work organizations are already having a global impact. Across the world, national governments with very different systems of vocational education and training are having to adapt them to the demands for skills from organizations with new ways of organizing production. In developing countries, the same forces are at work leading governments there to seek ways of forming their emergent systems to meet these new demands. It is also clear that there is no one best solution that all governments can adopt. Each country is learning to adapt its own system to best meet these new demands. In this respect, the solution adopted in the Republic of Korea will be very different from that adopted in Anglo-Saxon or Germanic countries. However, within these broad categories, there is a great deal to be learned from each other in terms of which practices work and which may not be worth pursuing.

The issues of equity

The development of new forms of work organization raises serious questions of equity, precisely because many of the new skills required appear to be acquired in the workplace. The UK Skills Survey (Ashton et al., 1998) found that those groups who do not have access to new HPWOs are not developing communication, problem-solving, IT and teamworking skills to the same level as those who are employed in them. In addition, we can confidently expect that the level of technical skills will be higher among those in the HPWOs precisely because of the greater investment in training associated with these organizations. In analysing the results of the UK Skills Survey, Felstead et al. (2000a) found that those who are excluded comprise a number of distinct groups; namely those in traditional organizations, part-time workers (primarily women), the self-employed, older workers and temporary workers. To this list, we can also add the informal sector workers in many developing countries.

The extent of this problem of exclusion will be determined by two main factors. First, it will not be a significant problem where there is a high proportion of the population already in knowledge-rich occupations, since the professionals, scientists, technicians and managers will be constantly under pressure to update their knowledge and skills by virtue of their occupational position. In those occupations, continuing professional development is already well entrenched as a professional requirement. The second determinant is the extent to which HPWPs have been adopted in a country. In HPWOs, ordinary workers are also under pressure from the work context to continue acquiring and using knowledge. The problem is greatest for those in Taylorist organizations who, as we have seen, have few if any opportunities to develop skills through their work. To these workers, we add the workers identified by Felstead et al. together with informal sector workers, and we have some idea of the size of the problem in each country. All these are at risk of exclusion from the new economy.

There are a number of ways in which this issue is being tackled. Employers in some countries have produced exemplary practices, unions have also sought to become involved in helping to provide opportunities for this group, and governments, especially in Scandinavia, have also developed imaginative schemes.

Employers and equity

In the Anglo-Saxon economies, one of the obvious ways in which companies can help individual employees is through the delivery of national vocational qualifications. By providing access to these qualifications, companies ensure that learning at work is certified and the individual employee obtains national recognition. This means that, should the company fail or the individual wish to move on, the learning he/she has acquired will be recognized in the national labour market. This was the route taken by Thorn, Ltd. which also devised a local scheme whereby unemployed youths in the region could register with the company for a pre-employment training course. This enables the company to identify potential new recruits, should suitable vacancies arise. In the meantime, it provides the unemployed with work experience and an additional achievement for their CV to help in their search for work.

A further way in which employers, even those using Taylorist forms of work design, can help promote employee development is through the use of employee development schemes. These provide funds for employees to pursue training or courses of learning of their own choice. One of the most famous of these is the Ford Employee Development and Assistance Programme (EDAP) scheme in the United Kingdom. This has been very effective in stimulating interest in learning among Ford employees in the United Kingdom. The UK Government has also used public funds to stimulate multi-employer schemes, especially among SMEs. Evaluation of all these schemes suggests that they are effective in stimulating learning among employees at the lower end of the workforce. However, they do need time to become established, usually between one and three years, and they do need to be linked to personal development as complementary to training linked to business goals (Department for Education and Employment (DfEE), 1998).

South African Breweries provides another example of the ways in which these HPWOs can use their resources and knowledge of performance management to address issues of equity. Here again, there are two areas where SAB has been active. The first used techniques of performance management to eradicate racial barriers to internal mobility. Here the company initiated a programme to encourage all employees to question the values associated with apartheid and to commit themselves to the new values of equality. This was then followed up with the use of performance targets for the recruitment of black South Africans into senior positions. Together, this resulted in considerable progress being made towards the goal of racial equality within the company.

The other way in which SAB tackled the equity issue was its method of dealing with problems of redundancy consequent upon the downsizing associated with the introduction of HPWPs. In 1996, SAB and the main union FAWU discussed their mutual concerns about employee security. The result was the birth of an initiative called Project Noah, aimed at developing alternatives for employees who have been retrenched. SAB and FAWU attended a workshop at the headquarters of the International Labour Organization (ILO) in Geneva, Switzerland. These interactions with the ILO, and with business and labour internationally, reinforced the realities of competitiveness and pointed to the need for creative strategies which focus on the development of small new enterprises as a global priority. A joint statement of intent emerged from this workshop as the rationale and principles for Project Noah, described in the box overleaf.

Project Noah

Project Noah established centres in cities or towns in South Africa, where retrenchments of SAB employees were anticipated. These centres were temporary, with a lifespan of about eight months, and were staffed with contractors who provided administrative, business and psychological support for retrenchees. While many obstacles and frustrations do occur, Noah is encouraged by the success it had achieved by 1999: 161 small, micro and medium-sized businesses have been initiated with retrenchees. These businesses cover a range of industries from farming to manufacturing and service businesses and have been of real value to both the employed and unemployed in South Africa. Additionally, Noah has also established a business incubator, which has the capacity to house and nurture over 20 small businesses at any given time. As a joint venture with Government, the community, and labour, SAB also initiated a rural micro incubator in the Eastern Cape, which has initiated in excess of 100 businesses over the past nine months.

Source: UNISON, 2001.

Trade unions and equity

Perhaps the most important role for unions is in promoting the adoption of HPWPs and ensuring that, when they are implemented, worker participation is effective. One of the dangers of high performance management techniques is that they can be used as another way of enhancing control over workers. Here, as we saw in Chapter 3, the work of Lowe (2000) has shown how in Canada some companies have used HPWPs to increase their control over worker behaviour and intensify the work rate. Workers may have initially bought into the process of change as they saw the benefits of multi-skilling and teamworking. However, when these and other techniques are just used to squeeze more work out of employees who are then excluded from the decision-making process, then commitment is withdrawn and performance benefits fail to materialize. Where unions exist, they help ensure that worker participation in decision-making is effective and that workers share in the benefits of enhanced productivity and profitability. In this way, they help ensure the commitment of employees to organizational objectives and to their own employment security.

In many respects, unions are in a strong position to reach those people with low-level education who may for one reason or another be reluctant to enter formal education programmes. In some cases, individual employees may have had a bad experience at school or they may distrust employers' attempts to provide help, but they may be willing to accept help from union colleagues who are perceived as more understanding of their circumstances. In partnership with employers, the UK public sector union UNISON has developed a Return to Learn (R2L) Programme which has successfully targeted this group.[6]

Unison's Return to Learn Programme

Launched in 1995, UNISON's Return to Learn (R2L) focuses on joint provision of an employee development programme at the workplace. R2L was initially intended for building basic skills for further learning. However, supported by wider workplace learning agreements with employers, R2L was later extended to higher levels of vocational and professional courses targeted at low-paid and under-qualified workers. Through the Open College (set up in 1994), a "passport approach" to learning was established. Individuals, mostly UNISON members, can engage in learning at one of four levels. Provision at the first three levels is free. Level 1 provides for very basic skills. The learning is recognized by further-education colleges and employers. At Level 4, UNISON members and non-members alike can study professional or vocational courses, although fees are charged at this level.

This system means that UNISON acts as both a provider and a facilitator of learning opportunities within a unified system covering the most basic level (literacy and numeracy) to degree-level qualifications. More importantly, provision is linked to employer support: financial support and time off for learning are often provided by employers. In addition, recognition by professional bodies means that the qualifications are beneficial to workers' employability in general.

By 1998, some 6,000 students had completed R2L. Eighty per cent of these students were women; 60 per cent had no qualifications; 42 per cent were part-time workers; 76 per cent earned less than £10,000 p.a.; 78 per cent were aged over 35 and 9 per cent had left school before 16. R2L was therefore regarded as successful in enrolling the targeted groups, many of whom had high proportions of ethnic minorities. R2L programmes were introduced to a wide range of industrial sectors, e.g. health trusts, social services, universities, and local governments. By 1999, there were over 120 schemes in existence.

In building on the success of schemes such as these, the UK Government has established a Union Learning Fund to increase the capacity of unions to encourage training and to support learning. These support the establishment of union learning representatives, appointed in the workplace to promote training. This has enabled a number of UK unions to create workplace representatives who have the capacity to provide non-traditional learners with front-line learning advice and guidance. In general, government-funded evaluations of these programmes reveal the following achievements: they help identify those with basic skills learning needs; they provide advice to those who are unwilling to approach their employer about training; they overcome resistance to learning; and they provide a source of expertise and an impulse to action by employers on organizational training. Further measures planned by the UK Government may provide statutory backing for unionized workplaces to appoint a part-time union learning representative (DfEE, 2000).

The role of government in dealing with equity issues

While there is clearly much that employers and unions can do, the main responsibility for dealing with equity issues usually rests with governments. Here the concern is with the unemployed, part-time workers, the self-employed, temporary workers and workers in the informal sector. In numerical terms, the largest group is part-time employees, the vast majority of whom are females.

As far as we are aware, no government has explicitly addressed the issue of provision for those excluded from HPWOs, although a number of governments are currently developing more general policies for those at risk of exclusion from developments associated with the "new economy" or the "knowledge economy", of which the spread of HPWOs is a constituent part. The question facing governments is therefore how to ensure that workers outside HPWOs can maintain their interest in learning and access at least some of the requisite skills in order to participate in the new economy, once such employment opportunities are available. The response of governments across the globe has been to try to develop a culture of lifelong learning.

Lifelong learning: Contrasting approaches to the problems of exclusion

In tackling the issue of lifelong learning, governments have tended to adopt two contrasting approaches. On the one hand, Anglo-Saxon countries have tended to focus on programmes to develop the work-related skills of those at risk. On the other hand, Scandinavian governments and others such as the Singaporean Government have adopted a more holistic approach which seeks to develop the broader skills of those at risk, for example skills used in the family and community. We examine both of these approaches below.

Lifelong learning: The Anglo-Saxon approach

The Anglo-Saxon approach, as epitomized by the United States and United Kingdom Governments, contains two main components. First, attempts have been made to rationalize existing government provision in order to create an infrastructure to provide better support for work-related learning - the United States though the Workforce Investment Act (1998) and the United Kingdom through the Learning and Skills Councils (2000). The aim of such rationalization is to make information on learning and training opportunities more readily available and accessible. In both countries, recent reforms have brought all the provision of government programmes under one body, the Workforce Investments Boards in the United States and the Learning and Skills Councils in the United Kingdom. These function at the regional or local level in partnership with other local providers in the public and private sector. In the United Kingdom, they work alongside "Learndirect", a publicly financed telephone helpline to provide information on learning opportunities. This is to be supplemented by the new University for Industry which will provide courses throughout the country, available through local learning centres using both traditional and modern ICT-based forms of delivery.

A second component of this approach has been the use of Individual Learning Accounts (ILAs). The idea behind these is that a given amount of public money is allocated to each individual to enable (empower) him/her to purchase his/her own training, thereby giving an impetus to the development of a strong training culture. In the United States, these are targeted at people taking government programmes (i.e. those at the lower end of the labour market) to encourage them to invest in their own learning. In the United Kingdom, the programme is not so highly focused on specific target groups. There, 1 million accounts have been made available on a first-come first-served basis, to be taken up by March 2002, for those over 19 years of age who are not engaged in education or who are unemployed. By February 2001, 740,000 accounts had been opened (DfEE, 2000a). It is the intention in the United Kingdom that employers should eventually contribute to ILAs, which in the initial programme were limited to £150 per individual.

A different approach has been adopted by the Australian Government. There the emphasis has been on making the delivery of training as flexible as possible. This has involved making sure that people from rural and remote areas gain equitable access to VET programmes, encouraging more adult upgrading of skills by providing more part-time, night-time, weekend, and alternative open-learning options to participate in training. It has also involved providing alternative learning options to disadvantaged groups such as indigenous peoples and those with special learning needs (C. Robinson, 2000).

Although all the Anglo-Saxon governments have suggested that lifelong learning should be about personal development and not just work-related learning, the general thrust of their policies so far has been focused on work-related learning.

Lifelong learning: The holistic approach

This is characterized by a more inclusive approach in which work-related learning is but one component of a broader concern with developing skills for family and community involvement. The main focus of these programmes is on the personal development of individuals as citizens. Lifelong learning policies are therefore primarily concerned with equity considerations. Through increasing the access of individuals to learning opportunities, the programmes are designed to increase the abilities of individuals to continue learning in all facets of life. These programmes provide opportunities for those whose work, or lack of it, would otherwise restrict their development. Once these broader goals are met, this is seen as increasing their employability and potential productivity, but this is a secondary consideration.

This approach has been developed in Denmark, Sweden and Norway, while Singapore has also recently pledged to follow this type of approach to lifelong learning. All these countries have a strong cultural concern for equity, and all are targeting their programmes at those at risk in the labour market, namely those with a low level of education, the unemployed and disadvantaged groups. They are distinctive in that that they are developed through partnerships between the central government (and local governments in the case of Norway and Sweden) and unions and employers and provide comprehensive coverage of all facets of learning, including formal education, the workplace and the community. They are also concerned to develop new technologies and techniques for the delivery of learning opportunities. In the case of the Scandinavian countries, all operate in a decentralized manner; for example, in Sweden the local municipalities play a key role by providing the infrastructure for partnership building in pursuit of building a culture of lifelong learning.

In Norway, the Government is currently implementing a policy to encourage adult learning through Competence Reforms introduced in the 1990s. These are summarized by the recent OECD report as follows:

> "The Competence Reform embraces the whole adult population, in and outside the labour market, and is focused on the needs of the workplace, society and individual. Adults' non-formal learning will be assessed and validated upon entry into a regular programme in the public sector. Recently much effort has been put into providing educational opportunities for groups of adults with particular difficulties, e.g. adults with inadequate schooling, mental or physical disabilities, reading and writing difficulties or an inability to speak Norwegian" (OECD, 2000: 2).

The Reform, initiated in 1999, is being implemented through cooperation between the Government, the social partners and various providers of education and aims to provide better opportunities for training and competence building. One objective is to develop strategies for adults who have a low level of education to enhance their competence. Another is to stimulate the development of user-adapted educational opportunities and flexible training programmes to improve access to adult learning. The Competence Reform is an extensive programme involving individual rights to primary and secondary education, recognition of non-formal learning, individual rights to study leave and financial support, competence building in the workplace, reorganization of the public education system (one-quarter of the higher-education students are over 30 years of age) and easily accessible information and guidance for adults on learning opportunities. Other points of focus are on closer collaboration between education and work, and flexible learning methods, including the use of ICT and distance education.

Sweden started a five-year programme to boost adult education in 1997, the Adult Education Initiative (AIE), out of which it expects a new system to emerge. The aim is to provide new learning opportunities which will enhance the individual's self-confidence and ability to find jobs, provide a foundation for learning at work in modern organizations, develop the capacity to play an active part in the community and provide the basis for lifelong learning. The primary target groups are those who left school early or are unemployed. The aim is to improve their earnings and so reduce income inequality and to promote workplace modernization and development. By boosting the supply of skilled labour, the initiative will promote economic growth.

The initiative is creating closer collaboration between local authorities and labour market providers to stimulate the provision of information, the use of information technology, new forms of work organization and the combination of work experience with theoretical training (the Delegation for Adult Education Initiative, 1997; Kearns and Papadopoulos, 2000).

Opportunities for all adults to finance their own needs for competence development are to be encouraged through the use of Individual Learning Accounts into which the State, employees and employers contribute. This is planned to come into operation in January 2002 (Swedish Government, 2001).

Given the recent development of these Scandinavian approaches to lifelong learning, there are few, if any, evaluations available. Our discussion of them has therefore had to be somewhat descriptive, but it has served to demonstrate a more comprehensive approach to the development of a culture of lifelong learning than is generally considered by the Anglo-Saxon countries. This broader approach also provides a more inclusive way to tackle the equity issues raised by the spread of HPWPs by promising to develop workers' skills in the context of the family and wider community.

Lifelong learning: Delivering IT skills

While approaches to lifelong learning differ substantially amongst countries, the approach to the delivery of technical skills, especially IT skills, does not. These can be delivered through either formal-classroom or computer-based instruction to those who have been denied access to them in the past. Thus, government and unions can and do provide IT courses for part-time workers, housewives wishing to return to the labour market, the unemployed and temporary workers. The problem here is usually one of funding and generating the interest among the "excluded" in acquiring these skills. Here programmes funded through trade unions have been effective in reaching some of these groups.

One promising solution to this problem for developing countries, highlighted in the ILO's World Employment Report 2001, is the use of community-based learning centres. These can be funded by a variety of agencies, governments, private enterprises, NGOs and charity organizations. In Malaysia, the Government funds the Demonstrator Applications Grant Scheme that finances access to Internet kiosks and seeks to raise awareness among the poor, orphans and paddy farmers in rural communities. In Benin, an agricultural NGO operates three community learning centres which offer training classes to entrepreneurs, students and members of NGOs. In Ghana, there has been rapid growth in community learning centres which provide public access to ICT tuition and which have become a significant skill-building force in Ghana (ILO, 2001:64). These offer low, often subsidized, Internet connectivity fees and digital literacy courses at below commercial rates and, crucially, are tailored to meet the educational needs of the local population.

Lifelong learning: Delivering soft skills

The main problem then remains that of developing expertise in problem solving, communication and teamworking among those groups whose paid employment is organized along more traditional lines, with a rigid division of labour, narrow and circumscribed job tasks and little or no chance of exercising discretion. These are all too often the characteristics of part-time employees. For those outside paid employment, the problem is even greater.

However, the work of Stasz (1998) offers some hope for both these groups. What she has sought to do is to identify, through a careful and detailed study of actual problem-solving groups and self-managed work teams, the generic component of such skills. She argues that the generic component can be transmitted through off-the-job courses, provided that the training simulates the work process. This means moving away from the didactic classroom tradition whereby trainees are instructed in the skills. Here we need to move toward a situation in which the learning context is structured in such as a way as to facilitate individual participation in group problem solving and teamworking. We can then start to move towards delivering these generic skills through formal programmes. Indeed, the CREST Programme in Singapore is already attempting this, as it seeks to develop these critical enabling skills among the existing employed population. For the unemployed and those seeking to return to work, there is no reason why such training should not be included in existing programmes.

Finally, it is worth pointing out that many of these skills - teamworking, communication, problem solving - are also skills which are utilized on a day-to-day basis in the context of the family and community work, churches, community groups, youth clubs, etc. in which people are involved outside the work context. There is a need to explore ways in which skills acquired there can be certified as part of a national skills recognition system. This would enable those outside the labour market to move towards an accumulation of credits which can be converted into a full-blown national qualification, thereby easing the transition from a non-work into a work situation. This is an area which the newly developed Danish system of lifelong learning is seeking to develop (Denmark, 2000).

Conclusions

Once again, we find ourselves concluding that when it comes to the variety of ways in which governments can help spread the use of HPWPs, there is no one best way. This is because the shape of the practices themselves are influenced by the national institutional structure and culture. In addition, the different ideological and philosophical positions traditionally adopted by governments provide the parameters within which the policy process operates, and this restricts the range of options. Moreover, the internal systems of politics and administration provide further limits on the type of policy interventions governments can make. Thus, the United States could not impose a centralized policy of apprenticeship or workplace redesign even if officials in the federal Government wanted to. The existing constitutional limits on the actions of the federal Government, together with the ability of the individual States to jealously guard their own powers, would make such an attempt futile. In these circumstances, and given the size of the country, the federal Government has to rely more on the operation of market forces. Other countries with more centralized administrative structures and a more pragmatic ideology have other possibilities. Thus, France may be able to use the training tax to develop workplace learning in a similar way to Singapore. Singapore has developed a range of mechanisms through which it seeks to influence employers' practices and the skills of the labour force. Like the other Asian Tigers, it is more pragmatic and less constrained by the Anglo-Saxon notions of individualism and voluntarism when it comes to labour market interventions.

In the Scandinavian countries, the strength of organized labour means that they are in a better position to use the social partnership mechanisms to deliver interventions in the form of comprehensive lifelong learning programmes. The possibilities this creates for supporting the spread of HPWOs are well summed up by Sohlman (1998) in his report for the OECD on the Swedish system.

> "At a more general level, one may say that the tripartite commitment to economic development - by the Government, the unions and employers - was creating a learning-rich environment where literacy was practiced both in civil society and at work. A good circle was created where more education made more advanced work organizations possible which in turn created more opportunities to develop new skills and maintain old ones."

All this illustrates the fact that governments have different levers available to them when it comes to developing programmes to support HPWOs and to deal with the associated issues of social exclusion. However, as we have tried to show here, the precise range of levers is partly determined by the existing institutional structures and cultures. In these circumstances, the straight-forward transfer of practices can be problematic. Transfer can be achieved but only after a period of adaptation and adjustment (Turbin, 2001). This is another reason why we have not sought to advocate one best set of practices. All we have tried here is to provide an overview of the range of policies to broaden and inform the thinking of policy-makers in governments, employers' organizations and unions who may be seeking to promote HPWPs.

Notes

[1] These issues are discussed in Ashton and Sung (2001).

[2] In the late 1990s, the company was bought out by Wassell which instituted short-term cost-cutting measures, but two years later (2000) it was sold to the German company Zumtobel, which because it was privately owned was able to concentrate on longer-term investments (Financial Times, 90.10.00).

[3] Details of the Singaporean programmes have been obtained through interviews and correspondence over the last two years with senior officials at the Singapore Productivity and Standards Board.

[4] The UK IiP has now entered its second phase with new standards introduced in 2000 in response to the evaluations and feedback received from the implementation of the first phase.

[5] These projects are documented at http://www.wawbl.com/resources_educators/skill_standards/sectioni_6.htm.

[6] Details of the UNISON programmes have been obtained through correspondence with senior union officials in 2001.

CHAPTER 7

CONCLUSIONS: PLACING HIGH PERFORMANCE WORK ORGANIZATIONS IN CONTEXT

Introduction

Having made the argument for taking HPWOs seriously, we want to use this final chapter to explore the wider potential of HPWOs within national and global markets and the limits which capitalist relations place on them. We do not wish to portray HPWOs as the solution to all our ills. There are limits to their use, some to do with the evolution of product markets and others to do with the ability of societies to provide appropriate basic skills in the labour force. However, while it is important to understand these constraints, we must take care not to over-emphasize their importance. For example, it is sometimes argued that HPWOs are not appropriate for developing countries because of their low levels of educational achievement. Here we show why this is not the case.

One of the problems with the analysis presented in this book is that we have had to be selective in the way in which we portray organizations. The reality is always more complex. This final section therefore enables us to highlight some of these complexities, but in doing so it also demonstrates the new opportunities that HPWOs open up to us.

The use of HPWPs in the global division of labour

We have seen how the origins or genesis of HPWOs lay in intensified competition as companies from different countries started to compete more directly after the Second World War. In one sense, this created a virtuous circle of competition. In rebuilding their industries, the Japanese learned management techniques such as statistical quality control from the United States, incorporating them into distinctive Japanese practices[1] to produce more productive ways of organizing human labour. In the face of competition from these more productive Japanese companies, the Americans and more recently the Europeans, Latin Americans and Asians learned to adapt their organizations by incorporating some of these practices. In the process, as we have seen, they too became more productive and produced distinctive national variants of HPWPs. The result of this process is that in world markets the base level of productivity required to compete effectively has been ratcheted up. This means that in many markets newcomers have to start from this new higher-base level of productivity if they are to compete effectively.

We have also seen that these changes in the way we organize human labour have been linked to corresponding changes in the markets for goods and services at the international level. One manifestation of this has been a shift in the basis of competition in some markets, away from a focus on price alone to the increasing importance of quality. This has resulted in the differentiation of markets and the growth of markets characterized by customized quality forms of production. Of course, some national markets, for example the German, have long been characterized by a demand for differentiated quality production. What has distinguished these last two decades has been the growth of global markets with these characteristics. As we have seen, it is for these markets which HPWOs are particularly well adapted. However, this is only one trend in the marketplace and not an invariant law.

The growth of high performance forms of work organization therefore does not spell the end of mass production for markets where the main basis of competition remains that of price. Such markets have also grown as national barriers to trade have been reduced. What is happening here is that the capital required for production in these markets is moving to the countries where labour costs are low and where governments are stable and sympathetic to capitalist forms of production. In markets where price is the overriding consideration, for example in the production of standardized forms of clothing and footwear and basic electrical goods, mass production and Taylorist forms of management continue to remain the most productive way to organize human labour. HPWOs can only exist in these markets if they can compete on the basis of features over and above that of price, such as fast turn-around times and rapid response to changing customer requirements.

Where price remains the overriding consideration, it is not surprising that production should move to those countries which offer disciplined labour at the lowest cost. Given the existing organization of both national and international markets, we are therefore unlikely to see the end of mass production and Taylorist forms of management. This is an important limitation to the growth of HPWOs for, while HPWOs may make inroads into some markets for mass produced goods, the emergence of HPWOs as the dominant form of production may have to wait until most markets are characterized by a demand for differentiated high quality goods and services. This then raises a number of other questions we must confront.

The first and most obvious is whether production for the markets for quality and differentiated goods and services will be the sole province of the older more "advanced" industrial societies – whether HPWOs are just another feature of the rich man's club. Such a scenario is presaged by the explicit commitment of many of the political leaders of these societies to the "high-skills" route of economic development and to the creation of an economy dominated by the use of highly skilled labour producing high quality goods and services for home consumption and export. This would leave the developing societies doomed to the production of mass-produced goods. However, such a scenario is not likely to materialize for the following reasons.

First, many of the domestic markets of the older societies still have a strong demand for mass-produced goods. Moreover, the increasing penetration of forms of shareholder capitalism is tending to emphasize the need for short-term gains which may well be reinforcing the perpetuation of these markets. For example, in the United States and the United Kingdom, many of the existing domestic markets are still characterized by goods and services for which price remains the overriding concern and where employers still compete using mass-production techniques and Taylorist forms of management. Even in the newer service sector, in addition to the notorious fast-food outlets which make extensive use of Taylorist work practices, employers are still finding ways of reducing costs through the use of variants of the older mass-production techniques. We saw in Chapter 5 that the deregulation of financial services and the introduction of new technology have enabled banks and insurance companies to make more extensive use of routine operations, in the form of call centres and ranks of VDU operatives, to drive down the cost of standardized motor insurance and banking services. There are many other sectors where similar deskilling processes are at work. What the introduction of HPWPs does is to provide a choice about how work is organized but, as we have seen, even in the wealthier industrial societies mass production is far from dead. What is happening in these societies is the co-existence of these older Taylorist forms of work organization with a smaller group of HPWOs operating in selected markets. Indeed, there is a strong debate in the West as to whether some of these older industrial countries such as the United States and the United Kingdom can ever become high-skill societies (Finegold, 1999; Finegold and Soskice, 1988; Crouch et al., 1999; Brown et al., 2001; Brown and Lauder, 2001). In other countries, such as Germany, there is a longer history of a demand for quality, differentiated goods and services, which has led to the use of higher-skilled labour for quality-differentiated production by wealthier and more discerning consumers (Keep and Mayhew, 1998).

This same contrast between the existence of different modes of organizing human labour is also to be found in the developing societies. Over the last three decades, capital has been flowing into countries such as Thailand, Indonesia, and China to fuel the growth of mass-production industries competing in world markets. Yet over time, this has not just meant the creation of routine, low-skilled jobs. Even within those developing economies where many MNCs now produce for world markets and where western retailers source many of the goods they sell, new domestic markets are emerging for which HPWOs are appropriate. Thus in China, MNCs producing for the domestic Chinese market are using HPWPs to drive up productivity. For example, Proctor and Gamble is using these techniques to produce toiletries adapted for the Chinese market. In the ITC market, Chinese entrepreneurs, such as USOFT, are using HPWPs to organize labour in the production of computer programmes to provide the software for the business infrastructure for Chinese companies.

Here it is important to remind ourselves that what has characterized the high-performing Asian economies, where economic growth has been unprecedented, is the ability to leapfrog stages in the developmental path. They have learned from the Western and Japanese companies and do not have to repeat the mistakes made in the past or to content themselves with the old technology. They have a steeper learning curve and the ability to adapt the latest ideas to their own circumstances. As we saw in Chapter 5, HPWOs are firmly established in developing societies – they also have a choice as to how they organize labour for production.

A further reason for believing that HPWOs are likely to figure more prominently in the future of many developing countries is the experience of those Asian Tiger economies which have made the transition from developing to developed status, for example Hong Kong, China; Taiwan, China, the Republic of Korea and Singapore. These are all societies which grew by reaping the advantages of disciplined, low-cost labour in the production of mass-produced goods for world markets. However, their very success in these areas led to pressures on wage costs and a subsequent shift into value-added forms of production where HPWOs are more appropriate (Verma et al., 1995; Ashton et al., 1999). The expansion of labour-intensive manufacturing has led to the creation of full employment, and this in turn put pressure on wages to rise so that living conditions improved. As the cost of labour increased and the next generation of developing countries emerged with cheaper labour, this has placed pressure on governments and employers to invest in skills and move into higher value-added goods and services in order to remain competitive. Economic growth is essentially a dynamic process, where change is constant and the use of HPWPs is now an integral part of that change.

All this is not to deny that developing societies face special problems when it comes to the introduction of HPWOs. One of the most immediate is the lack of basic literacy and numeracy skills among the labour force, a task for the education system to provide. However, as HPWOs are still in a minority in all countries, the demands they make on the education system are not that great, at least in the early stages. Providing some young people achieve a basic secondary education, this offers a firm basis on which to build HPWOs.

Once these basic educational levels have been achieved, then the issue is one of raising the technical and soft skills of employees. As we have seen, this can be expensive for employers and is one of the reasons often given why many employers in the Anglo-Saxon countries have refrained from introducing HPWPs. However, set against that is the fact that labour costs are lower in developing societies. Thus, although employers may have to spend more in upgrading the skills of their employees, those skills eventually are much cheaper to produce and sustain than they are for comparable employees in developed economies.

Another strategy that has been adopted by employers in developing countries is to restrict recruitment into HPWOs to those with a high level of secondary education. This was the strategy originally adopted by the Japanese employers (Dore, 1973). It is also the strategy some employers in China are adopting; for example, Proctor and Gamble only recruits graduates of higher education for its operations in China. The only circumstance in which a lack of basic education is likely to become a problem for HPWOs in developing countries is where the economy has reached full employment. As long as they remain a minority of organizations and can offer better conditions than other local employers, then the question of a lack of basic education among recruits is not likely to deter them.

Maximizing the spread of HPWPs within societies

The problem facing governments in both types of societies is therefore one of maximizing the spread of HPWOs. If this task is left purely to the market, there is a danger that the use of

HPWPs will continue to be restricted to a limited range of companies. They become islands of good practice. As we have seen in Chapter 3, there are many forces at work which can counter the use of HPWPs: changes in ownership and product markets and failure of the business leaders to develop an appropriate strategy for the organization as a whole; as well as unexpected innovations and changes in the product market. As we also saw in Chapter 6, government programmes can do much to spread this "good practice", but even beyond this there is a need for the skills required for the use of HPWPs to become embedded in the wider institutional network of which government workforce development programmes are only one part. Here we are talking of the need for societal learning or collective intelligence (Brown and Lauder, 2001) to become embedded in the nation's institutions. In the same way that organizations "learn" through mechanisms which collect and distribute information, knowledge and skills, so too do societies. In this instance, it is essential that the knowledge, information and skills required for the maintenance and growth of HPWOs is embedded in our national institutions and practices.

In sustaining HPWOs, this societal learning can take a number of forms. For example, reform of the education system may help create and sustain a high level of academic and technical skills. Government programmes can help persuade employers of the value of HPWPs and provide them and their employees with the requisite skills to implement and sustain them. However, there is a also a need for local employers' organizations to be aware of the benefits of HPWPs and to use their own information and training resources to sustain them. Similarly, there is a need for trade union organizations to learn to value these practices as a means of enhancing the quality of the working life of their members. This may mean using the collective-bargaining process to push employers into considering the use of these practices and using any consultative machinery to encourage better training provision. Similarly, business schools should be making the management of the learning process an integral part of management training.

Once embedded in this broader network of institutions, both public and private, new employers would then start to incorporate the assumptions behind HPWPs into their thinking when designing and managing working practices. We have already seen a similar process working in Germany and Japan. In Germany, any employer seeking to create a new company will be faced with a labour market structured around the occupations which form the basis of the German apprenticeship. This not only provides the employer with a supply of highly skilled labour, but it also constrains management to organize the production process around those trades and skills, hence the wider span of control of supervisors in Germany and the more extensive use of skilled labour. Add to this the legal system which obliges employers to consult workers over redundancies and training, and we can see how these "external" constraints start to shape the "internal" structure of the organization.[2]

It is not difficult then to move one step forward and look at the ways in which these external institutions could be used to make it easier for employers to utilize HPWPs. The government could enact legislation which encourages employers to focus on the long-term returns from their capital to take account of the interests of all stakeholders. It could introduce a national programme of workforce development which focuses on providing employers with incentives to introduce teamworking and a training system which delivers the appropriate skills for IT and communication in addition to the technical skills. Add to this employers' organizations that are capable of delivering the technical support to introduce appropriate management practices and unions that see such practices as one means of furthering their members' interests, and we have a powerful coalition of interests. Once this is in place, then the skills for the development and maintenance of HPWPs are in place, and the system becomes self-sustaining. Under these circumstances, the use of HPWPs would be the obvious first choice, part of the manager's everyday reality, and other forms of organizing production would only be used as a second or last resort.[3]

HPWPs and the growth of SMEs

One further area of concern within economies has been the change in the size composition of firms which has taken place in part as a consequence of the introduction of modern management practices. In Chapter 1, we saw how the forces of competition and the need to increase productivity have led companies to downsize their operation. This has led to an increasing concern among governments with the need to support SMEs as a major source of growth. As part of this general concern with SMEs, the question has also been raised as to whether these HPWPs are equally applicable to smaller organizations. This is a question on which we have touched upon but not directly addressed.

The answer is that HPWPs are just as applicable to SMEs as they are to larger organizations. We saw this in Chapter 2 with the example of Comfort Driving Centre in Singapore, but this is just one example; it could be the exception. In fact, there has been little research done on this but what exists is encouraging. Work by Cosh et al. (2000) in the United Kingdom, cited in Chapter 1, found that SMEs which use HPWPs are more likely to grow and create jobs than are conventional firms. Other research by the Centre for Labour Market Studies in the United Kingdom (Sung et al., 2000) has shown that the same HPWP practices are used to organize work in SMEs as are used in the larger companies. The only difference is that in SMEs this is done in an informal manner. This is especially the case in organizations with fewer than 50 staff.[4]

Among these smaller organizations, less use is made of formal communications mechanisms precisely because there is less need for them. It is much easier for the manager/owner to speak to all the staff and to listen directly to their concerns. The use of teamworking, self-managed work groups, appraisal and multiskilling may indeed be easier to implement in smaller organizations where there are fewer obstacles to the establishment of trust between senior and junior staff. In these small SMEs, there is less room for specialist HR personnel, which means that line managers are used to training subordinates and supporting learning. It also follows that major decisions about the use of labour and the development of staff are often made informally but, providing they are in the spirit of encouraging, supporting and rewarding the development of employee skills and these are linked to business objectives, then the principles of HPWPs are just as valid.

Conclusions: Placing high performance work organizations in context

Imposing order on a messy reality

Throughout this book, we have tried to bring home to the reader the distinguishing characteristics of HPWOs. In order to keep our message clear, we have deliberately focused on those organizations which exemplify the full range of characteristics of HPWOs. Our case studies reported in Chapter 2 were selected with this in mind. Many companies and organizations were approached which, on further investigation, failed to meet the full range of our criteria. These we deliberately excluded in order to avoid confusing the reader. We could then contrast the full- blown HPWOs with companies and examples drawn from the literature which are at the other extreme and epitomize Taylorist forms of management and work design. Yet, as we are all no doubt aware, in reality the majority of organizations are somewhere in-between the polar cases we have documented. In reality, the picture is more messy.

On the one hand, we have some organizations which make extensive use of HPWPs, but these are only applied to some parts of the organization and not others. These are usually the "core" functions and employees. Other parts may be organized along Taylorist lines. In other organizations, some HPWPs may be applied throughout but make little impact on the practice of management or the work and opportunities available to the employees. Thus, we know from the research cited in Chapter 5 that many organizations use just one or two HPWPs. In the United Kingdom, the vast majority of employers report the use of one practice such as appraisals and suggestion schemes. However, this does not necessarily mean that these organizations are on the road to being full HPWOs. Indeed, the contrary may be the case. These are often companies which may have adopted the practice because it is fashionable to do so or, in the public sector, because they are expected to do so. Yet very often the management does not know how to implement them effectively. For example, the managers may have no training in appraisal techniques, and employees may not know what the objectives of the exercise are. In these circumstances, the exercise becomes a mere formality and often a waste of time on the part of both manager and employee. Similarly, with regard to suggestion schemes, management puts out a box with the promise of rewarding good suggestions, but this is not done in a systematic manner. Some suggestions may be implemented, but if the scheme is not operated in a systematic and transparent manner or employees are not adequately rewarded, they then soon cease to bother. Taken on their own, these types of practices are perfectly compatible with Taylorist forms of management.

In other organizations, especially those in the public sector, they may make use of performance targets, with managers' performance measured against them. However, if they are not supported by other HPWPs and operate in a blame culture, then again little can be expected. There, decision-making is often centralized and departments or units are instructed to implement decisions taken centrally, with neither the managers nor other employees having much discretion in the ways in which they conduct their work. Because decisions are taken centrally, local initiative is not rewarded and blame and sanctions are heaped on those who fail to deliver specific objectives. Here employees learn that they have to comply but, beyond that, commitment is minimal. We could go on citing instances of the multifarious ways in which organizations are run, but here we are only concerned to demonstrate that many are still not run along the lines of HPWOs, although ostensibly they may have some of the characteristics.

Another consequence of our attempt to seek order in a messy reality is that we have concentrated on the role of human resource management practices in creating improvements in performance; that, after all, is one of the objectives of the book. However, because of this, we are always in danger of over-emphasizing the importance of these HPWPs in relation to the other factors which affect the success of organizations in both the public and private sectors. As we mentioned earlier, there are numerous factors which determine the success of organizations, not least of which is the quality of the leadership, their grasp of the market, the behaviour of competitors and so on. No matter how good our work and management practices are, unless we can continue to satisfy customers or unless we receive unconditional support from government, the organization ceases to exist. All we can claim is that the use of these practices has now been demonstrated to enhance the likelihood of success in achieving organizational objectives. This means that perhaps for the first time we can see that the way in which we treat our fellow workers can be a major determinant of success.

Our aim throughout has been to demonstrate that the introduction of HPWPs has created an opportunity for a major improvement. No doubt, the reality will remain messy. Many of us, if not the majority, will continue to experience work as exploitative. Indeed, the very organization of work in traditional organizations in which management retains knowledge of the process while workers are assigned to narrowly defined tasks and rewarded only for the performance of those tasks virtually guarantees that work will be experienced as alien and exploitative by most employees. In these organizations, the points of mutual interest between employees and senior managers or owners are minimal. Both rely on the continued existence of the organization as a source of income. Beyond that, the very structure of the organization often serves to remind workers and managers of their differences. The inferior status of workers is demonstrated by differences in the conditions of their contract of employment; they are paid by the hour, not by the month, and they are provided with inferior opportunities for eating and performing the most basic of bodily functions. All this serves to emphasize the fact that these groups have few shared interests.

The contrast with HPWOs could not be greater. There, employees share the same contract of employment; they experience the same conditions at work, the same eating and toilet facilities, the same prospect for receiving rewards if the organization performs well and the same tightening up if it does not. Such organizations have been designed to maximize the shared interests of all employees. Differences of interest still exist between owners of capital and those who labour, but these are now contained within a much broader range of shared interests.

The other major advantage of HPWPs from the point of view of employees is that they offer the possibility of continuous development. These organizations ask more of their employees, but they offer more in terms of the opportunities they provide for continuous growth. By increasing the skills of employees, they enhance their ability to continue to learn. By presenting employees with new challenges in the workplace on a day-to-day basis, they encourage continuous problem solving and learning. Of course, there are catches; they usually do not support any form of learning, unless they have a well-resourced self-development programme. In this sense, they are not a "learning organization", i.e. an organization which promotes learning for learning's sake - we have universities for that. In HPWOs, learning is strictly linked to individual and organizational performance improvement. But compared to the old traditional organization where opportunities to learn at work were minuscule, this is a major step forward in terms of the possibilities which we provide to our citizens to engage in lifelong learning.

Indeed, without the more widespread adoption of these forms of HPWPs, the aspirations of many contemporary governments to create a "learning society" or a society of lifelong learning will remain precisely that - an aspiration. There are, of course, other areas apart from work where we can as citizens engage in lifelong learning, for example in our family and community activities, in churches, clubs, special interest groups and sporting activities. However, for the majority of us, work will continue to take up a minimum of eight hours per day. To be starved of opportunities and supports for learning during that period can, as we now know, have serious consequences for the development of our ability to learn and indeed for the development of our personality. For the first time in decades, we now have the opportunity of ensuring that those eight hours can be the basis for meaningful activities which can contribute to our growth as human beings.

Notes

[1] There is still a debate as to whether these management practices are a distinctive product of Japanese culture or merely a rational response to the circumstances facing Japanese business after the Second World War (see Koike and Inoki (1990) for the latter view.)

[2] There is now a substantial body of literature which demonstrates the impact of national institutional structures on the internal structure of organizations, for example the work of Dore on Japan, Streeck in Germany and the "societal school" in France as well as the National Institute for Economic and Social Research in the United Kingdom. All we are doing here is applying the lessons from that literature to show how these institutions can be used to embed support for new forms of work organization in the society at large.

[3] These ideas have been developed by Finegold et al. using "game theory".

[4] This figure is arbitrary. Here we are talking of very small companies which range from micro enterprises of one-five staff to small enterprises with between six and 50 staff. Once an organization approaches 30-50 staff, it usually requires the introduction of more formal techniques of management. These may or may not be HPWPs.

APPENDIX

THE THEORY OF LEARNING IN HIGH PERFORMANCE WORK ORGANIZATIONS

Introduction

The purpose of this brief appendix is to document the theory of how learning contributes toward performance improvements in HPWOs. It provides an opportunity to explore the criticisms levelled at studies of high performance work organizations as well as a chance to identify the mechanisms through which learning is transformed into improvements in performance.

Criticism of the theory

There are a number of criticisms that have been levelled at studies of high performance working practices and high performance work organizations, both at the theoretical and empirical levels. First, there is confusion over the name. Many people are still not familiar with the terminology. For some, the notion of high performance working practices still has a Tayloristic flavour to it: the idea that the emphasis on performance implies a concentration on "hard" measures, e.g. statistical measures of performance, and a neglect of the "softer" issues originally raised by the human relations school, such as its concern with the people side of management, e.g. group cohesion and employee satisfaction. However, as we have indicated earlier, HPWPs are equally concerned with developing the abilities and commitment of the individual employees as they are with the issues of performance management. In this respect, HPWOs represent a unique combination of the two facets of management. We have already drawn the reader's attention to the fact that the practices which constitute high performance working are sometimes referred to as high involvement or flexible working practices. We have chosen to use the term high performance working practices because it is the most widely used and does itself reflect the fact that these practices can produce higher levels of performance.

At a theoretical level, the main thrust of the criticisms is that the theory is confused. At the risk of some oversimplification, we can (following Guest, 1997) identify three major differences in current approaches to HPWPs. The first argues that there is one best fit of HPWPs to company strategy. Youndt et al. (1996) found that in a sample of manufacturing plants there is a link between the use of HPWPs and a quality strategy. Others, such as MacDuffie (1995), could not find such a link in the automobile industry. A second approach is to argue that there is one best internal fit in that the more practices a company has, the higher the level of performance, as indicated by labour turnover, productivity and financial performance. As Guest (1997) points out, this is the most widely tested and strongly supported type of fit. However, we must be wary in that most of the work has been done on manufacturing establishments or companies. More recently, Wood et al. (2001) have argued on the basis of an extensive UK survey that it is not just the number of practices that are important but an underlying management orientation to the use of high involvement practices. This is manifest in the use of certain bundles of practices which are linked to improved performance across a range of indicators.

The third theoretical approach assumes that there is no one best fit, but rather a series of bundles of practices that produce improvements in different aspects of organizational performance. The empirical task is then to identify the precise nature of these bundles and their constituent elements and then to establish how they produce the desired impact on the various indices of performance. This raises the possibility that different bundles may be effective in producing different performance outcomes. Thus, some bundles may produce better human relations outputs, for example employee commitment and low labour turnover, but not necessarily better financial performance. Thus, Guest and Hoque (1994) found that companies with low levels of HPWPs have poorer human relations outcomes but no differences in productivity and quality. Applebaum et al. (2000) found that the gains from team sewing in textile plants come from the ability of the company to respond quickly to customer requirements and therefore build longer-term, more profitable relationships with retailers, in spite of the fact that the time spent sewing is not reduced. They also found that the use of HPWPs reduces down time in other companies, leading to enhanced productivity, while in others this enables the company to reduce the number of employees. As a result of these studies, we are now fully aware of the fact that we need to differentiate the various types or bundles of practices and the range of indices we use to measure performance.

We can now return to the critical point that proponents of HPWPs are unclear in their theoretical orientation.[1] While it would be premature to assert that these differences in theoretical orientation have been resolved, it is nevertheless becoming clear that the weight of evidence is pushing in the direction of further research concentrating on how the bundles of practices impact on different aspects of performance. In this respect, the initial differences in theoretical orientation can be seen as an essential part of the research process through which alternative hypotheses are debated and tested through field research, which then leads to a progressive enhancement of our knowledge. However, at this stage in the development of our knowledge, we cannot be dogmatic about the precise nature of the relationship between these bundles of practices and performance, apart from the statement that a relationship has been shown to exist

158

in a series of different studies. We see the purpose of further research as to help refine our knowledge about the nature of that relationship.

We certainly do not believe that there ever will be one "best fit" or set of uniform practices which can then be applied in all circumstances in the sure knowledge that performance improvements will follow. To begin with, the practices take different forms in different cultures; we know that bundles are important, but the exact constituents of each bundle may vary from one context to another. As the case studies show, the constituents of the bundles that produce the improvements in performance may also vary from one industry or sector to another. At this stage in the development of our knowledge, we can only provide the practitioner with guidance, not precise instructions. We still have much to learn about the nature of the relationships involved, but we do believe that at a theoretical level we have sufficient knowledge about the mechanisms involved in creating these improvements in performance to offer useful guidance to the practitioner.

Methodological criticisms

At a methodological level, there are a number of important criticisms, some of which we have already encountered. First, it is argued that there is little agreement among the proponents of this approach about what practices should be included within the ambit of the term HPWPs. If the proponents of the thesis cannot agree, how can others be expected to take it seriously? Legge (2001:25) points out that of "15 high-commitment practices" identified in the UK WERS 98 study, only seven appear in US studies. At first sight, this does suggest real confusion among the researchers. Indeed, the lack of a consensus among researchers within societies is a real problem; for example, within the United States where highly developed internal labour markets are a characteristic of the traditional, Tayloristic form of work organization, it is common to see internal promotion systems, but some researchers within the United States now use the existence of a system of internal promotion as a characteristic of HPWOs. However, this confusion may well reflect the fact that we are still in the early stages of research into what is a comparatively new way of organizing and managing the production of goods and services. Once we know more about HPWPs, we may well be in a position to ascertain whether internal labour markets are a fundamental characteristic of both forms of work organization or just one.

The lack of agreement on what constitutes the essential characteristics of HPWPs in different types of societies is less of a problem. As we have already shown, HPWPs do take on slightly different forms in each society, and therefore we would not expect researchers in the United States to be looking at exactly the same practices as researchers in other societies. In this respect, rather than speaking all the time in terms of specific practices, we have introduced the idea of different dimensions, which are reflected in different practices, but with the precise characteristics of the practices varying between societies. Thus, teamwork as a form of organizing work will vary in its manifestion between societies, as we have already shown. Nevertheless, we can still talk of teamwork as a recognizable approach to the organization of work. Thus, teamwork forms one of the underlying dimensions of work organization and employee involvement that we use to characterize HPWOs.

In view of the above, some of the other criticisms levelled against the HPWP school, if we can call it such, become less important. Thus, Legge argues that studies of HPWPs show further confusion in their approach, in that individual practices such as contingent pay are measured in different ways by different researchers. She cites the example of Huselid (1995) and Arthur (1992) where Huselid measures it using the proportion of the workforce covered by profit sharing, gain sharing and merit pay, and Arthur uses the percentage of employment costs accounted for by bonus or incentive payments (Legge, 2001:25). We can of course argue over whether one of these is a better measure than the other, but as a general point we are primarily interested in whether the use of forms of remuneration which reward individual or group performance are linked to organizational performance. The fact that researchers have used different measures does not in itself detract from the validity of the findings that these forms of reward are linked to improvements in company or organizational performance. To us, that is not a problem, providing that the pay is perceived by the employee as rewarding performance. Social science is never such an exact science that we must always have universal agreement on the precise way in which we specify the operationalization of our concepts.

Where much HPWP research lays itself open to criticism is on the grounds that a great deal of it has been quantitative and that in order to achieve the large numbers required for statistical analysis many of the surveys rely on one respondent within the organization to respond in a quick-fire manner to questions about practices that operate throughout the organization. Thus, Purcell (1999) questions whether one senior manager is in a position to know what practices are used throughout the organization, especially in firms with diversified structures. This is a very valid criticism, and if we only relied on large-scale surveys of organizations it would be a very damaging one. However, as we have shown in this book, much research has sought to use both quantitative and qualitative methods to obtain data, while yet others (Applebaum et al., 2000) have triangulated their methodology, using surveys of employers and employees together with case studies. Other researchers have sought to minimize the risk of respondents having inadequate information by restricting their sample to establishments rather than organizations. However, we need to keep this criticism in mind when dealing with data from large-scale surveys of organizations.

Another serious methodological criticism is that, while respondents may have knowledge of the existence or otherwise of a certain set of practices, they may not have a very adequate knowledge of the effectiveness of those practices. Thus, I may know that my organization has an appraisal system, but I may not have any solid knowledge of the extent to which the system is systematically implemented or, indeed, how effectively it is implemented in the case of specific departments. Many of these practices are only used for some groups within the organization and not others. Thus, the UK Training and Development (2001) Survey found that, while most establishments use coaching and mentoring, it is only used extensively for managers and white-collar workers, not for manual workers. Moreover, with that research being based on a survey, it cannot tell us how effective the coaching and mentoring are. It may be that some establishments merely nominate a person as a mentor or coach, but in practice this may mean very little as the "mentor" may have neither the knowledge nor the inclination to pursue effective mentoring. Again, this criticism can be countered through the use of triangulation, but that is a very expensive methodology. However, we do have numerous case studies which do suggest that, while the practices may vary in both the extent and effectiveness of their implementation, the use of them nevertheless does have an impact on behaviour.[2] Moreover, as we are concerned with the impact of bundles of such practices rather than single practices, the effectiveness with which any one practice is implemented is of less central importance.

Some of the most serious criticisms which have been directed at studies of HPWPs concern the nature of the link between the use of these practices and organizational performance. As Guest (1997) has already highlighted, many of the early US studies relied on single measures of financial performance and productivity. More recent studies, including those of Guest (1999), Applebuam et al. (2000) and Wood et al. (2001), have used a much broader range to include employee satisfaction, employee stress, labour turnover rates, customer satisfaction, client retention and so on. These recent studies have tended to focus more on the impact of these practices on the employees, as it is here that the theory suggests one of the crucial links is made between learning and performance. The hypothesis is that employees respond to these practices by developing higher levels of commitment to the organization, higher levels of motivation and by using their tacit knowledge to introduce continuous improvements, thereby increasing productivity and other organizational outcomes. As critics such as Legge have frequently pointed out, it is at the level of causality that most of the attacks on the validity of research on HPWPs has been concentrated.

The most frequently cited criticism is one we have already encountered in Chapter 1, namely that most studies are of a cross-sectional nature. This means that all we observe is a correlation between these practices and performance, but such correlations do not constitute a proof of causation. Because the two are found together does not mean that one causes the other. It may be that both are a product of a third factor; for example, there will be a correlation between the sales of ice cream and tarmac melting on roads, both as a result of hot weather, but apart from that they are not related in any other way. This is clearly an important criticism, but in the last decade this problem has been resolved through the use of longitudinal studies. These have enabled researchers to establish that it is the use of HPWPs that leads to the improvements in performance and not vice versa. Where we are still relatively ignorant is in our knowledge of the mechanisms through which this is brought about. This is the focus of the next section.

What does current theory tell us about how HPWPs operate?

At a theoretical level, a number of authors including MacDuffie (1995), Patterson et al. (1997), Guest (1997), Becker and Huselid (1998) and Applebaum et al. (2000) have suggested ways in which the process may operate. However, while there are some similarities in their models, there are also some areas of disagreement. As yet, we have no consensus on the mechanisms involved in translating the use of HPWPs into improved performance. Guest (1997) following MacDuffie (1995) suggests that expectancy theory may provide the link between the practices and performance, with the link taking the form of employee motivation.

MacDuffie argues that HPWPs operate effectively when workers possess knowledge and skills which managers lack, when employees are motivated to apply these skills through discretionary effort and when the firm's business strategy can only be achieved through mobilizing this discretionary effort. Guest (1997:268) takes this one step further and argues that selection and training practices deliver the appropriate skills; employee involvement and possibly performance-related pay provide the motivation; and job design, teamworking and extensive communication and feedback provide the appropriate role structure and perception, i.e. the (functional) flexibility required by HPWOs. Together these facilitate high levels of individual performance which in turn produce the high performance outcomes, in the form of productivity and low labour turnover, that result in the financial outcomes. For him, the key feature linking HR practices and worker outcomes such as job satisfaction, perceived job security and motivation is the psychological contract between employer and employees, in which employees provide the high commitment in return for job security and satisfying work.

Guest (1997) also argues that we need to locate the impact of HPWPs within the overall context of the other factors which impact on the organization's performance. He has made a start on this by his insistence on the importance of the role of external context and strategy on outcomes. He makes a distinction among three types of strategy: product differentiation or innovation, a focus on quality, and cost reduction. For him, the human relations model (HRM) practices identified above of selection and training, job security and rewards, communication and employee involvement lead to the HRM outcomes of commitment, quality and flexibility respectively; the behavioural outcomes of effort, cooperation, involvement and organizational citizenship; and a range of performance outcomes in the form of high productivity, quality and innovation and low absence, labour turnover, conflict and customer complaints.

Patterson et al. (1997) follow a similar line of reasoning and hypothesize that the human relations management (HRM) practices involved in high performance working can improve company performance by increasing employee skills and abilities; promoting positive attitudes and increasing motivation; and providing employees with expanded responsibilities so that they can make full use of their skills and abilities. These are seen as the three "causal routes" from HRM to performance. However, in the same report Patterson et al. also argue that organizational culture is an important variable in determining performance and profitability. If this is the case, then we will have to extend their theory to include a specific type of organizational culture. Thus, Patterson et al. found that higher levels of performance are associated with the use of the HRM as the dominant management framework, where the primary emphasis is on the organizational values associated with belonging, trust and participation, the improvement of motivation through attachment, cohesiveness and group membership. More explicitly, in this type of culture the organization provides support and concern for employee welfare, making the employees feel valued and trusted, providing them with autonomy through job design and providing support in the acquisition of skills through training and guidance from supervisors.

While Patterson et al. place HR practices at the start of the causal chain, Becker and Huselid (1998:59, 93) start the process with the stress on business and strategic objectives.

They see strategic objectives as leading to the design of an HRM system which produces the requisite job design and work structures, which in turn produce higher levels of employee skills and motivation. This high level of skills and motivation then leads workers to produce more discretionary effort and creativity, which in turn leads to increased productivity and operating performance. From this flow increased profits and growth and thereby increased market value. This is a longer and more complex chain than that suggested by Patterson et al., with Becker and Huselid placing more of an emphasis on the importance of business strategy in driving the process.

The most recent attempt to develop this theory is that of Applebaum et al. (2000). Following the work of Bailey (1993), they suggest that factors which make the bundles of practices effective can be summarized in terms of the three components: motivation, skills, and opportunity to participate. They argue that variants of the three components are to be found in the conceptual approaches of many of those currently working in this field. They point out that Delery et al. (1997), when reviewing the literature, identified the main HRM practices that produce the desired effect on workforce characteristics in the following quotation: "Selective recruiting and staffing procedures and training enhance workforce skills and higher base pay and benefits attract better-qualified workers. Recognizing employee contributions, as well as soliciting employee input and encouraging employees to participate in decisions, is expected to enhance employee empowerment" (Applebaum et al., 2000). These are seen by Delery et al. as the HRM practices which comprise the work system that enables employees to use their skills and motivation to maximum benefit.

Applebaum et al. argue that these are, in general, the same points made by MacDuffie (1995) and Becker and Huselid (1998). For them, HPWOs to be effective require three basic components: opportunities for substantive participation in decisions; appropriate incentives; and training and selection policies that guarantee an appropriately trained workforce (Applebaum et al., 2000:39). The opportunity to participate in substantive decisions is important because front-line workers can only contribute to organizational performance when they have the power and authority to solve problems. Applebaum et al. argue that the precise form this takes, whether this is self-directed work teams or quality improvement teams, does not matter, providing the decision-making is decentralized and workers are involved. They also argue that workers will need considerable autonomy and the ability to access resources from the wider organization if they are to make effective decisions.

Policies to guarantee adequate skills are necessary to ensure that workers have the skills in breadth and depth as well as the necessary soft skills, while selective recruitment provides an alternative means of increasing the skill level of the labour force. However, many of the skills will be firm-specific because of the importance of tacit knowledge.

Finally, incentives are necessary to elicit the requisite discretionary effort from the workforce. Individual incentives such as piece rates tend to promote the individual rather than the group or collective interest; therefore, group incentives are favoured such as gain sharing or team-based piece rates. Other forms of incentive come from developing trust in employees through considerate supervisory behaviour and making employees shareholders, as well as the eradication of symbols of status differences such as different terms and conditions and extreme wage differentials. Applebaum et al. summarize their theoretical approach in terms of the following diagram.

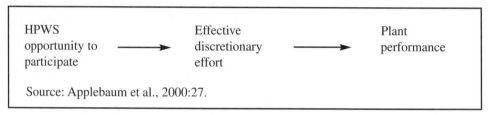

Source: Applebaum et al., 2000:27.

In building on this work, we suggest that there is a need to increase the dimensions around which bundles cluster to incorporate four dimensions: work design/employee involvement; support for performance; information and communication; and reward for performance, This is because, as we have already argued, these dimensions relate to different but complementary mechanisms which are responsible for ensuring that performance is enhanced. Thus, work design and employee involvement may take a number of forms including multi-skilled teams and self-managed work groups. What is important is that the design provides the opportunity for the person to develop skills and be involved in the process of decision-making. To develop the skills requires support from superiors and colleagues to learn and practice skills, hence the support for performance practices. These take the form of access to training courses for technical skills and feedback from managers and colleagues (mentors/coaches) to support the learning process and the continuing application of such skills through time. Moreover, individuals can only use their skills effectively if they have the requisite information from management, hence the importance of mechanisms such as team briefings, regular meetings of the workforce, etc. which convey business information and knowledge to the workforce. Finally, action on all these fronts will not be fully effective unless the product of that effort and creativity put in by the individual is rewarded. This can be either in the form of individual or group-based monetary rewards, but it may also take the form of prizes, trips to conferences and symbolic rewards.

While we have concentrated on specific practices, we would stress that the research surveyed in this book has also pointed to the importance of the establishment of trust between the employer and employee and management and workers. This may be manifest in different ways: it may take the form of guarantees of employment security or openness in communication or sharing the same values. What we can be certain of is that without this trust the learning required for the improvements in performance to be realized is unlikely to take place. In view of this, we argue that organizational culture which embeds trust should be treated as a pre-condition for the successful establishment of these bundles of practices.

Some unresolved issues

In this brief discussion, we would not wish to pretend that all is rosy. There are many issues which remain unresolved. One such concerns the utility of conceptualizing the problem in terms of a linear model of causality. This is implicit in the Becker and Huselid model and more explicit in the Applebaum et al. model. Given that we are talking of a complex web of interdependent practices and behaviours, it may make more sense to think in terms of feedback loops between the factors or variables involved, or figurations, to use the term polarized by Elias (1978). This enables us to speak in terms of the properties of specific collective forms or figurations, which essentially is what characterizes high performance organizations and differentiates them from traditional Taylorist forms of organization.

It is the co-existence of these practices that is important, not their order of precedence. Given the complex nature of human interaction, the output in the form of enhanced performance is not just the result of individual motivation, leading to the application of employee discretion. Motivation itself is a function of prior trust in relationships, of the opportunities to learn, of support from others in the process of learning, of the availability of appropriate information and knowledge for that learning and of knowledge that the application of that learning through appropriate behaviours will be rewarded. Some of the bundles in which these practices are manifest may carry greater weight than others in influencing the outcomes, but that has to be a matter for empirical enquiry.

A second issue concerns the importance of locating the use of HPWPs in the context of the wider range of factors which influence organizational performance. These include the market strategy adopted by the company, whether it is focused on innovation and differentiation, low cost or quality, as Guest has suggested. Other factors such as the level of investment in new technology and the expenditure on research and development, to name but a few, are all important in determining whether an organization is successful in the market. Thus, the most effective HPWPs may be in place, but if the company gets its product market strategy wrong or if the market is lost through political changes, then the best HPWPs in the world will not help them to survive. For public sector organizations, these factors are not as important, but the quality of service they deliver and the effectiveness with which it is delivered are increasingly important as governments seek to enhance the performance of public sector organizations. Here we must not forget that we are only dealing with one determinant of longer-term performance and sustainability of organizations.

It should also be remembered that HPWPs are only one route to financial success and profitability. Traditional methods of organizing production remain the norm. They are still capable of delivering high levels of profitability in many industries (Ashton and Green, 1996). Indeed, we still do not know the extent to which HPWPs are only appropriate for certain types of industry or product market strategy. These all remain open research questions.

Another area where our knowledge is weak is the cost of implementing high performance working practices. As our analysis suggests, in many traditional organizations the costs of this exercise can be very high. Indeed, in one of the companies we interviewed in Hong Kong as a possible case study, it had successfully implemented a team approach to the design and sales of office equipment, providing a total ICT solution to the business. However, the costs of labour turnover involved in replacing those who were opposed to change, in training and multi-skilling existing sales personnel and in changing all the company's procedures to support the new teams meant that it was having second thoughts on whether or not to go down the same road with its service engineers. It is always a delicate balancing act between the cost of change to a new system and the benefits expected to derive from the changes. At the moment, our knowledge of this is thin. It may be that the costs involved are so high that it pays companies operating in low value-added markets to remain with the old system. Until we have more detailed research, we will not be able to specify the exact costs involved.

One area where we can make a start on this task is in further differentiating the impact of the different bundles of practice on the various indices of performance. As we mentioned above, most of the studies have, for understandable reasons, focused on the financial benefits of HPWPs and the high levels of profitability associated with them. More recently, researchers have started to broaden the range of indices they are looking at to include benefits such as enhanced quality of the goods or service produced, the rate of absenteeism, employee satisfaction, client retention, employee commitment and employee wages, to name but some. Certainly, from an employee's point of view, while it may be that overall productivity does not rise as a result of the introduction of HPWPs, if there are significant gains in work satisfaction and personal development, then the exercise is well worth while.

Notes

[1] See Legge (2001) for an elaboration of these criticisms.

[2] Bowey and Thorpe (1986) found that it is not the practice itself which affects behaviour but the process of implementation. In their case, it is the fact that workers are consulted about a proposed payment system that is important, not the precise form of the payment system itself.

BIBLIOGRAPHY

AFL-CIO 1994: *The new American workplace: A labor perspective,* Washington, DC, AFL-CIO.

Applebaum, E.; Bailey, T.; Berg, P.; Kalleberg, A.L. 2000: *Manufacturing advantage: Why high performance work systems pay off,* London, Cornell University Press.

Applebaum, E.; Batt, R. 1994: *The new American workplace: Transforming work systems in the United States,* London, ILR Press.

Arthur, J.B. 1992: "The link between business strategy and industrial relations systems in American steel minimills", in *Industrial and Labor Relations Review,* 455, pp. 488-906.

Ashton, D.; Davies, B.; Felstead, A.; Green, F. 1998: *Work skills in Britain,* Oxford and Warwick Universities, ESRC Centre on Skills, Knowledge and Organisational Performance.

—; Felstead, A. 2000: "From training to lifelong learning: The birth of the knowledge society?", Ch. 9, in Storey, J. (ed.): *Human Resource Management: A critical text,* second edition, London, Routledge, pp. 165-189.

—; Green, F. 1996: *Education, training and the global economy,* Cheltenham, Edward Elgar.

—; Green, F.; James, D.; Sung, J. 1999: *Education and training for development in East Asia: The political economy of skill formation in East Asian newly industrialized economies,* London, Routledge.

Ashton, D.; Sung, J. 2001: *Lessons from abroad,* report for the PIU Project on Workforce Development, UK Cabinet Office.

—; —: 2000: *Skill recognition systems: The US, UK and European experience,* paper prepared for the ILO/APSDEP/Japan Regional Meeting on Workplace-Based Skills Recognition and Training, OVTA, Chiba, Japan, 7-10 Mar., p. 19.

—; —: Raddon, A.; Powell, M. 2001: *National frameworks for workplace learning,* paper delivered to the CIPD Seminar on Workplace Learning, London, 1-2 Apr.

—; —: Turbin, J. 2000: "Towards a framework for the comparative analysis of national systems of skills formation", in *International Journal of Training and Development,* (4)1, pp. 8-25.

ASTD 2000: Mary McCain, *High performance workforce investment systems for the new economy,* talk prepared for the Centre for Labour Market Studies Conference: Implementing High Performance Work Practices, Dublin, 6 Sep. 2000.

—: 2000a: *State of the Industry Report,* Alexandria, VA, ASTD.

—: 1996: "Training industry trends 1996", in *Training and Development,* Alexandria, VA, ASTD, Nov.

Bacon, N.; Blyton, P. 2000: "Industrial relations and the diffusion of teamworking: Survey evidence from the UK steel industry", in *International Journal of Operations and Production Management,* 20(8), pp. 911-31.

Bailey, T. 1993: "Organizational innovation in the apparel industry", in *Industrial relations,* 32, pp. 30-48.

Baldry, C.; Bain, P.; Taylor, P. 1998: "Bright satanic offices: Intensification, control and team Taylorism", in Thompson, P.; Warhurst, C. (eds.): *Workplaces of the future,* London, Macmillan Business, pp. 163-83.

Barnard, M.E.; Rogers, R.A. 2000: "How are internally oriented HRM policies related to high performance work practices? Evidence from Singapore", in *International Journal of Human Resource Management,* 11(6), pp. 1017-1046.

Becker, B.E.; Huselid, M.A. 1998: "High performance work systems and firm performance: A synthesis of research and managerial implications", in *Research in Personnel and Human Resource Management,* Vol. 16, Stamford, JAI Press, Stamford, CT, pp. 53-101.

Becker, B.E.; Huselid, M.A.; Pickus, P.S.; Spratt, M. 1997: "HR as a source of shareholder value: Research and recommendations", in *Human Resource Management,* 36, pp. 39-47.

Beer, M. 1997: "The transformation of the human resource function: Resolving the tension between a traditional administrative and a new strategic role", in *Human Resource Management,* 36, pp. 49-56.

Berg, P.; Applebaum, E.; Bailey, T.; Kalleberg, A.L. 2000: "Modular production: Improving performance in the apparel industry", in Ichniowski, I.; Levine, D.I.; Olsen, C.; Strauss, G.: *The American Workplace: Skills, Compensation and Employee Involvement,* Cambridge, Cambridge University Press.

Bertrand, O.; Noyelle, T. 1988: *Human resources and corporate strategy: Technological change in the banks and insurance companies,* Paris, OECD.

Betcherman, G. 1997: *Changing workplace strategies: Achieving better outcomes for enterprises, workers and society,* Government of Canada and OECD.

Betcherman, G.; Leckie, N.; McMullen, L. 1997: *Developing skills in the Canadian workplace,* Ottawa, Canadian Policy Research Networks, Inc

Bowey, A.; Thorpe, R. 1986: *Payment systems and productivity,* Basingstoke, Macmillan.

Boxall, P.; Purcell, J. 2000: "Strategic human resource management: Where have we come from and where should we be going?", in *International Journal of Management Reviews,* 2(2), pp. 183-203.

Braverman, H. 1974: *Labour and monopoly capital,* New York, New Left Books.

Brown, P.; Green, A.; Lauder, H. 2001: *High skills: Globalization, competitiveness and skill formation,* Oxford, Oxford University Press.

Brown, P.; Lauder, H. 2001: *Capitalism and social progress: The future of society in a global economy,* Basingstoke and New York, Palgrave.

Business Decisions Limited 2000: *Government support programmes for new forms of work organisation,* report for DG Employment and Social Affairs, Jan., available on http://europa.eu.int/comm/employment_social/soc-dial/workorg/ewon/survey_final.pdf.

Cappelli, P. 1996: "Technology and skill requirements: Implications for establishment of wage structures", in *New England Economic Review,* May-June, pp. 139-54.

—: 1998: "Technology, work organisation and wage structures", The Wharton School, quoted in OECD, 1999.

—: Rogobsky, N. 1994: "New work systems and skill requirements", in *International Labour Review,* No. 2, pp. 205-20.

CIPD 2001: *Training and Development 2001, Survey Report,* London, Chartered Institute of Personnel and Development.

Coleman, S.; Keep, E. 2001: *Background literature review for Performance and Innovation Unit project on workforce development,* UK Cabinet Office.

Cosh, A.; Hughes, A.; Weeks, M. 2000: *The relationship between training and employment growth in small and medium-sized enterprises,* Nottingham, DfEE Publictions.

Crouch, C.; Finegold, D.; Sako, M. 1999: *Are skills the answer?,* Oxford, Oxford University Press.

Crysdale, S. (ed.) 1988: *Youth's stormy launching from home and school to work in the information age,* McGill-Queens University Press.

Cully, M.; O'Reilly, A.; Woodland, S.; Dix, G. 1999: *Britain at work: As depicted by the 1998 Workplace Employee Relations Survey,* London, Routledge.

Darrah, C.N. 1996: *Learning and work: An exploration in industrial ethnography,* New York, Garland.

Dehnbostel, P.; Molzberger, G. 2001: "Combination of formal learning and learning by experience in industrial enterprises", in Streumer, Jan. N. (ed.): *Perspectives on learning at the workspace,* Proceedings of the Second Conference on HRD Research and Practice across Europe 2001, University of Twente Enschede, the Netherlands, 26-27 Jan. 2001, pp. 77-88.

Delery, J.E.; Gupta, N.; Shaw, J.D. 1997: "Human resource management and firm performance: A systems perspective", paper presented to the 1997 Southern Management Association Meeting, Fayetteville, Department of Management, University of Arkansas, quoted in Applebaum et al. 2000.

Dench, S.; Perryman, S.; Giles, L. 1998: *Employers' perceptions of key skills,* University of Sussex, Institute of Employment Studies.

Denmark Government 2000: *Adult education and continuing training in Denmark,* http://www.uvm.dk/eng/publications/factsheets/veureform.htm.

Department for Education and Employment (DfEE) 1998: "The role of employee development schemes in increasing learning at work", in *Research Report,* No. 73, Aug.

—: 2000a: *Individual Learning Accounts Newsletter,* Feb.

—: 2000b: "A second evaluation of the Union Learning Fund", in *Research Brief,* No. 208, New York Consulting, July.

Dore, R. 2000: *Stock market capitalism: Welfare capitalism - Japan and Germany versus the Anglo-Saxons,* Oxford, Oxford University Press.

—: 1973: *British factory, Japanese factory: The origins of national diversity in industrial relations,* London, George Allen and Unwin.

Drago, R. 1988: "Quality circle survival: An exploratory analysis", in *Industrial Relations,* 27, pp. 336-51.

Dunlop, J.T.; Weil, D. 2000: "Diffusion and performance of modular production in the US apparel industry", in Ichniowski, C.; Levine, D.I.; Olson, C.; Strauss, G.: *The American Workplace: Skills, Compensation and Employee Involvement,* Cambridge, Cambridge University Press, pp. 38-61.

Dybowski, G. 1998: "New technologies and work organisation: Impact on vocational education and training", in Tessaring, M. (ed.): *Vocational education and training - the European research field,* Background Report, 1998, Vol. 1, Thessaloniki, CEDEFOP.

Easton, G.S.; Jarrell, S.L. 2000: "The effects of total quality management on corporate performance: An empirical investigation", 172-233 in Ichniowski, C.; Levine, D.I.; Olson, C.; Strauss, G.: *The American Workplace: Skills, Compensation and Employee Involvement,* Cambridge, Cambridge University Press.

Elias, N. 1978: *What is sociology?,* London, Hutchinson.

Engestrom, Y. 1996: *Innovative learning in work teams: Analysing cycles of knowledge creation in practice,* San Diego.

—: 1993: "Developmental studies of work as a testbench of activity theory: The case of primary care medical services", in Chaiklin, S.; Lave, J. (eds.): *Understanding practise: Perspectives on activity and context,* Cambridge, Cambridge Univiersity Press.

Eraut, M.; Alderton, J.; Cole, G.; Senker, P. 1998: "Learning from other people at work", in Coffield, F. (ed.): *Learning at work,* Bristol, Policy Press.

Evans, K.; Heinz, W.R. 1991: "Career trajectories in Britain and Germany", in Bynner, J.; Roberts, K. 1991: *Youth and work: Transition to employment in England and Germany,* London, Anglo-German Foundation, pp. 205-28.

Felstead, A.; Ashton, D. 2000: "Tracing the link: Organisational structures and skill demands", in *Human Resource Management Journal,* Vol. 10, No. 3, Nov., pp. 3-21.

—; —: Green, F. 2000a: "Are Britain's workplace skills becoming more unequal?", in *Cambridge Journal of Economics,* (24)6, pp. 709-27.

Financial Times 09.10.00: p. XII, report by Robert Taylor based on the Task Force on Reconstructing America's Labor Market Institutions, Institute for Work and Employment Research, Massachusetts Institute of Technology, iwer@mit.edu.

Finegold, D. 1999: "Creating self-sustaining, high-skills ecosystems", in *Oxford Review of Economic Policy,* 15(1), pp. 60-81.

—: Soskice, D. 1988: "The failure of training in Britain: Analysis and prescription", in *Oxford Review of Economic Policy,* 4(3), pp. 21-53.

—: Wagner, K. 1998: "The search for flexibility: Skills and workplace innovation in the German pump industry", in *British Journal of Industrial Relations,* 36(3), pp. 469-87.

Fleming, D.; Soborg, H. 2001: *Proactive human resource development policies in Malaysia,* paper presented at the Conference on Global Change, Global Governance and National Economic Restructuring, Arresodal Conference Centre, Denmark, Oct.

Frazis, H.; Gittleman, M.; Horrigan, M.; Joyce, M. 1997: "Formal and informal training: Evidence from a matched employee-employer survey", in Libecap, G.D. (ed.): *Advances in the study of entrepreneurship, innovation and economic growth,* Greenwich, JAI Press.

Froud, J.; Haslam, C.; Johal, S.; Williams, K. 2000: "Restructuring for shareholder value and the implications for labour", in *Cambridge Journal of Economics,* 24, pp. 771-97.

Furlong, A.; Cartmel, F. 1997: *Young people and social change,* Buckingham, Open University Press.

Gephart, M.A.; Van Buren, M.E. 1998: *Building synergy: The power of high performance work systems,* Alexandria, ASTD.

Gill, C.; Krieger, H. 1999: "Direct and representative participation in Europe: Recent survey evidence", in *International Journal of Human Resource Management* 10(4), pp. 572-91.

Green, F.; Ashton, D.; Felstead, A. 2001: "Estimating the determinants and supply of computing, problem-solving, communication, social and teamworking skills", in *Oxford Review of Economic Policy,* 53(3), pp. 406-33.

Guest, D.E. 2000: "HR and the bottom line: Has the penny dropped?", in *People Management,* 20 July 2000, pp. 26-31.

—: 1999: "Human resource management - the workers' verdict", in *Human Resource Management Journal,* 9(3), pp. 5-25.

—: 1997: "Human resource management and performance: A review and research agenda", in *International Journal of Human Resource Management,* 8(3), pp. 263-490.

—: Hoque, K. 1994: "The good, the bad and the ugly: Human resource management in new non-union establishments", in *Human Resource Management Journal,* 5(1), pp.1-14.

—: Michie, J.; Sheenan, M.; Conway, N.; Wetochi, M. 2000: *Effective people management: Initial findings of the future of work study,* CIPD Plymouth Distributors.

Guthrie, J.P. 2001: "High involvement work practices, turnover and productivity: Evidence from New Zealand", in *Academy of Management Journal,* (44)1, pp. 180-90.

Hackman, J.R.; Wageman, R.; Ruddy, T.M.; Charles, L.R. 2000: "Team effectiveness in theory and practice", in Cary, L.; Cooper; Locke, E.: *Industrial and Organizational Psychology,* Oxford, Blackwell.

Harrison, R. 2000: "Learning knowledge productivity and strategic progress", in *International Journal of Training and Development,* 4(4), pp. 244-58.

Heckscher, C.; Schurman, S. 1997: "Towards jobs and justice: Can labour-management cooperation deliver jobs and justice?", in *Industrial Relations Journal,* 28(4), pp. 323-30.

Heinz, W.R. 1999: "Job-entry patterns in a life - Course perspective", in Heinz, W.R. (ed.): *From Education to work: Cross-National Perspectives,* Cambridge, Cambridge University Press, pp. 214-31.

Hendricks, K.B.; Singhal, V.R. 2000: "Implementing effective total quality management programs and financial performance: A synthesis of evidence from the quality award winners", in Ichniowski, C.; Levine, D.I.; Olson, C.; Strauss, G.: *The American Workplace: Skills, Compensation and Employee Involvement*, Cambridge, Cambridge University Press, pp. 234-72.

Herman, A.M. 1999: *Future work: Trends and challenges for work in the 21st century*, report of the US Department of Labor.

Hill, S. 1991: "Why quality circles failed but total quality might succeed", in *British Journal of Industrial Relations*, 29(4), pp. 541-68.

—: Wilkinson, A. 1995: "In search of TQM", in *Employee Relations*, 17(3), pp. 8-25.

Hirschhorn, L. 1984: *Beyond Mechanisation: Work and Technology in a Postindustrial Age*, Cambridge, Mass., MIT Press.

Hunter, L.W. 1999: "Transforming retail banking", in Cappelli, P. (ed.): *Employment Practices and Business Strategies*, New York, Oxford, pp. 153-94.

Huselid, M. 1995: "The impact of human resource management practices on turnover, productivity, and corporate financial performance", in *Academy of Management Journal*, 38, pp. 972-91.

Huselid, M.; Becker, B. 2000: "Methodological issues in cross-sectional and panel estimates of the link between human resource strategies and firm performance", in Ichniowski, C.; Levine, D.I.; Olson, C.; Strauss, G.: *The American Workplace: Skills, Compensation, and Employee Involvement*, Cambridge, Cambridge University Press, pp. 111-36.

Huseman, R.C.; Goodman, J.P. 1999: *Leading with knowledge: The nature of competition in the 21st century*, London, Sage.

Ichniowski, C. 1990: "Human resource management systems and the performance of US manufacturing businesses", in *National Bureau of Economic Research Working Paper*, No. 3449, Washington, DC.

—:1992: "Human resource practices and productive labor-management relations", in Lewin, D.; Mitchell, O.; Sherer, P. (eds.): *Research frontiers in industrial relations and human resources*, Madison, WI, Industrial Relations Research Association.

—: Kochan, T.A.; Levine, D.I.; Olson, C.; Strauss, G. 2000: "What works at work: Overview and assessment", in Ichniowski, C.; Levine, D.I.; Olson, C.; Strauss, G.: *The American Workplace: Skills, Compensation and Employee Involvement*, Cambridge, Cambridge University Press, pp. 1-37.

—: Shaw, K. 1995: "Old dogs and new tricks: Determinants of the adoption of productivity-enhancing work practices", in *Brookings Papers on Economic Activity: Microeconomics*, Spring, pp. 1-65.

—: Shaw, K.; Prenushi, G. 1997: "The effects of human resource practices on productivity: A study of steel finishing lines", in *American Economic Review,* 87(3), pp. 291-313.

ILO 2001: *World Employment Report: Life at Work in the Information Economy*, Geneva, International Labour Office.

—: 1998: *World Employment Report: Employability in the Global Economy: How Training Matters*, Geneva, International Labour Office, 1998-99.

IPD 1999: "Training and development in Britain 1999", in *IPD Survey Report*, London, Institute of Personnel and Development, London.

C: 1998: "Changing the role of the trainer", in *IPD Internal Draft Report.*

Katz, H.C.; Kochan, T.A.; Keefe, J.H. 1987: "Industrial relations and productivity in the US automobile industry", in *Brookings Papers on Economic Activity*, 3, pp. 688-715.

Kearns, P.; Papadopoulos, G. 2000: *Building a learning and training culture: The experience of five OECD countries*, NCVER, Leabrook, South Australia (www.ncver.edu.au).

Keep, E. 2000: "Creating a knowledge driven economy - Definitions, challenges and opportunities", in SKOPE Policy Paper No. 2, Sep., ESRC Centre on Skills, Knowledge and Organisational Performance, University of Warwick.

—: Mayhew, K. 1998: "Was Ratner Right? - Product market and competitive strategies and their links with skills and knowledge", in *Employment Policy Institute Economic Report*, 12(3).

Kelley, M.R. 1989: "Alternative forms of work organization under programmable automation", in S. Wood (ed.): *The Transformation of Work*, London, Unwin Hyman, pp.235-46.

Kelly, J. 1978: "A reappraisal of socio-technical work systems and firm performance", in *Monthly Labor Review*, May, pp. 1069-99.

Kessels, J. 1996: "Knowledge productivity and the corporate curriculum", in Schreinemakers, J.F. (ed.): *Knowledge management: Organization, competence and methodology*, Proceedings of the Fourth International ISMICK Symposium, 21-22 Oct., Rotterdam, Wurzburg, ERGON Verl.

Kirkman, B.L.; Lowe, K.; Young, D.P. 1999: *High-performance work organizations: Definitions, practices, and an annotated bibliography*, Greensboro, North Carolina, Center for Creative Leadership.

Kling, J. 1995: "High performance work systems and firm performance", in *Monthly Labor Review*, May, pp. 29-36.

Kohn, M.L.; Schooler, C. 1983: *Work and personality: An inquiry into the impact of social stratification*, Norwood, NJ, Ablex.

Kohn, M.L.; Slomczynski, K.M. 1990: *Social structure and self-direction: A comparative analysis of the United States and Poland*, Oxford, Blackwell.

Koike, K. 2000: "Workers' skills on the shop floor and government role", paper presented to ILO Tripartite Regional Meeting, Bangkok, 12-14 Dec., p. 18.

—: 1997: *Human resource development*, Tokyo, Japan Institute of Labour.

—: 1995: *The economics of work in Japan*, Tokyo, LTCB International Library Foundation.

—: Inoki, T. (eds.) 1990: *Skill formation in Japan and Southeast Asia*, Tokyo, University of Tokyo Press.

Krahn, H.J.; Lowe, G.S. 1993: *Work, industry and Canadian society*, Scarborough, Nelson, Canada.

Krogt, F.; Warmerdam, J. 1997: "Training in different types of organizations: Differences and dynamics in the organization of learning at work", in *International Journal of Human Resource Management*, 8(1), pp. 87-105.

Lauder, H. 1999: "Competitiveness and the problem of low skill equilibria: A comparative analysis", in *Journal of Education and Work*, (12)3, pp. 281-94.

Lave, J.; Wenger, E. 1991: *Situated learning: Legitimate peripheral participation*, Cambridge, Cambridge University Press.

Lawler, E. 1986: *High-involvement management*, San Francisco, Jossey-Bass.

—: Mohrman, S.A. 1987: "Quality circles: After the honeymoon", in *Organizational Dynamics*, 15(4), pp. 42-55.

—: Mohrman, S.A.; Ledford, G.E. 1998: "Strategies for high performance organizations", in *CEO Report*, San Francisco, Jossey-Bass.

Leelaratne, P.M. 2000: *Work-based skills training and recognition in Sri Lanka*, paper delivered to the ILO/APSDEP Conference on Workplace-Based Skills Recognition and Training, OVTA, Japan, Mar. 2000.

Legge, K. 2001: "Silver bullet or spent round? Assessing the meaning of the high commitment management/performance relationship", in J. Storey (ed.): *Human resource management: A critical text*, second edition, London, Thomson Learning, pp. 21-36.

Levine, D. 1998: *Working in the 21st century: Government policies to promote opportunity learning and productivity*, Armonk, NY, Sharpe.

—: 2000: "Public policy implications", in Ichniowski, C.; Levine, D.I.; Olson, C.; Strauss, G.: *The American Workplace: Skills, Compensation and Employee Involvement*, Cambridge, Cambridge University Press, pp. 273-82.

Lewis, K.; Lytton, S. 1997: *How to transform your company and enjoy it*, Chalford, Management Books.

Lloyd, C. 2000: "High involvement work systems: The only option for UK high skill sectors?", in *SKOPE Research Paper*, No. 11, Winter, University of Warwick.

Lowe, G.S. 2000: *The quality of work: A people-centred agenda*, Don Mills, Ontario, Oxford.

Lynch, L.M.; Black, S.E. 1998: "Beyond the incidence of employer-provided training", in *Industrial and Labor Relations Review*, No. 1, pp. 6-31.

MacDuffie, J.P. 1995: "Human resource bundles and manufacturing performance: Organizational logic and flexible production systems in the world auto industry", in *Industrial and Labor Relations Review*, 48, pp. 197-221.

—: Kochan, T.A. 1995: "Do US firms invest less in human resources? Training in the world auto industry", in *Industrial Relations*, 34(2), pp. 147-68.

—: Frits, K.; Pil, F.K. 2000: "The Adoption of High-Involvement Work Practices", in Ichniowski, C.; Kochan, T.A.; Levine, D.I.; Olson, C.; Strauss, G. 2000: *The American Workplace: Skills, Compensation and Employee Involvement*, Cambridge, Cambridge University Press, pp. 137-171.

Mason, G. 1999: "Product strategies, work force skills, and 'high-involvement' work practices", in P. Cappelli (ed.): *Employment practices and business strategies*, New York, Oxford, pp. 193-216.

Matlay, H. 1999: "Employers' perceptions and implementation of S/NVQs in Britain: A critical overview", in *International Journal of Training and Development*, Vol. 3, No. 2, pp. 132-141.

McMurrer; Van Buren, M.; Woodowell, W.H. 2000: *The ASTD State of the Industry Report*, Alexandria, VA, ASTD.

OECD 2001: *Science, technology and industry scoreboard 2001*, Paris, OECD.

—: 2000: "Is there a new economy?", in *First Report on the OECD Growth Project*, Paris, OECD.

—: 2000a: "Thematic review on adult learning, Norway", in *Background Report*, Paris, OECD, June.

—: 1999: *Employment Outlook*, Paris, OECD, June 1999.

—: 1996: *Technology, productivity and job creation: Best policy practices*, Paris, OECD.

Onstenk, J. 1997: "Innovation work teams and learning on-the-job", paper for EU Seminar on Knowledge and Work, Amsterdam, cited in Stern and Sommerlad: *Workplace learning, culture and performance*, IPF/IFTDO, London, IPD, 1999.

O'Reilly, J. 1992: "Where do you draw the line? Functional flexibility, training and skill in Britain and France", in *Work Employment and Society*, 6(3), pp. 369-96.

Osterman, P. 1998: "Work reorganization in an era of restructuring: Trends in diffusion and impacts on employee welfare", Sloan School, The MIT Press, mimeo., quoted in OECD, 1999.

—: 1998a: "Changing work organisation in America: What has happened and who has benefited?", in *Transfer*, 2, pp. 246-63.

—: 1995: "Skill, training and work organisation in American establishments", in *Industrial Relations*, Vol. 34, No. 2, Apr., pp. 125-46.

—: 1994: "How common is workplace transformation and who adopts it?", in *Industrial and Labour Relations Review*, 47(2), pp. 173-88.

Patterson, M.G.; West, M.A.; Lawthorn, R.; Nickells, S. 1997: "The impact of people management practices on business performance", in *IPD Issues in People Management*, No. 22, London.

Payne, C.; Lloyd, C. 2001: *Towards a political economy of skill?*, paper presented at the Labour Process Conference, London, Royal Holloway, Mar.

Pepitone, J.S. 1995: *Future training: A roadmap for restructuring the training function*, Dallas, AddVantage Learning Press.

Pfeffer, J. 1998: *The human equation: Building profits by putting people first*, Boston, Harvard Business School Press.

Pil, F.K.; MacDuffie, J.P. 2000: "The adoption of high-involvement work practices", in Ichniowski et al (eds.): op. cit.

—; —: 1999: "Organizational and environmental factors influencing the use and diffusion of high involvement work practices", in Cappelli, P.: *Employment practices and business strategy*, Oxford, Oxford University Press, pp. 81-106.

Pollard, S. 1965: *The genesis of modern management*, Harmondsworth, Penguin.

Porter, M. 1985: *Competitive advantage*, New York, Free Press.

Purcell, J. 1999: "Best practice and best fit: Chimera or cul-de-sac", in *Human Resource Management Journal*, 9(3), pp. 26-41.

Raper, P.; Ashton, D.; Felstead, A.; Storey, J. 1997: "Towards the learning organisation? Explaining current trends in training practice in the UK", in *International Journal of Training and Development*, Vol. 1, pp. 9-21.

Robinson, C.: 2000: *Developments in Australia's vocational education and training system*, paper presented to the Central Institute of Vocational and Technical Education, Beijing, PR China, Aug.

Robinson, D.G.; Robinson, J.C. 1995: *Performance consulting: Moving beyond training*, San Francisco, BK Publishers.

Robinson, P. 1996: *Rhetoric and reality: The evolution of the new vocational qualifications*, London School of Economics, Centre for Economic Performance, mimeo.

Roethlisberger, F.J.; Dickson, W.J. 1939: *Management and the worker*, Cambridge, MA, Harvard University Press.

Roy, D. 1952: "Quota restriction and goldbricking in a machine shop", in *American Journal of Sociology*, 60, pp. 255-66.

Rugman, A.M. 2000: *The end of globalisation,* London, Random House Business Books.

Savage, P. 1999: *The New Work Organisation in Ireland Programme - An innovatory partnership action programme at enterprise level*, paper delivered to ESF Workshop on Work Organisation, Brussels, Dec. 1999, pp. 1-15.

Scarbrough, H.; Swan, J.; Preston, J. 1998: *Knowledge management and the learning organisation*, report prepared for the Institute of Personnel and Development, London.

Schuck, G. 1996: "Intelligent technology, intelligent workers: A new pedagogy for the high-tech workplace", in Starkey, K. (ed.): *How organisations learn*, London, International Thomson Publishing.

Sisson, K. 1999: "A new organisation of work: The EU Green Paper and national developments", *EIRONLINE, Mar.*, http://www.eurofound.ie/1999/03/study/tn990321s.html.

—: 1997: *New forms of work organisation: Can Europe realise its potential?* Dublin, European Foundation for the Improvement of Living and Working Conditions.

—: 1994: "Paradigms, practice and prospects", in Sisson, K. (ed.): *Personnel management: A comprehensive guide to theory and practice in Britain*, Oxford, Blackwell.

—: 1993: "In search of HRM", in *British Journal of Industrial Relations*, 31(2), pp. 201-10.

Smith, A.; Hayton, G. 1999: "What drives enterprise training? Evidence from Australia", in *International Journal of Human Resource Management*, 10:2, Apr. 1999, pp. 251-72.

Sohlman, A. 1998: *The culture of adult learning in Sweden*, Paris, OECD.

Spilsbury, M.; Moralee, J.; Hillgate, J.; Frost, D. 1995: "Evaluation of Investors in People in England and Wales", in *Institute of Employment Studies Report*, No. 263, Brighton, Institute of Manpower Studies.

Stasz, C. 1998: "Do employers need the skills they want? Evidence from technical work", in *Journal of Education and Work*, Vol. 10, No. 3, pp. 205-23.

—: Ramsey, K.; Eden, R.; Melamid; Kaganoff, T. 1996: *Work skills in practice: Case studies of technical work*, Santamonica, Rand.

Stern, E.; Sommerlad, E. 1999: *Workplace learning, culture and performance*, London, Institute of Personnel and Development.

Stevens, J. 2000: *High performance working is for everyone*, London, Institute of Personnel and Development.

—: Ashton, D. 1999: "Underperformance appraisal", in *People Management*, Vol. 5, No. 14, London, Institute of Personnel and Development.

Streeck, W. 1989: "Skills and the limits of neoliberalism: The enterprise of the future as a place of learning", in *Work, Employment and Society*, (3)1, pp. 89-104.

Sung, J.; Raddon, A.; Ashton, D. 2000: *Learning and training in small and medium-sized enterprises*, Leicester University, Centre for Labour Market Studies.

Taylor, S. 1998: "Emotional labour and the new workplace", in Thompson, P.; Warhurst, C. (eds.): *Workplaces of the future*, London, Macmillan Business, pp. 84-103.

Thompson, M.; Templeton College, Oxford 2000: "The competitiveness challenge", in *The Bottom Line Benefits of Strategic Human Resource Management*, 2000, final report, The UK Aerospace People Management Audit.

Thompson, P.; Wallace, T.; Flecker, G.; Ahlstrand, R. 1995: "It ain't what you do, it's the way that you do it: Production organisation and skill utilisation in commercial vehicle", in *Work, Employment and Society*, 9(4), pp. 719-42.

Tung-Chun Huang 1997: "The effect of participative management on organizational performance: The case of Taiwan", in *International Journal of Human Resource Management*, 8(5), pp. 677-89.

Turbin, J. 2001: "Policy borrowing: Lessons from European attempts to transfer training practices", in *International Journal of Education and Training*, 5(2), pp. 96-110.

Unwin, L. 2000: *Delivering key skills effectively*, London, Department for Education and Employment.

Van Buren, M. 1999: *A yardstick for knowledge management*, Alexandria, ASTD.

—: King, S.B. 2000: *The 2000 ASTD International Comparisons Report*, Alexandria, ASTD.

Verma, A.; Kochan, T.A.; Landsbury, R.D. 1995: *Employment relations in the growing Asian economies*, London, Rutledge.

Wang, Xiaojun 2000: *Profile of Chinese enterprise training and intra-enterprise appraisal*, paper delivered to the ILO/APSDEP Conference on Workplace-Based Skills Recognition and Training, OVTA, Japan, Mar. 2000.

Wan Seman Bin Wan Ahmad 1999: *Country Paper: Malaysia*, delivered to the ILO Asian and Pacific Tripartite Consultative Meeting on Human Resource Development and Training, Singapore, 30 June-2 July.

Weinstein, M. Kochan, T. 1995: "The limits of diffusion: Recent developments in industrial relations and human resource practices in the United States", in Locke, R.; Kochan, T.; Piore, M. (eds.): *Employment relations in a changing economy*, Cambridge, MA, MIT Press.

Whitfield, K. 2000: "High-performance workplaces, training, and the distribution of skills", in *Industrial Relations*, 39(1), pp. 1-25.

Whitley, R. 1999: *Divergent capitalisms: The social structuring and change of business systems*, Oxford, Oxford University Press.

Wickens, P. 1999: *Energise your enterprise*, London, Macmillan.

Womack, J.P.; Jones, D.T.; Roos, D. 1990: *The machine that changed the world*, New York, Rawson Associates.

Wood, S. 1999: "Human resource management and performance", in *International Journal of Management Review*, 1(4), pp. 367-413.

Wood, S.; with de Menezes, L.; Lasaosa, A. 2001: *High involvement management and performance*, paper delivered at Centre for Labour Market Studies, University of Leicester, May 2001.

Youndt, M.; Snell, S.A.; Dean, J.W.; Lepak, D.P. 1996: "Human resource management, manufacturing strategy, and firm performance", in *Academy of Management Journal*, 39(4), pp. 836-66.